for use with Starter Book B

Longman Scienceworld

Teachers Book B

GENERAL EDITOR: BRENDA PRESTT

SCIENCE THROUGH INFANT TOPICS

ENID HARGRAVE AND JANET BROOKS

Longman

General Editor:
Dr Brenda Prestt MBE
who was a member of the APU Science Steering Group and editor of ASE Language in Science. She is a contributor to the Open University Primary Science course, and is Director of the Centre for Industry, Science, Technology Education Liaison based at Manchester Polytechnic.

Authors of the infant material in *Longman Scienceworld*:
Enid Hargrave
who was formerly Head Teacher
and
Janet Brooks
who is Deputy Head
of Chuckery Infants School, Walsall, West Midlands.

Illustrators: Ann Baum, David McKee and Mark Peppé and Chris Williamson
Cover photograph: Chris Wright

LONGMAN GROUP UK LIMITED
Longman House, Burnt Mill, Harlow, Essex CM20 2JE, England
and Associated Companies throughout the world

First published 1986
Second impression 1987
ISBN 0 582 18821 0
Typeset in Monophoto Univers 689
Produced by Longman Group (FE) Ltd
Printed in Hong Kong

CONTENTS

LONGMAN SCIENCEWORLD

This science scheme covers the Primary years – from when a child enters school up to the age of eleven. The books for the scheme are:

Infant

Year 1 *Starter Book A* accompanied by *Science through Infant Topics Teachers' Book A* and *Record Sheets*

Year 2 *Starter Book B* accompanied by *Science through Infant Topics Teachers' Book B* and *Record Sheets*

Year 3 *Starter Readers* (set of four) accompanied by *Science through Infant Topics Teachers' Book C* and *Record Sheets*

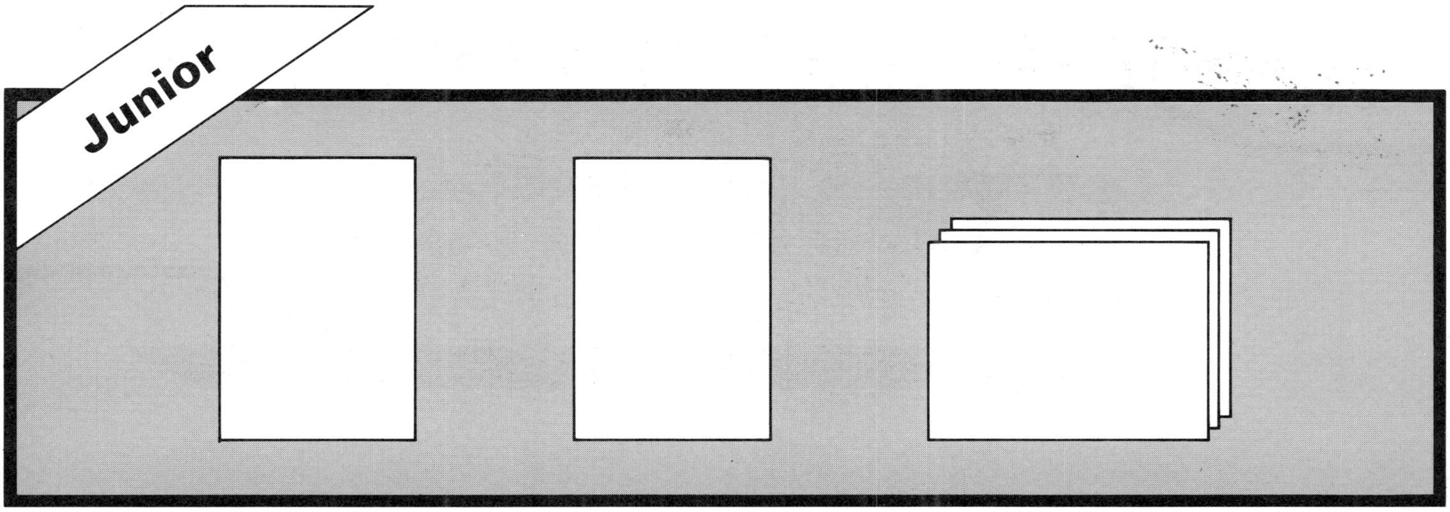

Year 1 *Junior Pupils' Book 1* accompanied by *Junior Teachers' Book 1 and 2* and *Record Sheets*

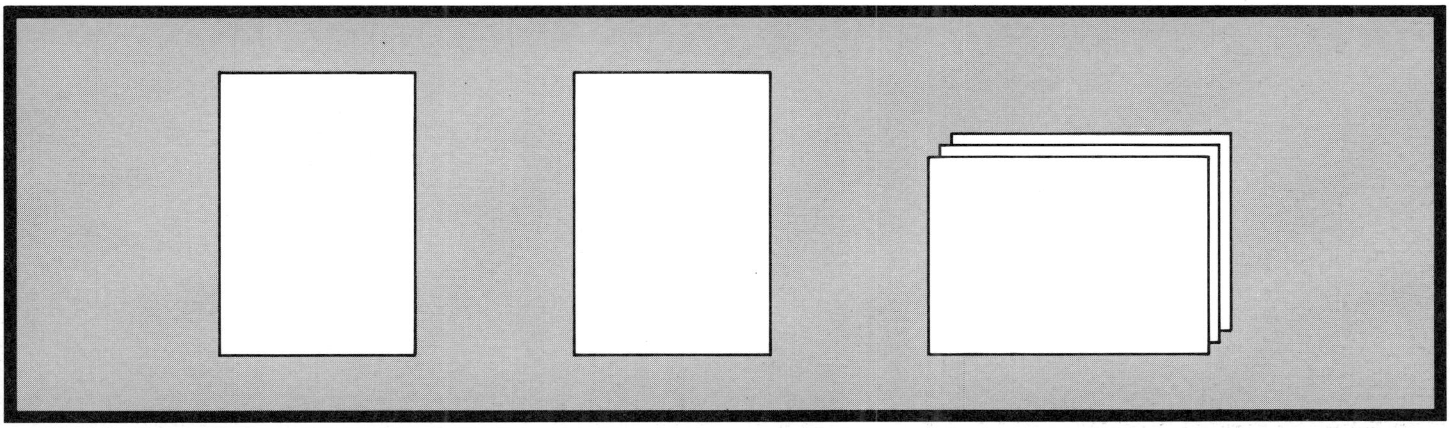

Year 2 *Junior Pupils' Book 2* accompanied by *Junior Teachers' Book 1 and 2* and *Record Sheets*

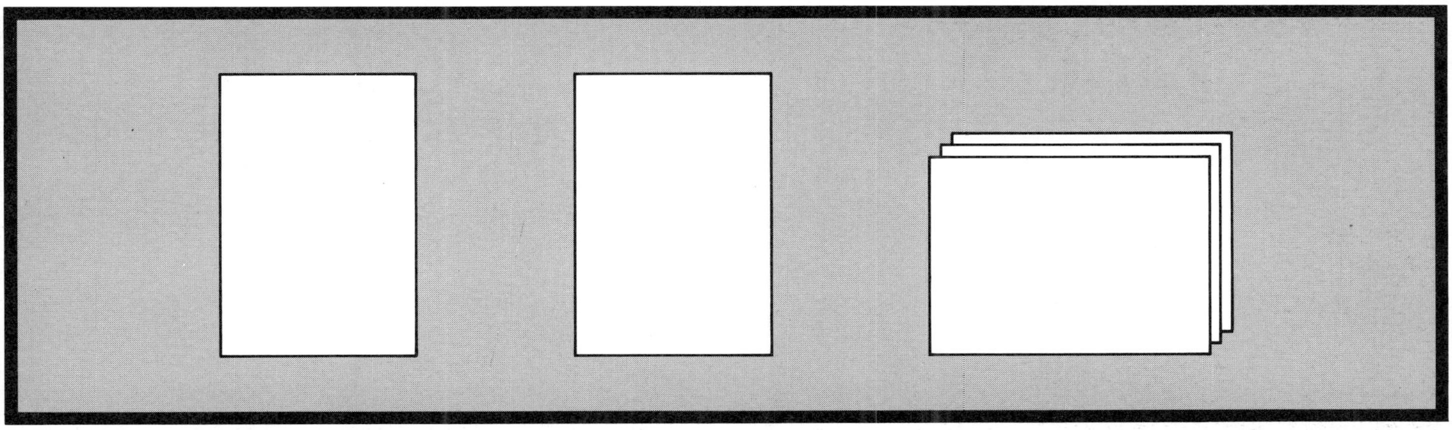

Year 3 *Junior Pupils' Book 3* accompanied by *Junior Teachers' Book 3 and 4* and *Record Sheets*

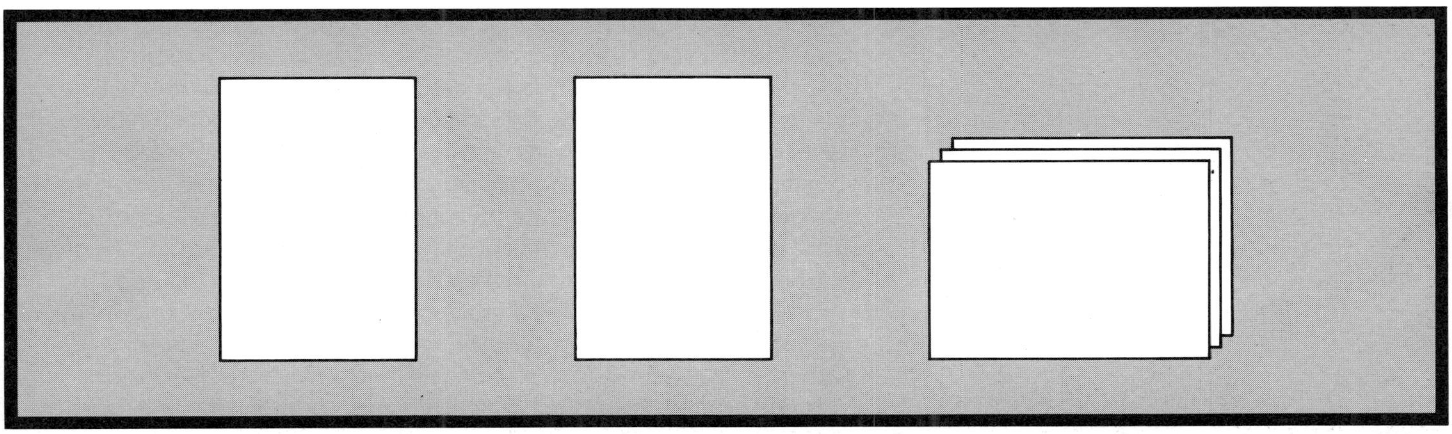

Year 4 *Junior Pupils' Book 4* accompanied by *Junior Teachers' Book 3 and 4* and *Record Sheets*

INTRODUCTION

This science scheme is firmly rooted in the infant curriculum of most schools. The topics have been carefully selected in response to children's interests, with the purpose of arousing their curiosity and fostering their enthusiasm.

Teachers use topic work to provide a wide range of learning experiences for children. The science which has always been there but has, too often, been unrecognised or neglected is presented here.

As the science in the scheme arises from familiar topics, you will be able to use the science activities in your curriculum without having to make uncomfortable changes or adjustments. Science must arise from the normal work of the infant classroom and be fully integrated with it if it is to become an accepted part of the infant curriculum and if it is to succeed. The link between science and mathematics is particularly close, so where appropriate, mathematical activities have been included. At each level, these have been carefully matched with the work normally covered in the infant classroom, where one of the more popular mathematics schemes such as *Nuffield Maths 5–11* is being used.

As you use the science activities with your children, you will find a wealth of opportunities for language work. Language is an important means by which understanding is explored and developed, and

Learning through water play

experiences shared and communicated. The development of science skills is inseparable from the development of language skills.

Not only should children experience science as an exciting way of investigating the world, but they should also grow up realising that science is always around us. With *Longman Scienceworld*, the children come to know the characters in a fictional street, Newton Street, which is used throughout the scheme. The different people in Newton Street use science in their everyday affairs and in their jobs.

Children are great inventors and take delight in making and doing. Their simple making and doing activities provide roots for the later development of technological ability. Making and doing continually raises questions about which materials to use and what they will do, how to make stronger structures and how to make things move – all questions which require scientific investigations to provide the answers. For young children, there is a lot to be gained by developing making and doing activities alongside science activities.

Helping the plumber

One of the joys of teaching young children is observing their progress and development. Children progress at very different rates and responding to the individual's needs makes great demands on the teacher. Perhaps even more difficult is the devising of appropriate activities which will help children to progress.

The activities over the three infant years are arranged so that there is a steady structured progression. In each year, the work is pitched at two levels, each corresponding to half a year. Within a level, the activities are of approximately equal difficulty, so that the topics can be used in an order different from that in which they are presented. It should be noted, however, that at each level it is assumed that the children have achieved the objectives of the previous level(s). Teachers who are starting to teach year 2 of *Science through Infant Topics* should refer to Extension A, Table 2 (i), page 108, which describes the skill levels which children who have followed year 1 of the scheme are likely to have achieved. A summary of the experiences provided by year 1 activities will be found in Extension C. Information about the achievement and experiences of individual children can be extracted from the *Record Sheets* for year 1, which will have been completed by the year 1 teacher.

The topics introduced in the infant years are described below.

	Homes	**People who help us**	**Special times**	**Shopping**	**General**
Year 1 Level 1			Harvest Bonfire night Christmas Winter	Clothes	What can I do?
Year 1 Level 2	The bathroom	The cook The caretaker	Spring School holidays		
Year 2 Level 1	Jobs in the kitchen	The post		The shoe shop The supermarket The sweet shop	Pets
Year 2 Level 2		The police The firefighter Milk	Easter		The park
Year 3 Level 1	In the garden Jobs in the house		Hallowe'en Celebrations	The newsagent	Sports and games
Year 3 Level 2				Fabrics	Transport Animals The farm Weather

Deciding whether children are ready to move from one level to another is not easy but we hope that the *Record Sheets* will help you to focus on specific aspects of the children's achievements and assist you in deciding where individual children need help.

As a final word, science for young children is about doing and finding out. Science for you is about providing the opportunities and sharing the children's enjoyment and enthusiasm.

The next pages describe the general structure of the books for *Science through Infant Topics*. Logically, you should carry on and read them but, if you have *Starter Book B* and you want to dive straight in, you could turn to Using the books, on page xii.

The rationale for our approach to science in the infant school is discussed more fully in the Extensions.

THE STRUCTURE OF THE BOOKS

Starter Books and Readers

The *Starter Books* for years 1 and 2 are teachers' books. They contain large pictures, each of which introduces a topic. Each picture is accompanied by a set of teachers' prompts which enables the teacher to introduce, in the context of the topic, science activities and short discussions about people and their jobs and occupations. In year 3, pupils' illustrated reading books replace the *Starter Books*. The four *Starter Readers* provide starting points for discussion and activities, in the same way that the pictures in the *Starter Books* did previously.

The *Starter Books* and *Readers* set the scene for science learning.

Teachers' Books

The *Teachers' Books* contain all the information needed by the teacher to:
carry out the Science activities,
introduce Making and doing activities,
and extend the topics with Further activities.
In addition, the *Teachers' Books* contain a discussion of the rationale for the scheme and other reference material.

Levels

The work for each year is set at two levels. The work of level 1 approximates to the first half of the year and level 2 the second half of the year.

Topics

In year 2, at level 1, the topics are:

Topic	*key letter*
The shoe shop	Sh
The supermarket	Su
Pets	P
The sweet shop	Sw
The post	Pt
Jobs in the kitchen	K

At level 2, the topics are:

Topic	*key letter*
Easter	E
The police	Po
The firefighter	F
Milk	M
The park	Pa

Topic guides

At the beginning of each topic in the *Teachers' Books*, you will find a diagram which sets out the main objectives of the Science activities based on that topic, and gives page references for these and for the Making and doing activities. Reference is also provided for the suggestions for Further activities. For discussion about People and their jobs and occupations, reference is made to the *Starter Book*.

Topic activities described in Teachers' Books A and B

Science activities

Title
Each Science activity has a short title, the main purpose of which is to aid staff room communication. The activity numbers in conjunction with the topic key letters provide a means of identifying specific activities.

Main objective
The main objective for each activity is clearly stated. It is these objectives which form the backbone of the scheme.

Materials required
These are listed as fully as possible; it is difficult to be precise about quantities since these will depend on the size of your group.

Description of the activity
The description provides a detailed guide to the presentation of the activity in the classroom and indicates points which should be emphasised. The implication throughout is that doing is only part of the activity; the talking throws light on the doing.

At some points where you might need further clarification about methods or presentation, there are references to the Extensions.

Very occasionally, it is suggested that children should taste items of food. Wherever this occurs, a warning is given in the text and you should make sure that the children understand that they should only taste what they know is food, and only if you, the teacher, give permission.

Making and doing activities

In each case, children are given a problem which has many possible solutions. All the problems require the children to make something. The presentation of the problem to the children is described step by step.

1 The problem
2 Exploring the problem
3 Ideas for solving the problem
4 Making
5 Evaluating

The sequence for problem solving is rarely as neat and tidy as this in practice, but it helps to establish a good approach to problem solving activity, which can be built on and developed. The suggested structure should be used as a guide rather than as a prescription. (The rationale for this approach to making and doing will be found in the Extensions.)

At a practical level, the materials required are specified as far as possible but quantities will depend on the size of your group.

Further activities

The topic guide which introduces each topic indicates that the science and other activities are part of a more extended scheme based on the topic. The section entitled Further activities is intended to give you some useful ideas which you might like to incorporate in your work in other areas of the curriculum. They are just ideas but it is hoped you will find them helpful.

Topic activities described in the Starter Books

People and their jobs and occupations

In these sections, the *Starter Book* pictures are used to bring out various aspects of what people do with their time. This is in itself of importance and interest but, in the context of the scheme, it is intended also to show how much people use and need science in everyday life.

Each of these sections has two parts. The first is a series of discussion points arising from the picture. By a series of numbers, reference is made to the second part, which consists of ideas to be developed.

Increasingly, there are links between the Science activities and what people need to be able to do or to understand in their lives. This is brought out not only in discussions about People and their jobs and occupations but also at appropriate points in the Science activities.

USING THE BOOKS

Preparation

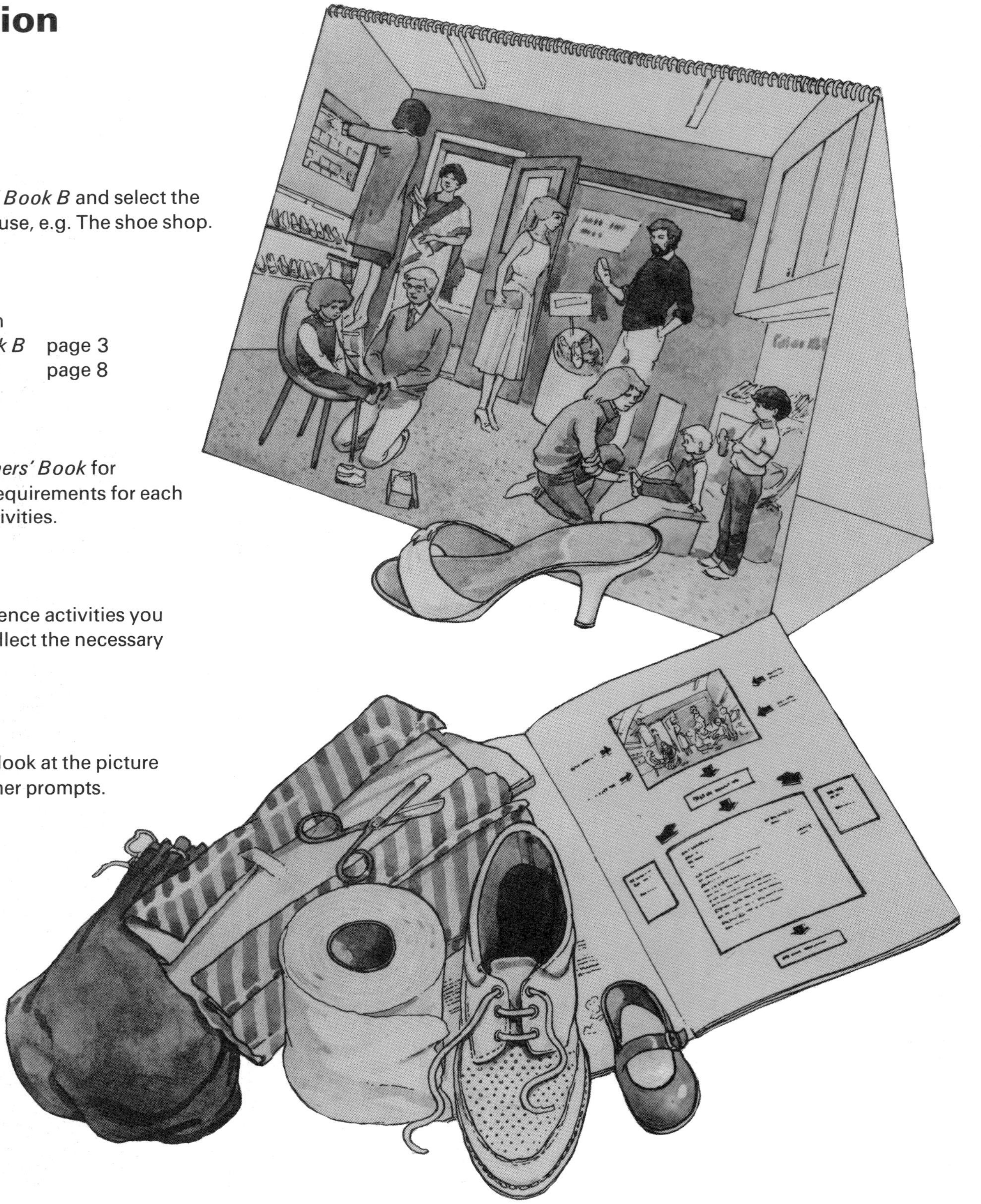

Step 1
Refer to *Teachers' Book B* and select the topic you wish to use, e.g. The shoe shop.

Step 2
Locate the topic in
a) *Teachers' Book B* page 3
b) *Starter Book B* page 8

Step 3
Refer to the *Teachers' Book* for instructions and requirements for each of the Science activities.

Step 4
Decide which Science activities you wish to do and collect the necessary materials.

Step 5
In *Starter Book B* look at the picture and read the teacher prompts.

With your class

Step 1
Show the children the picture in *Starter Book B* and use the Discussion points to introduce the discussion about People and their jobs and occupations. Extension G on page 136 offers guidance for this discussion.

Step 2
Use the Starting point which will lead you into the first of the Science activities which you have selected.

Step 3
Refer to the *Teachers' Book* for instructions for carrying out the activity with the children.
You can work through as many of the activities as you wish in a similar way.

Step 4
Refer to the *Teachers' Book* for instructions for the Making and doing activity associated with the topic.

Step 5
Refer to the *Teachers' Book* for suggestions for Further activities.

Recording progress

Ongoing accurate records are an essential part of ensuring that children's experience of science is progressive and developmental; to assist teachers in keeping records, sets of pupils' *Record Sheets* are available. There is a record sheet for each level so that a complete record of progress can be maintained for each pupil and accompany him or her from one class to the next. Extension H on page 138 gives fuller information about the *Record Sheets*.

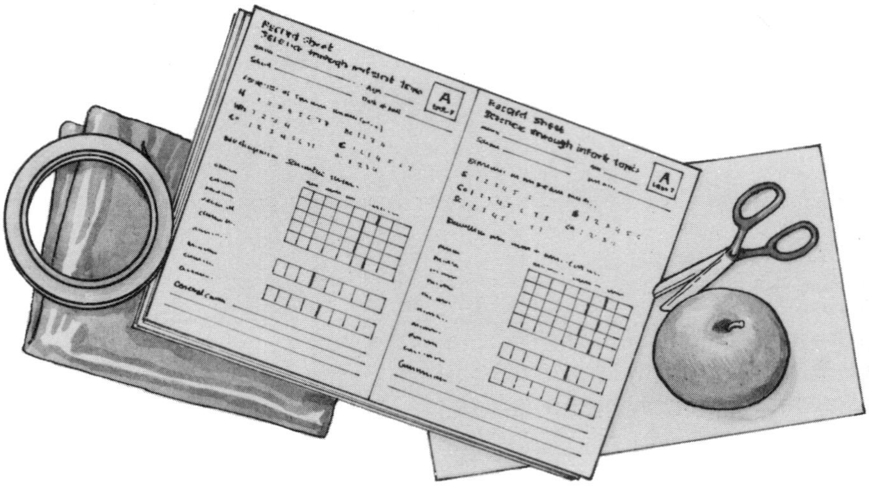

LEVEL 1: TOPICS

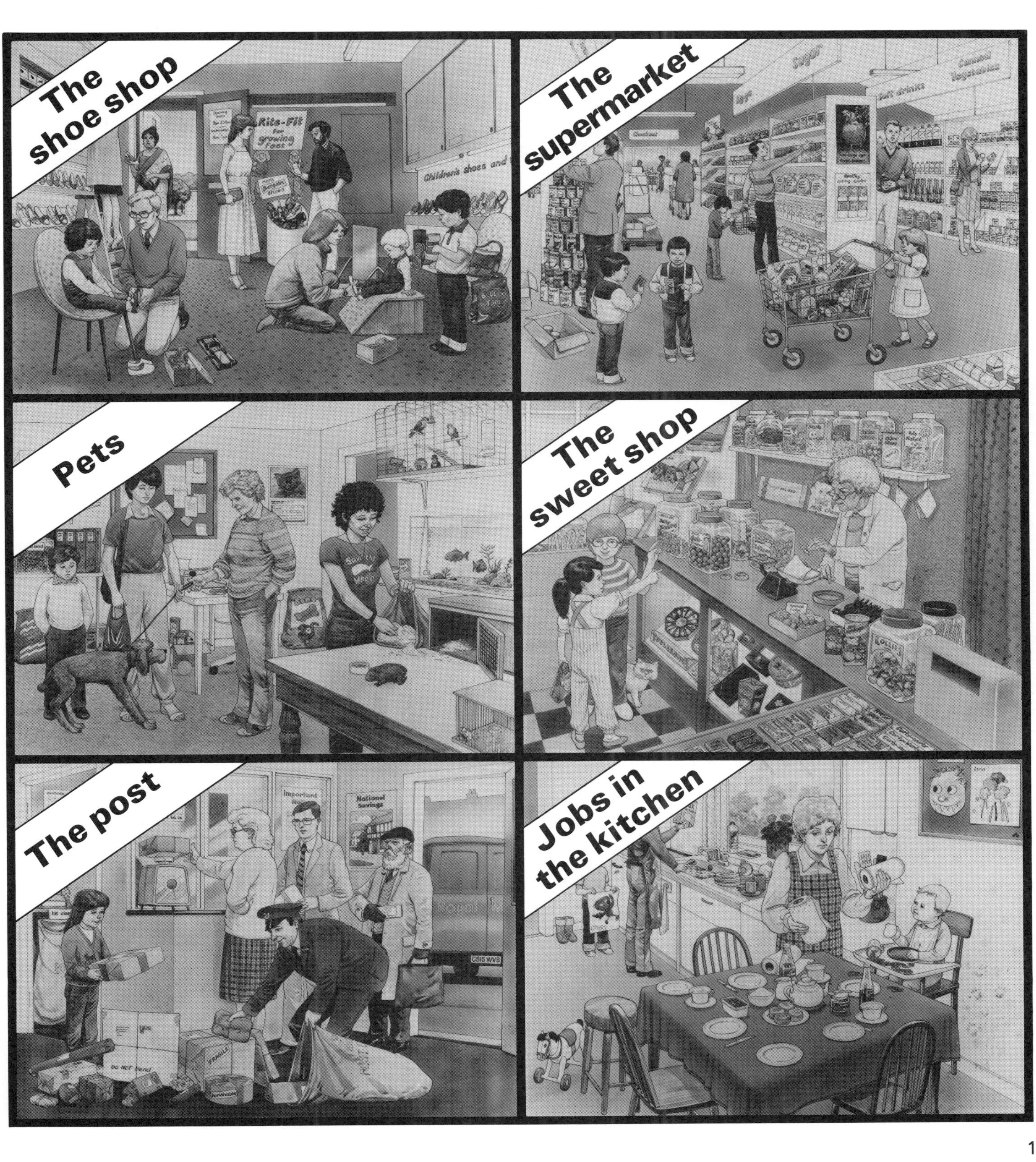

INTRODUCTION TO LEVEL 1

Children will now be familiar with a number of the ideas we are seeking to develop or, at least, with the approach we are using. As before, most of the onus for development rests with the teacher. Nevertheless we should now be encouraging the children, more and more, to make decisions whenever they are able to.

Where observations are made using more than one of the senses, or where use is made of more than one method of recording or communicating, children should be encouraged to consider which of the senses or methods used was most successful.

Children using different methods of recording

If you refer to Extension A, Scientific skills, on page 104, you will find a description of each of the identified skills at each level. Only the principal objective for each activity within the topics is listed. The objectives for the other skills are not made explicit but are woven into the fabric of the activities. Familiarise yourself with the descriptions of all the skills for the level at which you are working and take every opportunity to develop the skills as described.

Only you, as teacher, will be able to judge when a particular skill can be developed by a well-chosen word or question.

Language → The shoe shop

Mathematics → The shoe shop

Physical education → The shoe shop

Creative arts → The shoe shop

Science

People and their jobs and occupations

Starter Book page 8

Science activities

Making and doing

Teachers' Book page 7

Further activities

Teachers' Book page 8

Introduction

Science activities

Feet and shoes are always of interest to children and the activities in this topic give children opportunities to observe carefully their own feet and how they function. Ordering foot sizes and heights and investigating the relationship (if any) between the two introduces the idea of the variability of human beings. You can emphasise to the children that we expect people to be different even though we all have many characteristics in common.

Using observation to identify the material used for shoe uppers is a very practical demonstration of the importance of observing by feel and smell. The smell of leather is still the most valuable clue in identifying it.

Making and doing activities

The problem for the child is:

'Can you make a model of a shoe "lace-up" for practice in tieing shoe laces?'

Tieing shoe laces is one of the difficult tasks small children have to master at school. It is a very real problem for them and this activity provides the opportunity to make something which is directly useful.

The shoe shop   Science activities

Activity Sh1 — Feet and shoes

Observing and investigating feet; ordering sizes

You need:
some coloured or patterned wall-paper or used patterned wrapping paper; pairs of scissors; toilet paper for a height measure (see picture on page 5); an adult's shoe; a baby's shoe.

1 Ask the children to look at their own shoes and tell you in which ways both shoes in a pair are the same i.e. colour, size, material, shape, pattern, fastening. Encourage the children to give as full a description as they can.
2 Ask the children to tell you how the shoes are different. If they say that they are not different in any way, suggest that they put their left shoes on their right feet and right shoes on left feet. Ask them whether their shoes look right and whether they feel right. Now let each of the children put his/her shoes on a piece of patterned or coloured paper and draw round the shoes. Are the two drawings the same or different? How are they different? Let the children cut out the outlines. Can they put their feet prints one on top of the other so that they match? What do they have to do to make them match?
3 Let the children take off their socks and look at their own feet. How are their own two feet the same? How are they different?
4 Let two children compare their feet. How are their feet the same? How are they different?
5 Let each child use one of his/her shoes as a measure to measure a convenient distance. Record how many shoe lengths are needed for each child. Do they all get the same answer? Why not? What happens if an adult's shoe is used? What happens if a baby's shoe is used?
6 Let the children work together and draw round each other's bare feet and cut out the footprints. Ask them if they can suggest how to find out whether boys or girls have bigger feet. Use their suggestions (if possible). A chart showing footprints in order of size can form the basis of an interesting display.

7 Ask the children whether they think foot size is related to height. Do the tallest children have the biggest feet? Toilet paper is useful measuring paper for this purpose (see sketch) and the cut-off lengths can be mounted for a wall display. Is the order of heights the same as the order of footprints?

Activity Sh2—Shoe fasteners

Observing and sorting shoes

You need:
an opaque bag (shoe bag) for each child.

1 Ask the children to sit in a circle. Ask each of them to put one shoe in the middle of the circle. Each child should then select one of these shoes and put it in his/her bag so that nobody else can see it. Each child now puts his/her own other shoe into the middle of the circle and one child goes into the centre and is appointed 'chooser'. One of the children in the circle is asked to describe the shoe in his/her bag so that the 'chooser' can find the matching one from the collection in the middle. Each child can have a turn at being 'describer' and 'chooser'.
2 Ask the children to sit in a circle again and get them to look at the fasteners on their shoes. Ask all the children with laces to stand up and make a smaller circle in another part of the room. Tell them that they are a special 'shoe fastener' set. Ask them what is the same about every one in their 'shoe' set? How many are there in their set? Now ask the children what other 'shoe' sets could be formed: e.g. buckles, zips, no fasteners, etc. Let the children form these sets and count the numbers in their sets. How many shoes are there in each of the sets? Which kind of fastening is most popular? You could draw a block graph to show this as well as using the results for set diagrams.
3 If possible, you could repeat this investigation with another class.

Activity Sh3—Footprints

Observing and investigating footprints

You need:
a tray; talcum powder; dark-coloured sugar paper; scissors; hair lacquer; patterned paper and other paper for drawing round feet; scissors.

1 Introduce this activity by discussing with the children how they could find out if their shoes are big enough for their feet. Suggest that it might be possible to make 'paper patterns' of their feet to see if they fit their shoes properly. Tell them that they are going to make a pattern of their feet.
2 Dust the tray liberally with talcum powder and let one of the children step on to the tray with one bare foot. Then let the child step firmly on to a piece of sugar paper and leave a footprint as he/she walks across the paper. Then ask the child to step on the paper on tiptoe only so that a 'tiptoe' print is produced. Fix the footprints with hair lacquer spray. The other children can record their footprints in the same way.
   What is the difference between a 'walking' footprint and a 'tiptoe' print? Why? (The prints should show that although toes are very small they are very useful in walking normally and on tiptoe.)
3 Let the children work together in pairs. Ask them to draw carefully round their partners' bare feet to produce paper patterns, and then cut out the patterns of their feet. It is important that this is done accurately so some of them may need help.
   Let them next draw round their shoes (again care is needed). Then, making sure that feet are matched to the right shoes, let the children put the paper patterns of their feet on to the outlines of their shoes. Do their shoes fit? Is there room in their shoes for their feet?

Activity Sh4—Soles and uppers

Observing shoe materials

You need:
a collection of boots and shoes of different materials and intended for different purposes e.g. fur-lined boots, ballet shoes, high-heeled shoes, football boots, etc.; samples of shoe upper materials e.g. plastic, leather, canvas etc.; a tray of wet sand in which you have made sole prints of some of the boots and shoes in your collection; poster paint; paper.

1 Display your collection of boots and shoes for the children to see. Ask them to describe the items and encourage them to do this carefully and

systematically. Ask them if they can tell you the purpose for which each boot or shoe is intended. How do they know? How is it suitable for its purpose? (Who thought of making it like that?)

2 What are the shoe uppers made from? Can they tell by looking at them? Can they tell by smelling them? Can they tell by feeling them? Have your samples of canvas, plastic, leather etc. available so that the children can compare the shoe materials with these.

3 Ask them to look at the soles. What are these made from? What does the shoe designer do to make them non-slippery? Ask the children how they might make prints of their shoes soles. Let them try out their suggestions if possible. Show them how to make poster-paint prints of the soles to show the patterns. Why are the patterns different on different kinds of shoes? (There will be heavier, deeper patterning where there is more danger of slipping e.g. rubber boots, climbing boots.)

4 Show the children the sole prints you have made in the tray of wet sand and the collection of boots and shoes. See if they can match the soles to the prints. Can they suggest why the small high-heel went such a long way into the sand?

Making and doing activities

The problem for the children is:
'Can you make a model of a shoe 'lace-up' to practise tieing shoe laces?'

You need:
pieces of card; long boot or shoe laces; means of making holes in card; glue; scissors; hole reinforcers.

1 The problem — Can you make a model of a shoe lace-up on which to practise tieing shoe laces?

2 Exploring the problem — Tieing shoe laces is a problem with which young children are very familiar. In making the model, they need to realise it will be much more useful if the lace to be tied is in more or less the same position as a real shoe lace.

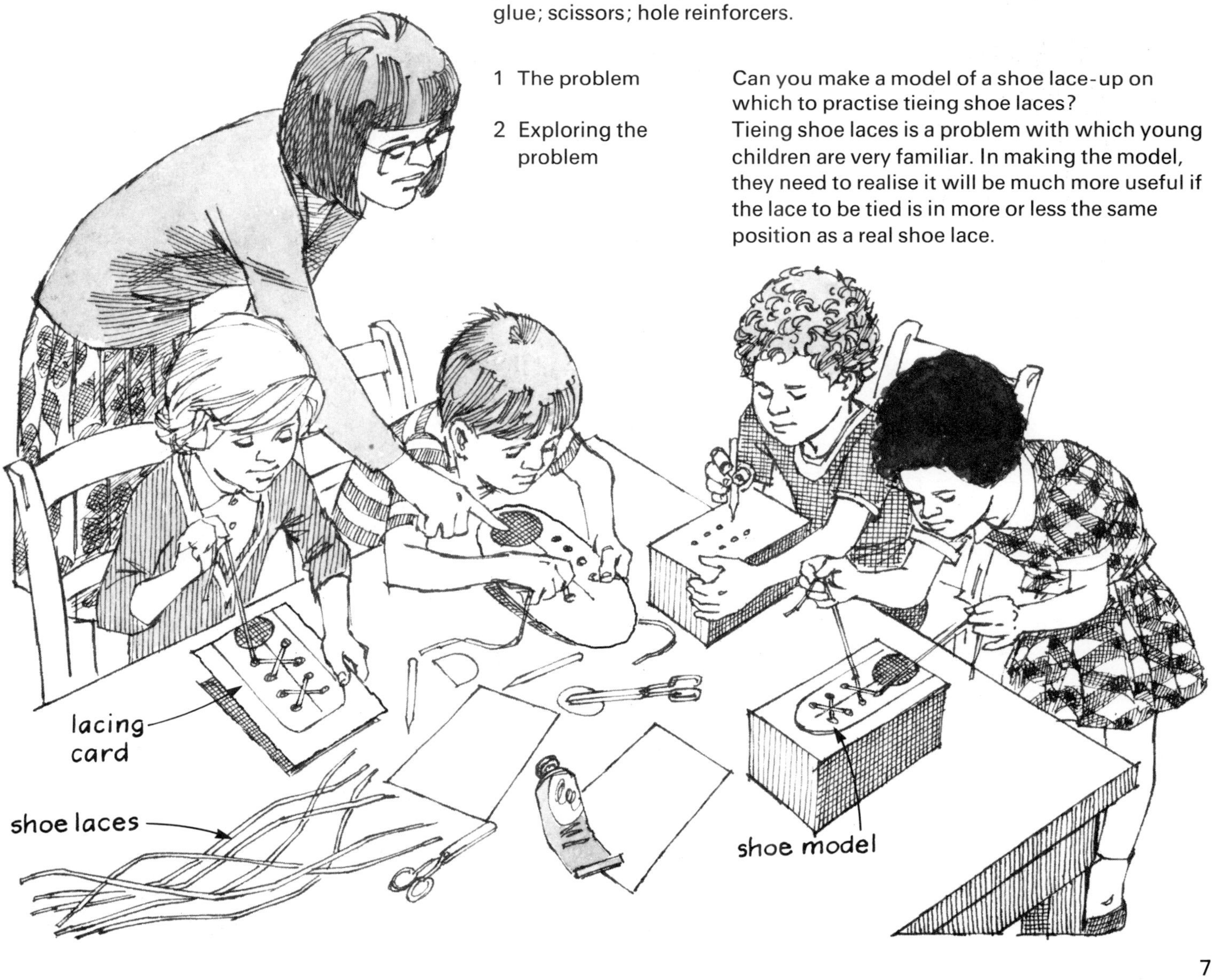

3 Ideas for solving the problem — Many children may already be familiar with lacing cards and have fixed ideas. Others may be more ambitious and want to produce more elaborate solutions. It will help if you steer them towards the possible constructions and keep in mind that the aim is to produce a model which is useful for practice rather than any other purpose.

4 Making — The difficulties here will vary according to how ambitious the ideas are. The main difficulty is likely to be in making the lace holes and positioning them in reasonable alignment. The hole reinforcers will help to improve their efforts.

5 Evaluating — The children can try using their own models and those which their friends have made. Which is easiest? Which is most useful for practising? Which is most like the real shoe-lacing problem?

You could have a display of the children's models and of shoes with different kinds of lace-ups.

Further activities

Some suggestions

1 Make a collection of things that come in pairs. Separate these into two sets – one set in which the two items of the pair are identical and one set in which there is a left and a right in each pair.
2 Invite someone from a shoe shop to come and show the children how feet are measured to decide on shoe sizes. The children could help measure each other's feet.
3 Reinforce the vocabulary used for P.E., including left and right.
4 Make a plaster cast of a heavily embossed shoe sole. Roll out a piece of plasticine big and thick enough to accommodate the shoe print and press the sole of the shoe into it. Build a plasticine wall about 1.5 cm

Making a plaster cast of a heavily embossed shoe sole

high round the print and pour Plaster of Paris into the mould thus formed. (Plaster of Paris is prepared by taking a container of water and then adding the powder until it comes level with the surface of the water. The mixture is then stirred before pouring into the mould.) The plaster takes some time to set. Don't remove the cast too soon. There is a time-lag between the plaster setting and being sufficiently strong.

As Plaster of Paris sets, it becomes warm and you can let the children feel this warmth. Can they suggest why it gets warm? (A 'right' or logical answer is unlikely but what they do suggest gives an insight into their thought processes.)

5 Let the children make a 'pretend' plasticine embossed sole for one of their shoes. Which way should the corrugations go to prevent slipping?

Would either the plaster sole or the plasticine sole be any good for real shoes? Why not? Discuss with the children what would be a 'specification' for real shoe soles.

6 Our shoes are usually made of leather, rubber or plastic. What else can shoes be made of and why? (Different purposes, different raw materials, different countries, different conditions.)

Language

Mathematics

Physical education

Creative arts

Science

People and their jobs and occupations

Starter Book page 10

Science activities

Making and doing

Teachers' Book page 19

Further activities

Teachers' Book page 20

Introduction

Science activities

The Supermarket introduces a number of simple investigations. Some of these are to do with food and cooking and the way in which foodstuffs change.

In Activity 5 the children are asked to investigate what happens when eggs are heated. We do not often think of this as chemistry but that is what it is. We are observing an irreversible change. There is no way of getting the white of an egg back in its original form once it has been cooked. This is in contrast to the reversibility of the change that occurs when, for example, lard is heated and then cooled; or water is frozen and then the resultant ice warmed.

The concepts involved are major ones, but through the children's observations we are helping them slowly to reach understanding and at the same time sharpening their ability to observe.

Making and doing activities

The problem for the child is:

'Can you make a timer using sand or water?'

This problem has two distinct aspects. One is an exploration of how we can measure the passage of time and the other is how to arrange available materials to allow sand or water to flow very slowly. Children of this age are unlikely to be able to measure the passage of time in minutes. In Activity 5 they are introduced to the egg timer. The time the sand takes to flow is related to the movement of the hands of the clock. This making and doing activity reinforces this experience and allows children to again explore the flow properties of sand and water.

The supermarket Science activities

Activity Su1—Containers

Sorting containers by shape, size and material

You need:
one or two large cuboids e.g. cornflakes packets; one or two small cuboids e.g. small tins or packets (stock cubes or similar); large cylinders e.g. washing up liquid, large soup can, etc.; small cylinders e.g. small milk can, tomato purée can; triangular prisms e.g. large and small Toblerone packets or similar packets. Make sure that the collection includes metal, cardboard and plastic items.

In addition you will need a matrix diagram large enough to put on the table and accommodate the objects being sorted. (See the illustration to the left.)

Matrix diagram

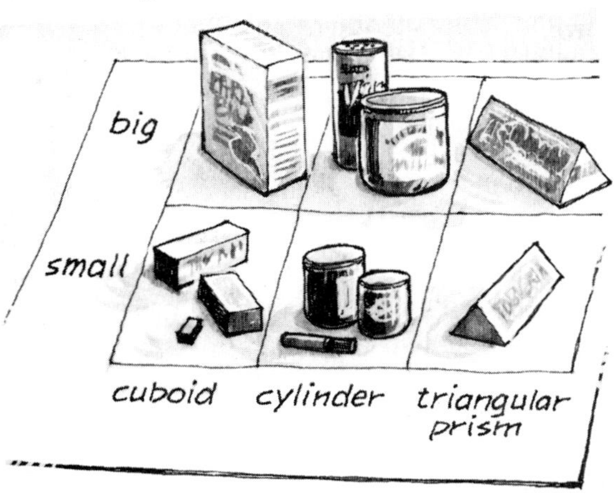

1 Let the children examine the containers. Ask them to name the shapes – cuboid, cylinder, triangular prism. Put the matrix you have drawn on the table and talk to the children about it. Point to the top row and ask the children to talk about the things which will fit in the top row. How are they the same? (All are big.) What about the things in the bottom row? (All are small.) What do they notice about the columns?

2 Now take one of your collection of containers and ask the children to tell you which square of the matrix it should go in. Ask them, 'What shape is it? Which column should it go in? Is it big or small? Which row should it go in? Which square should we put it in?' Then place the container in its correct place. Once you have done this with two or three containers, some of the children will be able to place the other containers correctly without further help. Others will need you to continue to ask the questions for all the containers.

3 Remove the matrix and choose a metal container. Ask the children to tell you about it. What does it feel like? Is it soft or hard? Is it shiny or dull? Is it rough or smooth? Does it feel cold or warm? What colour is it?

Ask the children to find other containers which look the same and feel the same. Put these containers together. Ask them why you can group these containers together. Encourage them through discussion to see that they are together because they are made from the same kind of material. Tell them that this material is called metal. You may also be able, whilst handling the containers, to give the children experience of some of the other properties of metals e.g. the ringing sound which metals make when they are struck or dropped.

We are trying to show the children that the word 'metal' is used to describe a material which has a recognisable set of properties: it is hard, shiny, smooth, feels cold, is silvery or coppery in colour, and makes a ringing sound when dropped. The word 'metal' signifies that the material has a range of properties which are common to the class 'metal' and the word 'metal' applied to a material indicates that the material will have the properties associated with the class 'metal'. That is, a material which is found to have a certain set of properties can be classified as a metal; a material which is labelled metal can be predicted to have the set of metallic properties.

Through the exploration of materials, we are encouraging in the children an understanding that if objects have the same set of 'material' properties, they are probably made from the same material.

4 Having discussed metals, follow the same approach with the cardboard containers and the plastic containers. With the children, explore the properties and build up sets of common properties associated with the materials of cardboard and plastic. Introduce the idea of 'rigid' and 'flexible' and start to use these words. Why do washing-up liquid bottles have to be flexible?

Activity Su2—Peas

Observing and investigating preserved peas

You need:
five small dishes; a packet of frozen peas; a packet of dried peas; a packet of dehydrated peas; a can of peas; some ready-soaked dried peas; small glass pans (five if possible); a hot plate; a can opener; scissors; teaspoons for tasting; kitchen paper; salt.

W

Warning

This activity involves tasting.
You must emphasise to the children that we only taste things that we know are food. We never taste anything else. They must *never* taste anything in the classroom unless you tell them to do so. Make sure that this activity is carried out under hygienic conditions – wash hands, use a tablecloth, etc.

1 Ask the children to look at the can and the packet of peas. What kind of peas are they? What do peas look like when they come from the plant? What has happened to these peas since they came from the plant? (They have been taken out of the pods and then canned, frozen or dried.) What are the containers made from? What shape are they? How do they open?
2 Open the can and the packets of peas and tip a few of each type of pea into the dishes, keeping the types separate. Ask the children what differences they can observe by just looking at the peas. Direct their attention to size, colour, surface appearance – smooth, wrinkled, wet, or dry. Then ask the children what differences can be found by touching them. They should notice the peas are hard or soft, rough or smooth, some are colder than others.
   Point out, in particular, the difference between the dried peas from the packet and those that have been soaked.
   Now ask the children what they need to put in the glass pans in order to cook the peas. Some peas will need water and salt added, and some need nothing.
3 Put the pans containing the peas with water and salt where necessary on the hot plate. Ask the children to watch very carefully what happens. The following questions may help them to notice the changes: Do the peas float or sink? Do the peas move about? Which peas start to move about first? What else can you see on the bottom of the pan? What do the peas start to do? What do the bubbles start to do? Explain that when water starts to behave like this, it is boiling. (Warnings about the dangers of boiling water and about not trying to do this at home are appropriate at this point.) Spend some time talking about the appearance of boiling water and make sure that the children notice the steam coming from the water. (No need to explain – just observe at this stage.) Which of the pans boiled first? Which was last?
4 When the peas are cooked, allow them to cool and let the children taste them. Do the different types of peas taste the same? Do they feel the same in the mouth? Which do the children like best? You could record your results by constructing a bar graph.
5 Put some water into a pan and let it come to the boil. Ask the children to describe what they see. Now add some frozen peas to the boiling water. What happens? Can the children suggest why?

Activity Su3—Liquids

Observing and investigating some properties of liquids

You need:
a variety of small dishes and other containers which will hold liquids (transparent preferably); teaspoons; several cut-off top halves of washing-up liquid containers; washing-up liquid; cooking oil; golden syrup.

1 Pour some washing-up liquid into dishes so that the children can observe it and examine it. Ask the children very carefully to tip their dishes and tell you what happens to the washing-up liquid. Does it move? Does it change shape or stay the same shape? What happens to the surface? Does it tip up or does it stay flat? What happens when the dish is put down? What happens to the surface when the dish is put down? Is it flat or lumpy? Is it smooth or rough? Is it dull or shiny? What does the surface feel like when you touch it? Can you touch it?

What happens to your finger when you try to touch it. Ask the children to carefully take out with teaspoons a small amount of liquid from their dishes. Tell them to let the liquid drip back gently into the dish. What happens to the drips? Do they stay in a lump on the surface? Can you find them again? Let the children label these dishes and put them on one side.

2 Take a dish of washing-up liquid. Tip it and touch its surface and again discuss with the children the properties which can be observed. Then pour the liquid into a container which is very different in shape from the dish. Discuss with the children what happens to the liquid – to its shape and to its surface. Reinforce this discussion by pouring the liquid into and from a number of containers of different shapes.

3 Let the children explore the properties of water when it is poured from one container to another. What happens to its shape? What happens to its surface? What happens to drips which are added?

4 Repeat 2, but this time use cooking oil and ask the children to 'predict' what will happen to the shape and surface of the oil as it is poured from one container to another.

Encourage the children to appreciate that although washing-up liquid, water and cooking oil have many different properties, they also have a set of properties which are the same – the properties of 'liquids'. Washing-up liquid is a liquid; water is a liquid; cooking oil is a liquid. All substances which have the set of properties identified are liquids. (These sentences indicate the direction in which you should be encouraging the children's thinking. Take it slowly.)

5 With your help, let the children explore the properties of golden syrup. Is it a liquid i.e. does it have the 'liquid' properties which you have identified? Does it behave in the same way as washing-up liquid, water and cooking oil? How is it different? (The children will be able to appreciate that it moves much more slowly than the other liquids.) Do washing-up liquid, water and cooking oil move at the same speed or do they appear to move at different speeds? Can the children think of a way of finding out? Pose this problem for the children to discuss and, if it is possible, use their ideas to set up a simple investigation of the comparative rates of flow of the four liquids. If the children do not have any ideas, talk to them about the possibility of finding out which liquid would run through a funnel most quickly and which most slowly. Show them the cut-off tops of the washing-up bottles and let them see how water will run through. Ask them how you could use your other washing-up bottle funnels to have a 'liquid race'. Discuss what you need to do. They will probably agree to set up the investigation as shown in this sketch.

The idea of putting in equal quantities may not emerge immediately but some children will undoubtedly see the need for this in order to make it a 'fair race'.

N.B. If the golden syrup is too slow, you can cheat a little by warming it up. You might like to show the children, in any case, how warm golden syrup flows more quickly than cold.

Activity Su4—Chocolate

Observing and investigating some properties of solids;
observing and investigating melting

You need:
a block of chocolate; margarine; cooking oil; a chocolate biscuit for each child; three glass pans; two transparent dishes; small polythene bags; a hot plate; paper kitchen towels; two or three wax candles.

Warning

This activity involves tasting.
You must emphasise to the children that we only taste things that we know are food. We never taste anything else. They must *never* taste anything in the classroom unless you tell them to do so. Make sure that this activity is carried out under hygienic conditions – wash hands, use a tablecloth, etc.

1 Offer each of the children a chocolate biscuit. Let them eat the biscuits and enjoy them. Encourage the children to discuss the taste, texture, sound of chewing, etc. When they have finished, draw their attention to their fingers. What has happened? What made the chocolate sticky?

2 Open the block of chocolate. Let the children break it into pieces and put the pieces into one of the pans. Ask the children if they think chocolate is a liquid. Why not? Can they remember what liquids do? Can they give you reasons why they do not think that chocolate is a liquid? Remind them if they have forgotten and again show them what water and washing-up liquid do.

Continue to explore the properties of chocolate. Can it be made into a liquid? Have any of the children ideas for how it could be done? How can they warm it? Let them suggest ways and, if possible, use their suggestions. Otherwise put the pan on a very low heat on the hot plate.

3 Ask the children to watch very carefully what happens. Which part starts to change first? How do they know it has changed? What does it do? Get the chocolate really runny and then tip the pan.

What does the chocolate do then? Very gently take the children through the following ideas. What has happened to it? What are its properties now? It has changed. It has changed from being solid to being liquid. The change is called melting. The change was caused by warming the chocolate.

$$\text{chocolate (solid)} \xrightarrow[\text{warm}]{} \text{chocolate (liquid)}$$

Is it still chocolate after it has melted? How do they know? Put the chocolate on one side to cool.

4 Repeat the sequence with margarine. Draw the children's attention to the change of colour as it melts. Put the margarine on one side to cool.

5 Put two or three candles in a polythene bag and put the bag into some very hot water so that the candles melt. Discuss with the children what is happening, as in the previous examples. When the wax is liquid take out the bag and show the children how, by squeezing the bag, the shape of the liquid always changes when the shape of the bag changes. Ask the children to watch the surface of the liquid very carefully. Can they describe what happens to the surface? (If they are very observant they will be able to tell you that the surface always stays flat and it always stays level.) You can crumple up the bag and then leave the wax to cool. You may like to repeat this sequence with

chocolate – children find it very interesting.

6 Get the chocolate and margarine which had been put on one side to cool. They should by this point have solidified. Ask the children what has happened. Ask them to describe the changes which have occurred. Encourage them to use words like solid, liquid, melting, cooling if they find these words useful in describing what they observe. Lead them towards understanding the sequence:

chocolate (liquid) ———→ chocolate (solid)
cool

Ask the children what is in each pan? Is it the stuff which you started with or is it different? How can they tell?

7 Put some cooking oil in a dish. Ask the children what it is. Is it a liquid or a solid? How do they know? Can they suggest a way of making it go solid? Can they think of:

liquid ———→ solid?
cool

Cooking oil will solidify if it is cooled in a refrigerator or a freezer.

Activity Su5—Eggs

Observing and investigating eggs;
observing an irreversible change

You need:
six hen's eggs of different colours and sizes in an egg box; a glass pan; two small plastic bags; a transparent dish; a plate; a knife; an egg timer; a clock with an easy to read minute hand.

Warning

This activity involves tasting.
You must emphasise to the children that we only taste things that we know are food. We never taste anything else. They must *never* taste anything in the classroom unless you tell them to do so. Make sure that this activity is carried out under hygienic conditions – wash hands, use a tablecloth, etc.

1 Show the children the box of eggs. Ask them what they think is in the box. Why do eggs come in this kind of box? Get the children to realise that eggs break very easily and they must be handled very carefully. Let the children remove the eggs from the box and place them in the centre of the table. Discuss similarities and differences – size, shape, colour, and surface texture.

2 Direct the children's attention to the shape of the eggs. Help them to notice that they are curved, have no corners, and are wider at one end than at the other. Do the children think that they will roll? Will they roll in a straight line? Can the children 'predict' how they will roll? (Do they remember what happened in 'Harvest' (*Teachers' Book A*) when they rolled a pear? How is a pear like an egg?) Let each child try gently rolling an egg. What happens? Were their predictions correct?

3 Let the children hold the eggs carefully. Is the shell solid or liquid? How do they know? Let one of the children crack an egg into a glass bowl or dish. What does the yolk look like? What shape is it? What colour is it? What colour is the other part of the egg? We call it the white. Is it white? Is it solid or liquid? Break the yolk. Can the children see the skin bag it was in? Is the yolk liquid or solid?

4 Do the children know how to cook a hard-boiled egg? Discuss this with them and explain that you are going to put the eggs into cold water and then heat up the water until it is boiling. Tell them that when the water is boiling you are going to use an egg-timer to make sure that

Exploring eggs

you cook the egg for long enough. Show them the egg-timer and let them see how it works.

Now let one of the children put some water into a glass pan and let another child put three or four eggs in their shells into the water. What do the eggs do? Do they sink or float? Do they stand on end or lie on their sides? Put the pan on the hot plate and let the children watch carefully what happens as the water is heated. They should notice the bubbles forming and rising; the eggs beginning to move; steam rising from the water. Remind the children that you are going to start the egg-timer when the water is boiling and that they must tell you when it is boiling. How will they know? What will they see? When the children tell you that the water is boiling, start the egg-timer. At the same time, point out to the children the position of the minute hand of the clock.

5 When the sand has run through the egg-timer, point to the clock again and say that, whilst the sand was running through, the egg cooked and the big hand of the clock moved that much. Put all except one of the eggs under the cold water tap to cool them and whilst you are doing this ask the children if they thought it took a long time or a short time to cook the eggs. What could *they* do in that much time? Suggest that later they might try to find out.

6 Take the hot egg and show it to the children. Has it changed in any way that they can see? Carefully peel it. Has the egg changed? Has it melted? (Having established that the egg is not liquid even when it is hot, you can use the cooled eggs and let the children pass them round and handle them.) Has the shell changed in any way that they can detect? Let the children crack the shells and peel the eggs. Do they notice the skin between the white and the shell? What has happened to the egg inside? Is it liquid or solid? Has it melted? How has it changed (colour, texture, liquid to solid)?

7 Cut the eggs up and let the children taste them. What does the white feel like in the mouth? What does the yolk feel like? Can they think of a way to make the egg go back to being liquid? Can they make it melt? Contrast this with the behaviour of chocolate and margarine.

8 You can let the children see the process of the white and the yolk hardening by separating an egg yolk from the white and putting these in separate plastic bags which are then sealed and placed in boiling water so that the changes can be observed.

Activity Su6—Dissolving

Investigating dissolving

You need:
granulated sugar; caster sugar; crystal coffee sugar; salt; four dishes; four jam-jars half-full of warm water; small labels; teaspoons; magnifying glass.

Warning

This activity involves tasting.
You must emphasise to the children that we only taste things that we know are food. We never taste anything else. They must *never* taste anything in the classroom unless you tell them to do so. Make sure that the activity is carried out under hygienic conditions – wash hands, use a tablecloth, etc.

1 Show the children the selection of substances in their original packets or containers. Start with the granulated sugar; pour some into a dish and label the dish 'granulated sugar'. Ask the children whether sugar is a solid or a liquid. Point out, unless they mention it, that you poured it out of its packet. Is it solids or liquids which can be poured? Discuss the various properties of the sugar and let the children look at it through a magnifying glass so that they can see the small particles of the sugar. Encourage them to appreciate that, though sugar is made up of very small *solid* bits, sugar can do some of the things that liquids do because the solid bits are so small.
2 Do the same thing with the other substances. How are they the same and how are they different? What about the crystal sugar?
3 Ask the children what we do with sugar. When someone suggests that we put it in tea, ask what happens to it. Why do we stir tea? Let the children discuss this and then tell them you will let them see what actually happens to the sugar. Half fill a jam-jar with warm water and ask one of the children to put a teaspoonful of sugar into the water. What does the sugar do? Does it sink or float? What happens when it is stirred? Can they still see all the sugar? Let the other children have a stir. Can they still see the sugar? What has happened to it? Where is the sugar? Has the water changed in any way? Does the water look different?
   Tell the children that because we know that we started off with water and we have only added sugar it is safe to taste it. Does the contents of the jar taste different from water? What does it taste of? Can they see the sugar? Where is it? Are they sure it is there?
4 Repeat the investigation with the other types of sugar and with the salt. Emphasise in each case that it is safe to taste because we are investigating things we *eat* and we know what is in the jars.
5 Discuss what has happened and draw their attention to the similarities of what has happened in each case. Introduce the word 'dissolve' as the word which describes the process which the children have been investigating.

Activity Su7—Plastic and glass

Sorting by material – plastic or glass;
sorting by rigidity or flexibility

You need:
a transparent plastic egg box; a clear plastic packet; a washing-up liquid container; a margarine carton and various plastic containers; some clear plastic bottles; clear glass bottles; two sorting circles, e.g. hoops.

1 Choose one of the containers and let the children examine it. What colour is it? What shape is it? What does it feel like? Is it hard or soft? Is it rigid or flexible? Can you see through it? What is the container made of?

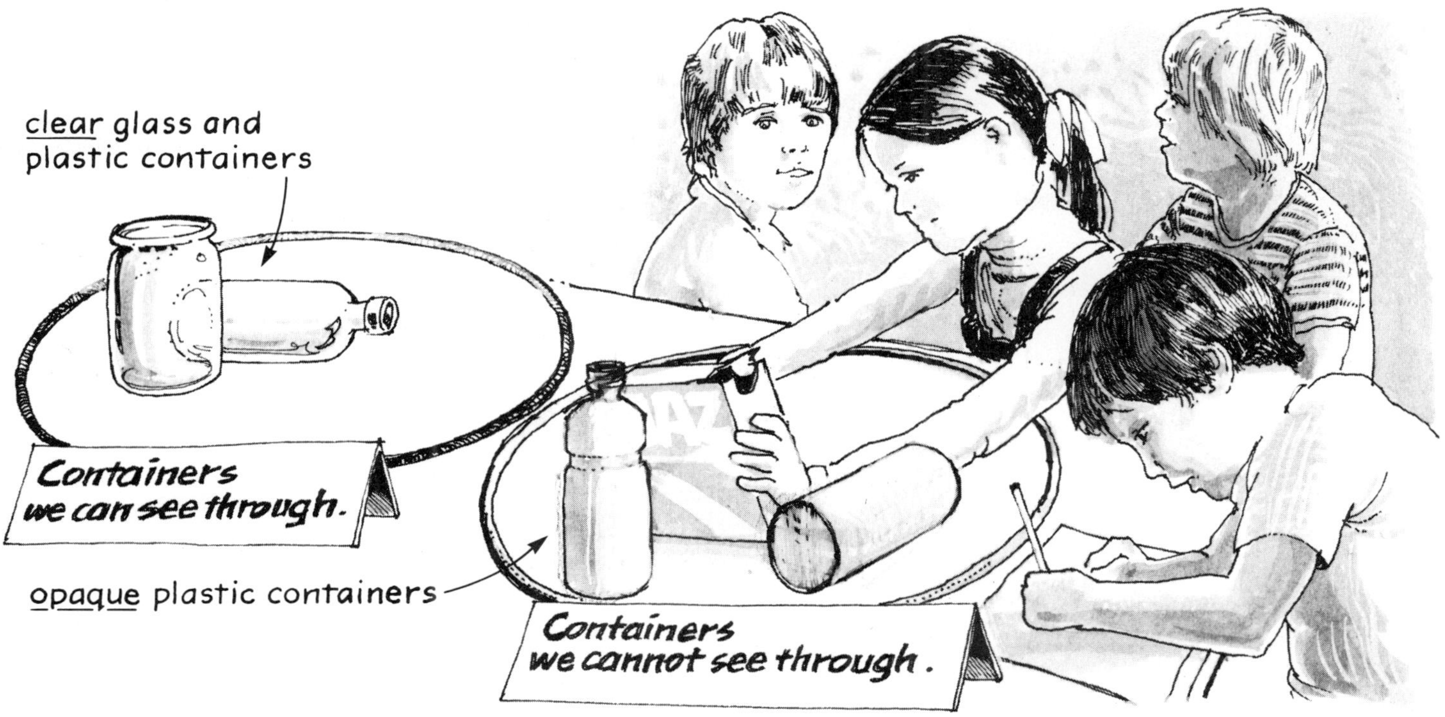

2 Put the sorting circles on the table and tell the children that one is for containers we can see through and the other is for containers we cannot see through. Ask the children where the first container should be placed and let them put it in the appropriate circle.
3 Get the children to examine and describe each container and then put it into the appropriate circle.
4 Take all the containers in the 'can see through' circle. Ask the children how they are the same and how they are different. Can they sort them into two sets, rigid and flexible? Do they know what the rigid ones are made from? Do they know what the flexible ones are made from? Is glass always rigid? Is plastic always flexible? Is 'see through' plastic always flexible? For which kind of container is glass most suitable and for which kind of container is plastic most suitable?
5 The children could investigate how to get water out of rigid and flexible containers. (We cannot get water out of glass containers by squeezing them.)

Making and doing activities

The problem for the child is
'Can you make a timer using sand or water?'

You need:
a sand egg-timer; fine dry sand; water; plastic containers; squeezy bottles sawn-off to make funnels; plastic bags; plasticine; aluminium foil; thread; scissors; meat skewers and darning needles may be requested and used with close supervision.

1 **The problem** — Can you make a timer using sand or water?
2 **Exploring the problem** — What do sand and water do? What property of sand does the egg-timer use? How can we make sand and water escape more slowly from a container? What can be used as a container? How can its outlet be restricted?
3 **Ideas for solving the problem** — Let the children examine the egg-timer and discover how it works. Let them explore and experiment with the materials which you have provided. What are the comparative advantages and disadvantages of sand and water? How can the flow be slowed down?

Water and sand timers

4 Making — The main problem will be how to produce a hole small enough to restrict the flow of sand or water. Holes in plasticine tend to clog with sand but may work for water. Holes in foil are more effective in this respect.

5 Evaluating — Can you use your device as a timer? What can you do whilst the sand or water is running out or in? For example, how many beads can you thread; how many peas can you pick up in the same time? What happens to the big hand on the clock whilst the sand or water is running out or in? By looking at each other's timers and the comparative times, the children may produce ideas about what makes the timer take a long or short time e.g. the size of hole, the amount of water or sand, etc.

Further activities

Some suggestions

1 Look at the lids of containers. How do they work? Do they screw, clip, hinge, or push in? What kind of opening is there? – is it big, small or are there several holes? Why? How do the contents come out – do the children use a spoon, pour or squirt? Make a collection of containers and sort them in various ways.

2 Melt some wax crayons in dishes on the radiator. Let the children paint with the liquid wax on kitchen paper. What happens to the wax – does it stay liquid?

The pictures have a translucent effect if mounted on the window.

3 Continue the investigation of plastic containers. How thick is the plastic? Can it be cut? Can it be torn? Can it be stretched?

4 Invite your local supermarket manager to tell the children how he or she decides on the arrangement of the items on a shelf in the shop. (What is the basis for sorting?)

5 Play a progressive memory game:

First child: I went to the supermarket and bought a cake.

Second child: I went to the supermarket and bought a cake and some soup.

Third child: I went to the supermarket and bought a cake, some soup and six eggs.
and so on.

6 Choose an item, e.g. butter, canned peas, bread etc., and discuss how it probably reached the supermarket shelves.

Language → Pets

Mathematics → Pets

Physical education → Pets

Creative arts → Pets

Science

People and their jobs and occupations

Starter Book page 12

Science activities

Making and doing

Teachers' Book page 30

Further activities

Teachers' Book page 30

Introduction

Science activities

This topic introduces the observation of a number of different creatures and the first very simple investigations of animal behaviour. It is suggested that the children try to find out what the animals like to eat – and no more than that is intended at this stage.

By studying a number of creatures in a sequence, the children are able to compare them more easily and to appreciate that, in spite of very obvious differences,there are many points of similarity. Encourage the children to talk amongst themselves and guide their discussion by pointed comment or question. They will recall differences and similarities more readily if, in answer to your questions, they 'discover' these features for themselves.

You will find notes about keeping animals and a list of resources in the section starting on page 147. It is essential that the children wash their hands after handling the small creatures.

Making and doing activities

The problem for the child is:

'Can you make a fan that looks like the fin of a goldfish?'

This will require careful observation of the action of the fin and an investigation of materials and constructions which will produce a similar effect.

Pets Science activities

Activity P1 — Fish tank

Investigating pouring water

You need:
an empty fish tank; aquarium gravel; clear plastic containers; jugs to hold water; water weed; one or more goldfish.

1 Produce the empty fish tank and tell the children that this is the tank which you are going to get ready for the goldfish. Ask them what they think needs to go into the tank. Establish that you will need water, gravel and weed. Ask the children whether they think that you should put the water or the gravel into the tank first. Suggest that it might be a good idea to find out before you start to fill the big tank.
2 Divide the children into groups of four or five and give each group a transparent plastic container, a jug of water and some gravel. Tell them that they must decide whether to put the gravel in first or the water in first. Let them try and observe what happens. Can they get an even layer of gravel on the bottom? What happens to the water? What does the water do to the gravel? Can they think of a way of stopping the water hitting the gravel so hard? The children may try holding the jug higher or lower. Why does this make a difference? They may try pouring more gently. You will probably need to pour the water off the gravel so that they can try out new ideas.
3 If the children do not think of it, suggest that they try putting something under the stream of water to stop it hitting the gravel so hard. They could try a variety of objects – a plastic saucer works very well. Once the groups have found something which they think works well, ask them to all come together for discussion.
4 Let the children discuss what they found out and tell each other about their solutions. Choose one of the solutions and let the children who discovered it fill the fish tank.

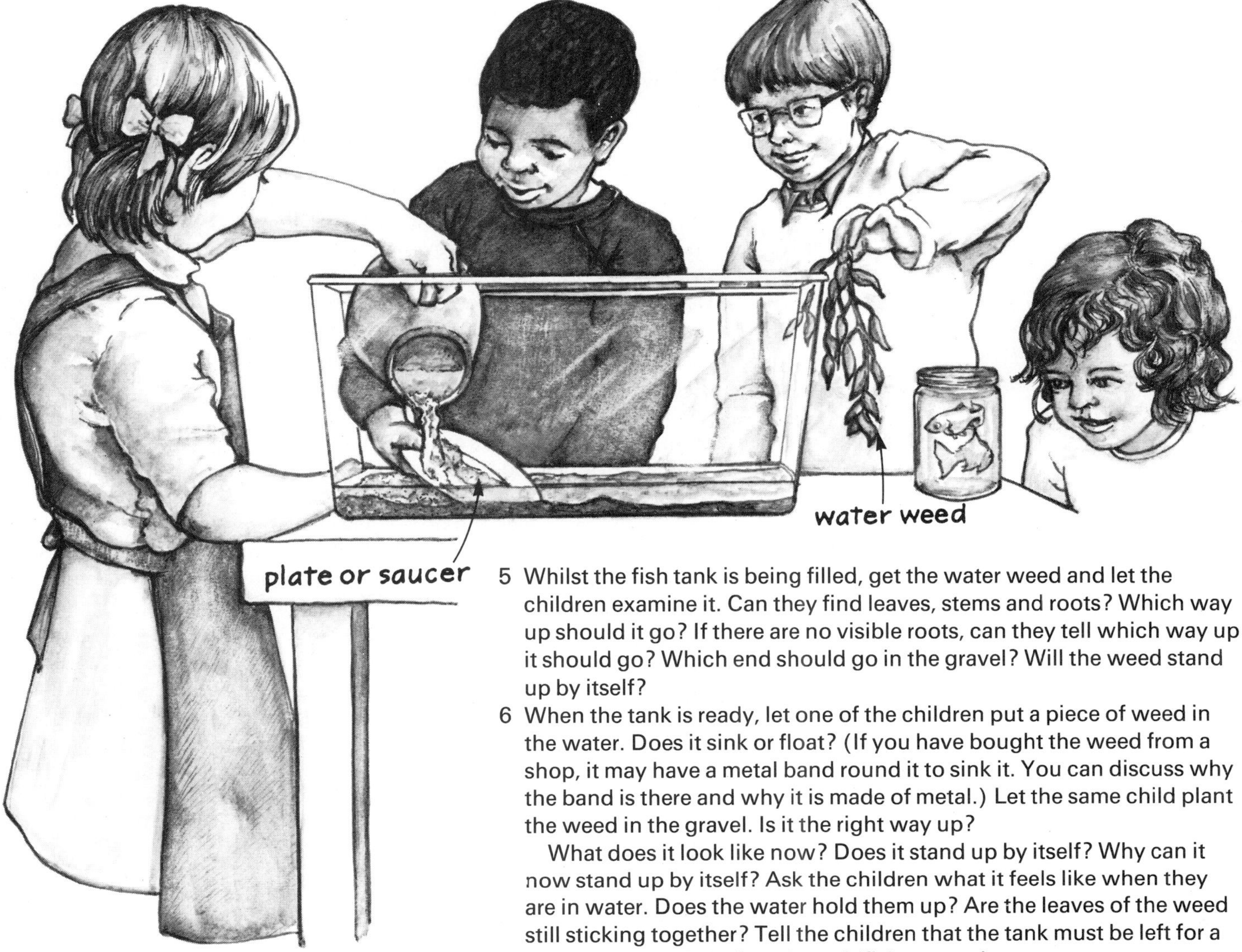

5 Whilst the fish tank is being filled, get the water weed and let the children examine it. Can they find leaves, stems and roots? Which way up should it go? If there are no visible roots, can they tell which way up it should go? Which end should go in the gravel? Will the weed stand up by itself?

6 When the tank is ready, let one of the children put a piece of weed in the water. Does it sink or float? (If you have bought the weed from a shop, it may have a metal band round it to sink it. You can discuss why the band is there and why it is made of metal.) Let the same child plant the weed in the gravel. Is it the right way up?

What does it look like now? Does it stand up by itself? Why can it now stand up by itself? Ask the children what it feels like when they are in water. Does the water hold them up? Are the leaves of the weed still sticking together? Tell the children that the tank must be left for a little time to settle before the goldfish are put in.

Activity P2—Fish scales

Observing goldfish; investigating fish scales

You need:
the goldfish; the tank prepared in Activity 1; a spare tank of water; two fish shapes for each child; glue; spatulas; 'scales' cut from foil; two prepared fish-shapes – one with its scales overlapping from head to tail and the other with the scales overlapping in the opposite direction (see sketch); skewers for holding the model fish.

Fish shapes

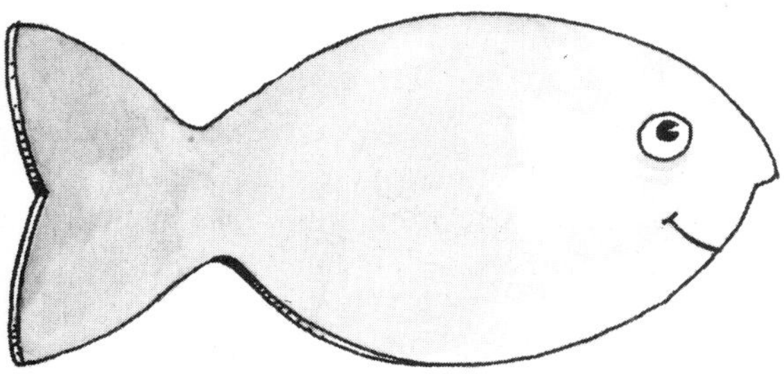

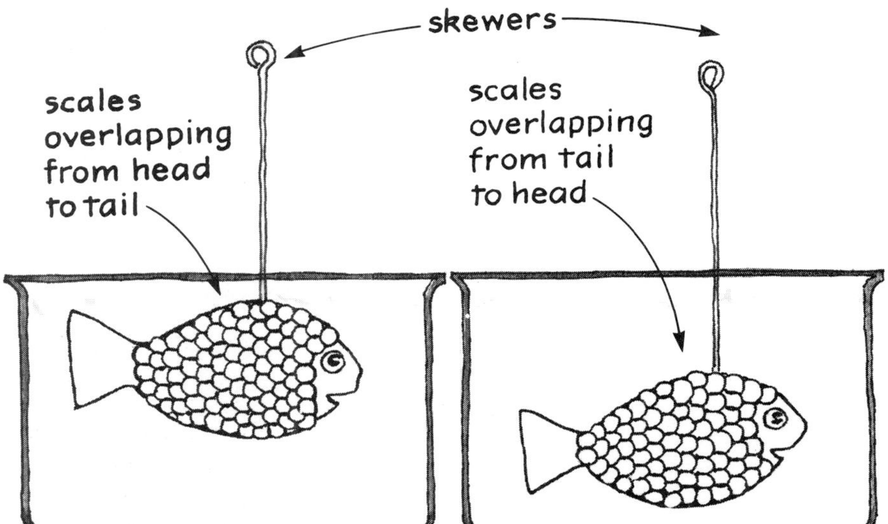

1 Put the goldfish into the tank. Let the children watch them. Where do they go? Can they move forwards, backwards, up and down? What colour are they? Are they the same colour all over? What colour are their eyes? What shape are their bodies? Are they long, wide, tall? Do they have straight lines? Do they have corners? Why do the children think they are this shape? Is it a useful shape for fish?

2 Now draw the children's attention to the fins. How many fins are there? Where are the fins (top, bottom, underneath, sides, left, right etc.)? What does a fin look like? Can the children see the ribs of the fin? What does a fin do? How does it move? Does it go from side to side, backwards and forwards or up and down? Can it open and shut? Does it make them think of anything else? (A fan?)

3 Now ask the children what is covering the body of the fish. Are the scales placed separately or do they overlap? (You may need to demonstrate what you mean with two of the foil scales.) Now give each child a fish-shaped card with a mouth and an eye marked. Give them some round scales cut from foil, some glue and a spatula and show them what you want them to do. Let the children decide whether to start at the head end or the tail end, but make sure that they do overlap the foil scales and do not just stick them side by side.

4 Ask the children to compare their fish with the goldfish. Are the scales going the same way? Does it matter which way they go? Give the children the two fish you have made. Which one has its scales going the same way as the scales on a real fish? What happens when you move it forwards in the water? Let one child hold the skewer and move the fish round in the water. Let the children try with the other fish. What happens to the scales? What makes them do that?

5 Give each child another fish shape, glue and foil scales. Ask if they started at the head or the tail last time. Do they know which end to start to make the scales overlap the same way as on a real fish?

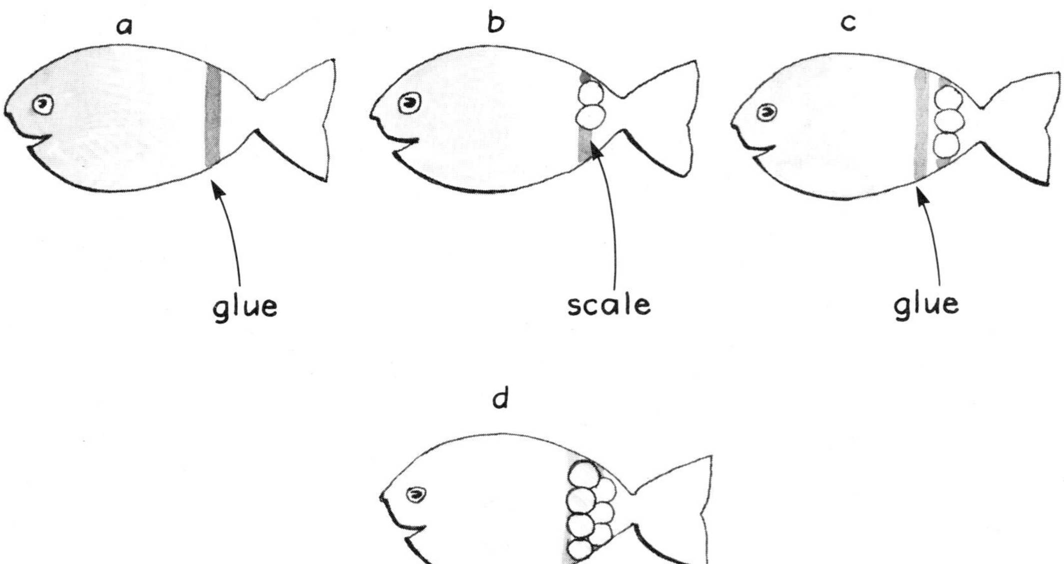

Putting fish scales on shapes

Activity P3—Budgerigar

Observing a budgerigar; investigating what it likes to eat

Note

Before embarking on activities which use budgerigars you should check whether your local authority has any specific guidelines about keeping budgerigars in school.

You need:
budgerigars in a large cage with a selection of toys (ladder, bell on a chain, ball with a bell inside); mixed bird seed; a small saucer; bits of

chickweed; groundsel; lettuce; dandelion; seed compost; yoghurt cartons (for seed planting).

1 Ask the children to observe a budgerigar carefully. What colour is it? What patterns can they see? What covers its body? Are the feathers all the same? What differences can they see? Where can they see a long feather? Where can they see a short feather? Which way do the feathers point? Do they overlap? Do they point towards the head or the tail?
2 Which body parts has it got? What can the children see on its head? What is on its head that isn't on the children's heads? What have the children got that it hasn't? Look at its feet. How many toes has it? Do they point forwards or backwards? How can it move? Can it walk, hop, run, climb, fly? Which parts of its body does it use to climb? Can the children use their feet like that?
3 Can they see its ears? Do they think it has any? Why do they think that? (The children may notice that it reacts to noises, copies noises and seems to like toys that make a noise.)

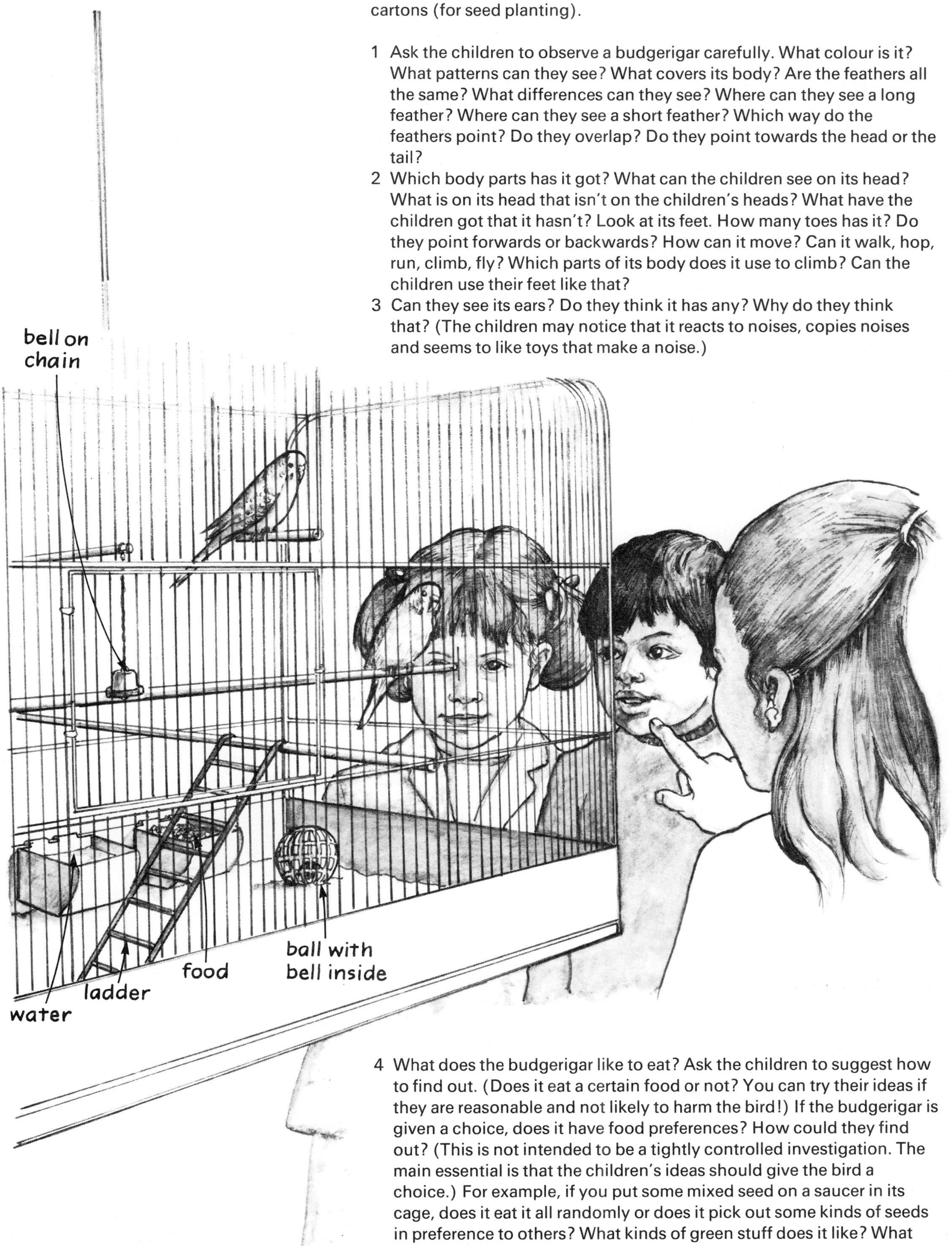

4 What does the budgerigar like to eat? Ask the children to suggest how to find out. (Does it eat a certain food or not? You can try their ideas if they are reasonable and not likely to harm the bird!) If the budgerigar is given a choice, does it have food preferences? How could they find out? (This is not intended to be a tightly controlled investigation. The main essential is that the children's ideas should give the bird a choice.) For example, if you put some mixed seed on a saucer in its cage, does it eat it all randomly or does it pick out some kinds of seeds in preference to others? What kinds of green stuff does it like? What kind(s) does it prefer? (Try chickweed, groundsel, lettuce, dandelion leaves.)
5 What is bird seed? Why is it called that? If it is a mixture of 'seeds' what would you expect them to do? Let the children plant some to see what happens.

Activity P4—Bird toys

Sorting toys by function
Before using this activity, you should read the note in Activity 3. page 24.

You need:
budgerigars in a large cage with the toys listed in Activity 3; also a mirror, swing, weighted rocking toy; an additional set of 'budgie' toys; three sorting circles; a selection of toys in the classroom which swing, rock or roll.

1 What do the budgerigars like to do? Let the children notice how they play with the toys in the cage.
2 Produce your collection of budgie toys and let the children examine them and talk about them. Ask the children how the budgerigars would play with them. What would they do with them? What are the toys made of? Which of them would make a noise?
3 When all the toys have been examined, ask the children to make a set of toys that would move when the budgerigars played with them and a set of toys that would not move. This is quite difficult and the children may need considerable discussion and trials before they can decide on which set to put the toys in.
4 Once the two sets are sorted, put the toys that do not move on one side and look with the children at the toys that move. Pick up the bell by the chain and swing to and fro. Ask the children how it moves. Swing it so that it swings backwards or forwards for them or from side to side. Put it in a sorting circle labelled 'These toys swing.' Can the children see another toy that moves in the same way? Let them put it in the same sorting circle.
5 Now roll the ball along. How does it move? What should the set to contain the ball be labelled as?
6 Look at the weighted plastic toy. Tap it so that it rocks. Get the children to describe its movement and label the set 'These toys rock.'
7 Let the children add to these sets by finding toys in the classroom or at home which swing, roll or rock.

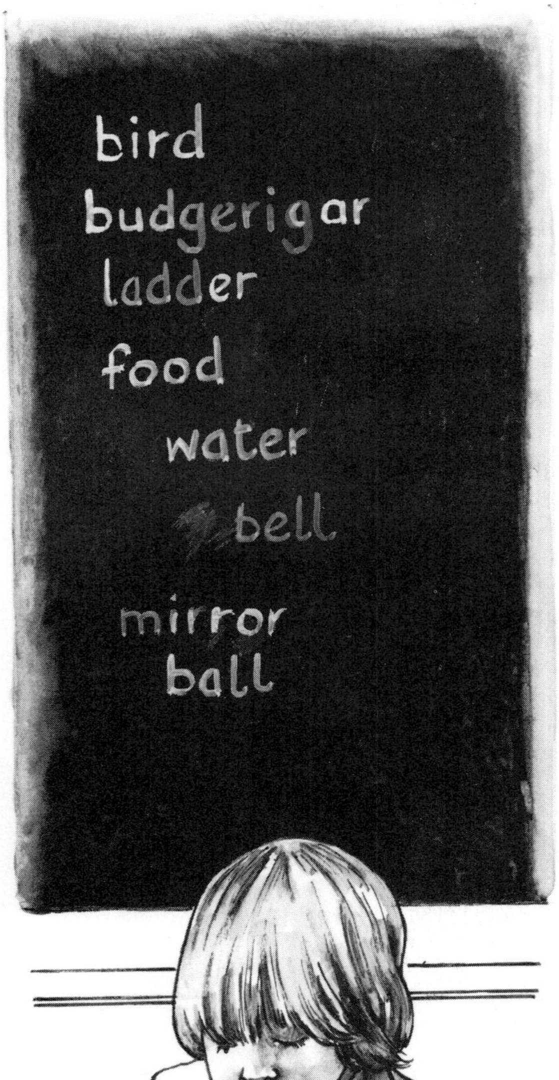

Which would move?

Activity P5—Tapping noises

Investigating the noises made by wood and metal
Before using this activity, you should read the note in Activity 3, page 24.

You need:
budgerigars in a large cage with mirror and bell; a selection of small plates made from the following materials – different metals, paper, plastic, glass, pottery, wood; a wooden spoon for each child; a selection of tuned wood and metal percussion instruments.

1 Get the children to listen when the budgerigars tap their mirror and when they tap their bell. (You may have to do this yourself so that the children can listen.) Do the mirror and bell sound the same? Look at the bell with the children. What hangs inside? What does it do when the bell swings? Do they know anything else that is made from the same material as the bell? What is it made of? (These questions are leading towards the idea that the sound indicates the material is a metal.)
2 Show the children a small metal plate. Ask the children to describe what it looks like. Encourage them to notice the properties which make it recognisable as metal. Ask the children if they know what it is made from? How do they know? Put it down on a hard surface and let one of the children tap it with a wooden spoon. Will it make a different sound if it is placed on other surfaces? Let the children try putting it on different surfaces. Ask them whether it is a hard or a soft surface. Does the surface make any difference to the sound made when the plate is tapped or does it sound the same? Can they tell you how it sounds different?

3 Now ask one of the children to pick up the plate and hold it by its edge with finger and thumb and let it hang down. What sound does it make when it is tapped? Which sound do the children like best?
4 Let each child choose a plate from the selection. Ask them to tap the plates when they are on different surfaces and held in different ways. When you think the children are ready, bring them all together again. Ask each child to tap his/her plate for the others to hear and then to tell the others what the plate is made of. Play a game – tap a plate where it cannot be seen by the children and ask them to tell you what it sounds like and what they think it is made of.

5 Now look at the selection of percussion instruments. Let the children look at the instruments and enjoy the sounds which they make. Encourage the children to talk about the kinds of sounds the instruments make. Draw their attention to the kind of material from which the instrument is made and encourage them to connect sound with material. Reinforce their experience and understanding of the differing sounds made by wood and metal. They should begin to make comments like, "It sounds like metal."
6 Choose a long and a short chime bar and let a child strike each in turn. Can the children tell you which gives a high note and which gives a low note? Get them to stretch up high when they hear a high note and curl up small when they hear a low note.
7 Do the same thing using the high and low notes on a wooden xylophone. If you have large and small triangles and cymbals you could try these. You may also be able to let the children hear steel drums and other percussion instruments which can be borrowed or which parents might play for the children.
8 Sing songs with the children and let them join in using the percussion instruments or plates.

Activity P6—Animal

Observing a small animal; investigating how small a space it can squeeze through

You need:
a small animal (mammal) – mouse, hamster or gerbil in its cage; a bucket balance; various drinks – milk, water, orange juice; various foods – meat, lettuce, cereals; a cardboard grocery box cut vertically down at the sides so that a card divider can be slid down to alter the size of the gap at the bottom.

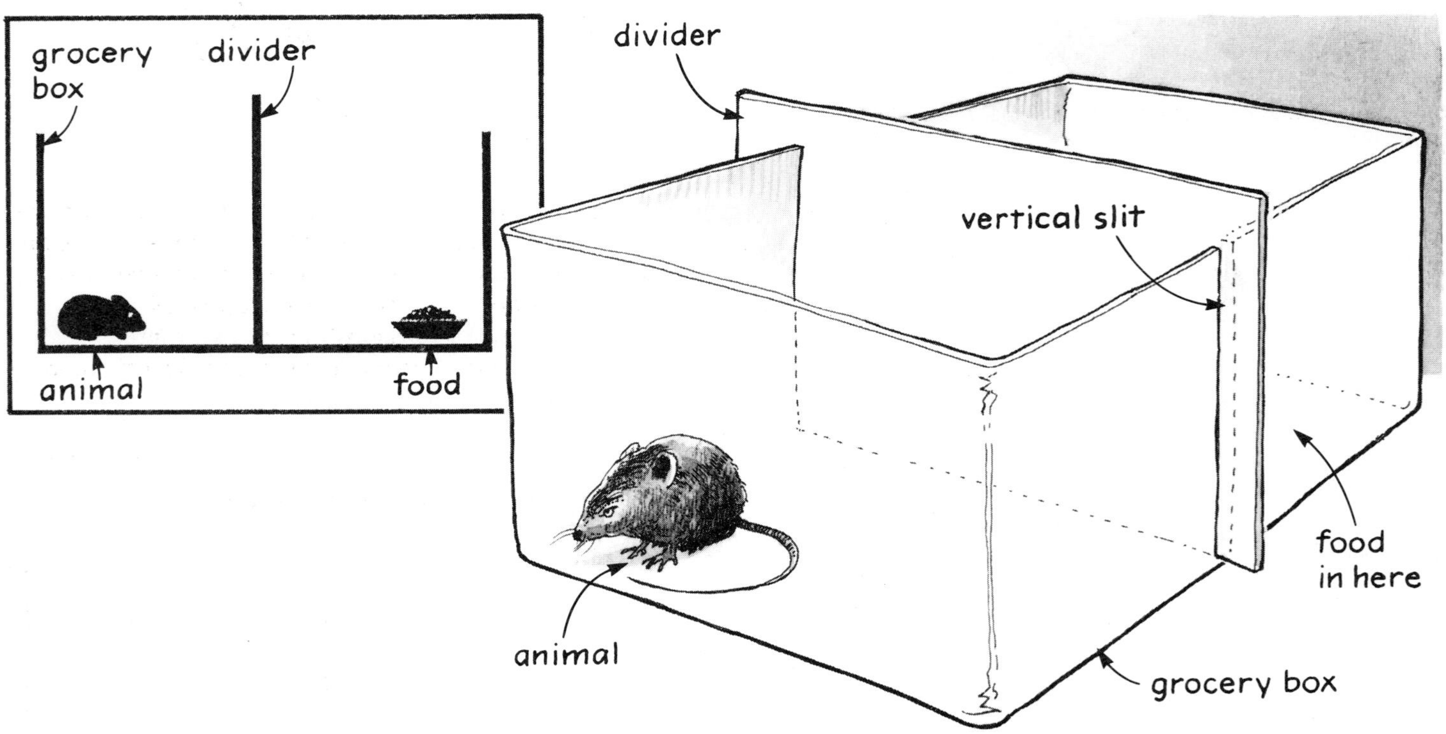

1 Let the children observe the animal in its cage. What does it do? Does it move slowly or quickly? What does it look like? Name its body parts with the children, paying particular attention to its head and feet. What covers the animal's body? Does the fur go straight up or does it lie in a particular direction? Which direction? Why do the children think it grows that way? Does it have a tail? How long is its tail? Is it longer than or shorter than the rest of its body? Whilst you are discussing the animal, ask the children questions causing them to compare the animal with the fish and the bird.

2 How heavy is the animal? Can the children find anything they think would weigh the same? Let them put the animal carefully and briefly in one bucket of the bucket balance and try the things that they have found in the other. Get the children to put them into sets, 'Things lighter than the animal', 'Things heavier than the animal' and 'Things which weigh the same as the animal'.

3 What does the animal like to eat and drink? You can let the children make suggestions and try giving the animal any of the foods which the children suggest which seem harmless.

4 Why are the bars of the cage so close together? How small a space could the animal squeeze through? Show the children the grocery box and divider and demonstrate how it works. Ask the children how you could use the divider to make different sizes of gaps. Suggest that the children find some things to rest the divider on so that it is held at various heights.

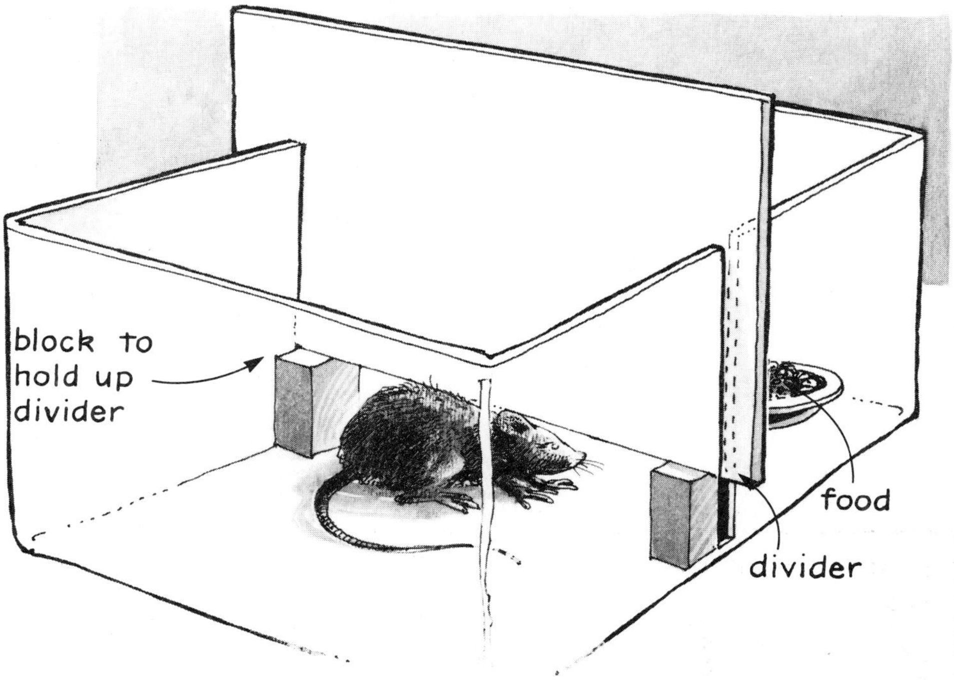

How small a space can the animal squeeze through?

Ask the children to put the blocks in order so that you can start with the gap quite large and then make it smaller and smaller. Put the divider on the highest blocks and put a little of the food which the animal 'likes' in one end of the box. Put the animal in the other end and watch what happens. Repeat this with the divider slightly lower and keep decreasing the gap until the animal cannot get through. The children can record the results like this:

5 You could use the box again with dividers of different heights pushed to the bottom to find out how high a wall the animal can climb.

6 In a P.E. lesson let the children find out how small a gap they can squeeze through using a cane and blocks.

Making and doing activities

The problem for the child is:
'Can you make a fan that looks like the fin of a goldfish?'

You need:
paper of different weights including tissue paper; different weights of plastic sheet (bags); plasticine; straws; fine canes; scissors; glue; fish pictures showing fins; any fans which you can collect.

Making fans that look like goldfish fins

1 The problem	Can you make a fan that looks like the fin of a goldfish?
2 Exploring the problem	What does a goldfish fin look like? What does it do? How does it move? What does a fan look like? How can a fan be made? How does it move?
3 Ideas for solving the problem	Could we make it just from paper? What would it look like? What can we use to make stiff ribs and for the flexible stuff in between? What can we use to hold it together?
4 Making	There will probably be a wide variety of solutions to various facets of this problem.
5 Evaluating	Does it work like a fish fin? Will it move like a fish fin? What can a fish fin do that your fan cannot do? You could have an exhibition of your pictures of fins, the collection of fans and the fans which the children have made.

Further activities

Some suggestions

1 Kittens can be observed in school. Make toys for the kittens, for example, a large button or screwed-up newspaper on a string. Does the kitten like them when the toys are still? Does it like them when they move? Why? What does the kitten do when it follows the toy? What things would it pounce on if it was outside?

Note

Check that your local authority does not have restrictions about bringing pet animals into school. Make sure that the children wash their hands after playing with the animal.

2 Let the children find out about the sizes and colours of the different animals studied. Also ask them to find out about caring for the animals. Make sure there are suitable books and pictures for the children to study.

3 Over a period of time, let the children weigh the food given to their pet and find out how much it eats in a day/week.

4 Invite someone to come to school to talk about caring for pets. The RSPCA might be able to help or a local pet-shop owner or boarding-kennel proprietor.

5 Ask the children to use the school and public library to find out the names of baby animals; what they can do when they are born; how they feed, etc.

6 Ask the children to make up a story about an unusual pet.

Language → | ← Physical education

Mathematics → | ← Creative arts

Science

People and their jobs and occupations

Starter Book page 14

Science activities

Making and doing

Teachers' Book page 38

Further activities

Teachers' Book page 39

Introduction

Science activities

The sweet shop topic gives an opportunity to let the children observe and investigate coloured light. We are concerned with simple direct observations but the use of transparent coloured sweet papers as light filters opens up a range of possibilities. The children can produce spots of coloured light and observe these and they can then investigate what happens when the colours are mixed and filters superimposed, giving a wide variety of results. It does not matter at all if you do not know what is supposed to happen, just join the children in finding out what does happen. Mixing coloured light does not give the same result as mixing the same colours of paints, so do not be surprised by this or think something has gone wrong.

Weighing sweets gives the children experience in estimating the relative weights of different kinds of sweets, although their estimates may be no closer than deciding whether one is heavier or lighter than the other, or a lot heavier or a lot lighter. This activity illustrates an approach to adopt on all suitable occasions i.e. to encourage the children to make a sensible 'guess'. Their guesses will slowly get better and eventually become real 'estimates'.

Making and doing activities

The problem for the child is:

'Can you make an icing sugar sprinkler?'

The main problem here is to produce holes of the right size and to discover that powdered sugar can be difficult to pass through holes which appear to be big enough.

The sweet shop Science activities

Activity Sw1—Sweets

Observing coloured light

You need:
sweets of various colours; some colourless sweets (do not include multicoloured sweets); sweet wrappers of various colours – some dull, some shiny, some see-through; four coloured shapes (red, yellow, blue and white) – so that the children can look at the colour through a coloured filter; six paper plates; three masks (red, yellow and blue cellophane); cling film; a large sheet of white kitchen paper; a collection of coloured see-through objects, prepared if necessary by wrapping coloured cellophane around colourless see-through objects – jelly cubes can be used as they are, melted to produce other shapes, or put into colourless transparent containers.

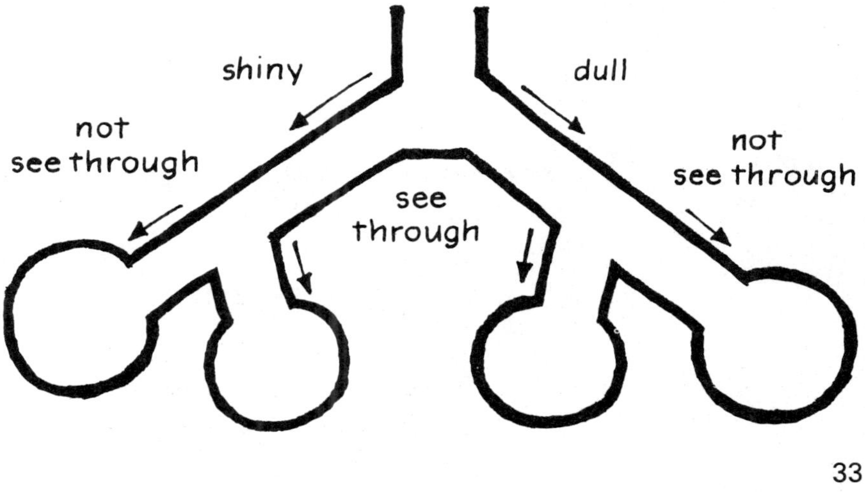

Sorting tree

Note
Read through the activity and check that your collection of sweets is suitable. You may need to wrap some in cling film to avoid stickiness. You may also decide to change the wrappings to give you the necessary variety. Useful sweets include chewy mints, glacier mints, clear fruit drops, fruit gums, or fruit chews depending on local availability.

1 Get the children to wash their hands. Spread the sweets on a large sheet of white kitchen paper and ask the children to talk about the colours. Give them the paper plates and ask them to sort the sweets on to the plates according to colour. (In the interests of hygiene, you might like to cover the sweets with cling film before the children begin sorting.)
2 Once the sweets are sorted, direct the children's attention to the range of colours within each group. How many different shades of red are there? Are there some sweets which are difficult to assign to a particular colour group? Where will they put them? What can the children tell you about the colourless sweets? Now look at the differences connected with light. Are any sweets shiny? Are any dull? Let the children hold the sweets up to the light. Do some of the sweets let the light pass through them? Can the children hold a sweet so that it produces a coloured light patch on a piece of white paper?
3 Now ask each child to cover one eye and look through the sweet with the other eye. Can the children see objects properly or can they just see lighter and darker areas? (By this stage some of the well-handled sweets can be disposed of and the children can wash their hands.)
4 Now produce your collection of sweet wrappers. Get the children to tell you about the colours and the patterns. Ask the children to sort the wrappers – shiny/dull, see-through/not see-through. Give them the sorting tree to help them. Talk to them about it before they start to use it. Ask them what the papers in each end-circle will look like. For example, point to one end circle and ask, 'Will these be dull or shiny?' 'How do you know?' etc. When the children have finished, you can ask them which set has the most papers (members) and which has the least. Reinforce the use of 'more than' and 'less than' – you may find that you have an empty set.

5 Let each child choose a coloured see-through paper. Can the children use these to produce a coloured patch of light on the white paper as they did with the coloured sweets? When seen through the coloured paper, can objects be discerned clearly or are just lighter and darker areas visible? What colour do things look?
6 Put the four coloured shapes on the table. Give the children the masks and let them look at the shapes. Which one(s) look a different colour through every colour of mask? What colour does each of the shapes look through the different colours of masks?
7 The children can 'find' other coloured objects that let light through if you 'stage manage' the placing of the other examples which you have collected or prepared. Whenever possible, encourage the children to find out what happens when the light passes through objects of more than one colour.

Activity Sw2—Fruit gums

Observing sweets dissolving

You need:
a packet of fruit pastilles; a packet of fruit gums; a selection of sweets including hard toffee, fudge, boiled sweets, hard mints; clear glass tumblers or jam jars; a teaspoon; hot water.

1 Look at the fruit pastilles with the children. Can they tell you what flavours they are? How do they know? Can they tell the flavours by taste alone? Ask the children to close their eyes and pop a fruit pastille into each of their mouths. Can they tell the flavour just by the taste? Were they right? What does a fruit pastille feel like in the mouth? Is it hard/soft, rough/smooth? If they just suck and don't chew, how does the sweet change?
2 Offer the children a selection of sweets including hard toffees, fudge, boiled sweets and hard mints. Let each of them take a sweet and suck it and say how it feels – hard/soft, rough/smooth. What does it taste like? What is happening to it? Is it getting softer/harder, rougher/smoother, larger/smaller? Is its taste altering or staying the same? (This is the last of the sweet-tasting activities. Talk to the children about the need to remove the stickiness from their teeth and show them how to use a drink of water to rinse their teeth.)
3 Ask the children to tell you what the insides of their mouths feel like. Are they wet/dry, warm/cold, soft/hard? Which parts are hard? Which parts are soft?
4 Get the tumblers or jam-jars and the fruit gums or clear boiled sweets. Let a child put a sweet into one of them. What did the sweet feel like? Was it hard/soft? Was it sticky? Now pour hot water over the sweet. Let one of the children stir the water gently to imitate the movement of the sweet when it is being sucked. What happens to the sweet? (It will become extremely sticky. After some time, sticky strands can be drawn from the sweet. These will harden as they cool.)

Activity Sw3—Weighing

Ordering sweets by weight

You need:
sets of balance scales; small packet of chocolate buttons or similar; five types of sweet (each type of a different weight e.g. small Mars bar, fruit drops, fruit chews, Smarties, jelly tots etc. (there should be enough of each type to balance the small packet of chocolate buttons or similar); small paper or plastic bags; card arrows; labels with 'is heavier than'.

1 Give the children the sets of balance scales and five types of sweet of different weights. Ask the children to put the sweets in order of weight, starting with the heaviest. If they are not sure how to do this, suggest that they choose the one that they think is heaviest and try to balance

each of the others against it in turn. If they find another which is heavier they must start again with that one. Once they have found the heaviest, they can repeat the process with the four which are left and then with the remaining three until they have ordered the five sweets. Give them the set of arrows and labels with 'is heavier than' and ask them to put these in place between the sweets.

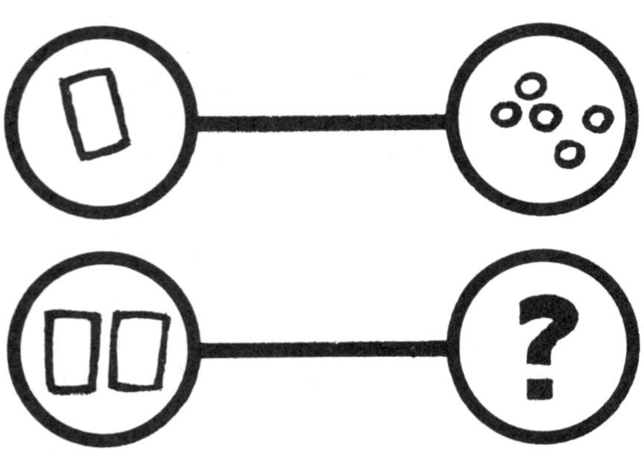

Balancing sweets

2 Now ask the children to put the heaviest sweet on one pan and find how many of the lightest sweets are needed to balance it. Emphasise that if they balance we say they weigh the same. The children can record their findings by drawing diagrams.
What do the children think would happen if they put two of the heaviest sweets on one pan? How many of the lightest sweets do they think would weigh the same? Can they find out if they were right?

3 Remind the children how many of the lightest sweets balanced one of the heaviest. Now put one of the heaviest sweets on the pan and select a sweet of intermediate weight. Can the children estimate (guess) how many of these will balance the heaviest sweet? Do they think that it will be more or less than the number of the lightest sweets? Let them find out and record what they have found. How many of these sweets will balance two of the heaviest sweets? Ask the children to guess first and then test their guess by using the balance.

4 Give the children the small bags and the small packet of chocolate buttons or similar. Ask them to make packets of each of the five sweets which they have been using which will weigh the same as the packet of chocolate buttons. You may need to help them with the first one by asking leading questions. Once they have made up their five bags of sweets ask them which is the heaviest. Can they tell you that they all weigh the same? Let them check this using the balance. Which sweets do they get most of in a bag? Which sweets do they get fewest of in a bag?

5 You can continue to develop these ideas if you have a classroom sweet shop stocked with 'sweets' made from play dough, papier mâché and small standard objects e.g. Lego blocks wrapped to represent sweets.

Activity Sw4—Sweet-making

Observing eggs; investigating whether colour affects taste

Note
This activity involves making marzipan. Other sweets which do not require cooking might be used for part of the activity e.g. coconut ice, fondant, etc.

You need:
for marzipan: the same weight of icing sugar and ground almonds (250g); one egg; four bowls (at least two of them identical – clear glass); a fork; a set of balance scales; a tablespoon; a few small rolling pins; a set of culinary colourings; absorbent kitchen paper and a clean work surface or pastry board for each child.

Warning

This activity involves tasting.
You must emphasise to the children that we only taste things that we know are food. We never taste anything else. They must never taste anything in the classroom unless you tell them to do so. Make sure that the activity is carried out under hygienic conditions – wash hands, use a tablecloth, etc.

1 Ask the children to wash their hands. Tell them that you are going to make marzipan and that you need equal weights of ground almonds and icing sugar. Give them the balance scales and the packet of ground almonds. Suggest that they put a clean piece of paper on each of the balance pans. Ask them how they can make sure that the two weights are the same. Once they have the ground almonds on one pan suggest that they use a spoon to put the icing sugar on the other pan until a balance is achieved.
   Put the ground almonds into one of the bowls and the icing sugar into another (not the paired glass bowls). Discuss with the children the differences between the two ingredients. Do they both leave a mark on the absorbent paper? Where have the children previously seen a mark like that produced by the ground almonds? (Fats/cooking oil) How do the icing sugar and the ground almonds pour into the bowls? Let the children rub a little of each between their fingers and then taste them. How do they feel different? How do they taste different?
2 Now let one of the children crack an egg into one of the clear glass bowls. What does it look like? Which is the yolk? Which is the white? Is it really white? Now give a child the fork to lightly beat the egg. What happens to the yolk? Does the yolk mix easily with the white? Can the children see any separate bits? Is the mixture all the same colour? Ask the children to put half the mixture into the other identical glass bowl. How can they tell whether they have half in each bowl?
3 Ask a child to add a tablespoonful of icing sugar to one of the bowls of egg and stir it gently with the fork. Does the icing sugar mix easily with the egg? Is the mixture all the same colour? Now ask another child to add a tablespoonful of ground almonds to the other bowl of egg and stir it gently. What happens? Does it do the same thing as the icing sugar? Now let the children add the icing sugar, a spoonful at a time, to the first bowl; counting the spoonfuls as they do so. A smooth yellow mixture will be produced when about half the sugar has been added. Ask the children what has happened. What does it look like? What does it feel like to stir? What has changed? Add the same number of spoonfuls of ground almonds to the other bowl and stir. Let the children compare the two mixtures – particularly colour and consistency.
4 Add the egg and almond mixture to the egg and sugar mixture and stir. Then let the children add the rest of the sugar and almonds. What happens? Is it easy to stir? Will it all mix in properly? (If the mixture is too crumbly you can add a few drops of water.)

5 Divide the marzipan into portions and use the colourings to colour the portions. The children can make their sweets of different colours either by rolling the marzipan into shapes on a board dusted with icing sugar or by rolling and cutting out shapes.
6 Can the children set up an investigation to find out if the colour affects the taste? (Children are given a small piece of marzipan of each colour to taste first and then given a small unseen piece of one of the colours. Can they tell its colour from its taste? Are there any colours which the children can identify? Do any of the colours taste different? (Are any 'right' guesses based on real differences in taste or are they just 'right' by chance?)

Making and doing activities

The problem for the child is:
'Can you make an icing sugar sprinkler?'

You need:
yoghurt cartons; 10 cm squares of various kinds of paper, foil, plastic, net curtain etc.; rubber bands of various sizes; scissors; a collection of sprinklers (pepper pots, sugar sprinklers, flour sifters, herb pots etc. as examples); access to a skewer or similar for making holes.

1 The problem	Can you make an icing sugar sprinkler?
2 Exploring the problem:	What must an icing sugar sprinkler do? What do people use them for? (You may have to demonstrate this. They may remember seeing you make patterns on the top of a cake by sprinkling sugar over a doily.) What is icing sugar like? How easily does it get through holes etc.?

3 Ideas for solving the problem:	It would be useful with this problem to let the children see some solutions. Show them the various sprinklers you have collected. Encourage the children to talk about the size of the holes in relation to the amount of sugar wanted and the fineness of the sugar. Let them talk about the possibilities in terms of the materials you have provided.
4 Making	The main difficulty to overcome will be in making holes of appropriate size and making the right number of holes.
5 Evaluating	Does it work? Does it sprinkle the right amount of sugar conveniently?

Further activities

Some suggestions

1 Use a packet of Liquorice All Sorts to sort for size and shape. Work also on roll/will not roll, etc.
2 Use cylindrical packets of mints and sweets and cuboid packets of sweets to show how circles, rectangles and squares build up to give cylinders and cuboids. Cube sugar and sweets of similar shape offer other possibilities.
3 Make other sweets which do not need cooking and take the opportunity to discuss the properties of the ingredients, (liquids and solids, pouring, melting, changes etc.).
4 Take sweet and chocolate boxes apart along edges and find out what shape the flat piece of card was. Make a display of boxes and the flat shapes from which they started.
5 Take every opportunity to discuss how too many sweets are bad for our teeth and our health generally.
6 Find out how some sweets are made e.g. Liquorice All Sorts, rock (with lettering), Smarties etc.

Language

Mathematics

Physical education

Creative arts

Science

People and their jobs and occupations

Starter Book page 16

Science activities

Making and doing

Teachers' Book page 44

Further activities

Teachers' Book page 45

Introduction

Science activities

Two particular areas are explored in this topic. The first activities enable children to explore further the properties of two- and three-dimensional shapes. The last activity introduces the puzzling non-relationship between size and weight. For children of this age a wide range of experience is required before they are able to accept with confidence that a very small object can be heavy and a very large object can be light.

Making and doing activities

The problem for the child is:
'Can you make an envelope?'

The post Science activities

Activity Pt1 — Parcels

Observing and investigating the properties of cuboids, triangular prisms and cylinders

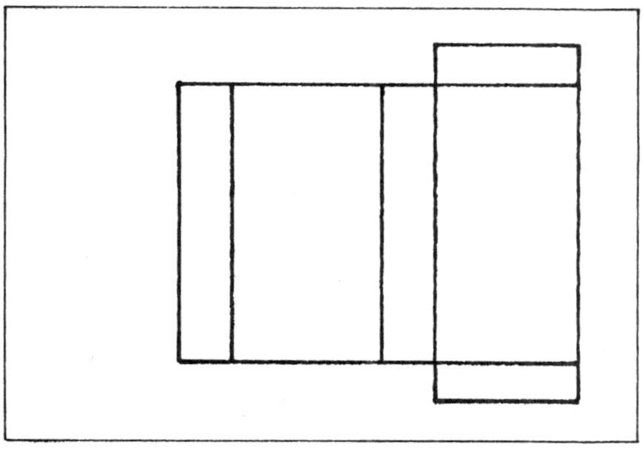

Flat view of a cuboid

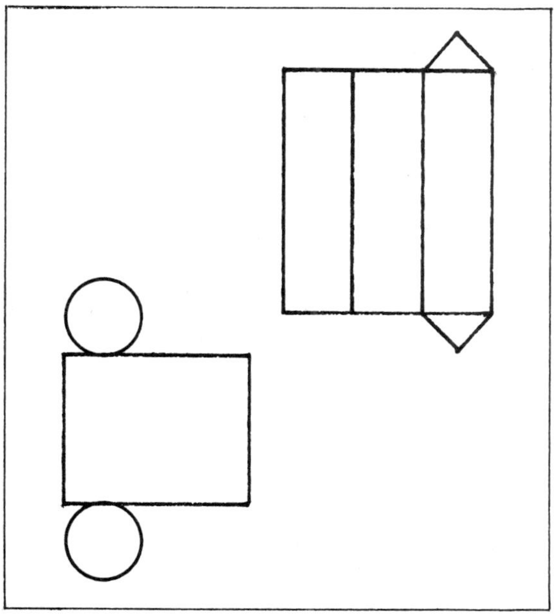

Flat view of a triangular prism and cylinder

You need:
the following wrapped as parcels – four cuboids of various sizes, four triangular prisms of various sizes e.g. Toblerone packets, four cylinders of various sizes e.g. Smartie packets; some small white and coloured sticky labels; some packets (a cuboid, a triangular prism and a cylinder) which can be cut to open out flat.

1 Let the children examine your collection of parcels. They will probably tell you what they think might be inside. They will try shaking to see if they can hear anything.
   Pick up a cuboid parcel and ask the children about its shape. How many faces are there? Use numbered white labels to stick on the faces as you count. Are the faces flat or curved? What shape is each face? Look at face 1. Put a coloured label on it. Can the children see another face which is exactly the same size and shape? Put the same colour label on this to match. Each of the pairs of faces can be identified and labelled in a similar way. Now ask the children to pick out the other cuboid parcels and put them together as a set. How are they all the same? How are they different?
2 Repeat this procedure with the triangular prisms. How many faces? Flat or curved? What shape are the faces? Find the matching faces. The children should be able to tell you that the three rectangular faces match and that the two triangular faces match. Call the shape a 'triangular prism'. The children will enjoy trying to say this. Ask them to pick out the set of triangular prisms and put them together. What is the same about all of them? What is different?
3 Look at the cylindrical parcels. How many faces are there? Are they flat or curved? Which faces match? What shape are they?
4 Cut a cuboid along the edges so that it will open out flat. Let the children count the faces, name the shapes and find the matching pairs. Can they fold it back into its cuboid shape?
5 Do the same thing with a triangular prism and a cylinder. Notice that the curved surface of the cylinder is now flat and it is a rectangle.

Activity Pt2—Post box

Observing and investigating the properties of cuboids, triangular prisms and cylinders (cont.)

You need:
a commercially produced 'posting box' and its set of shapes to post; three parcels (a cuboid, a triangular prism and a cylinder); a cardboard grocery box with holes cut in its sides to fit the parcels.

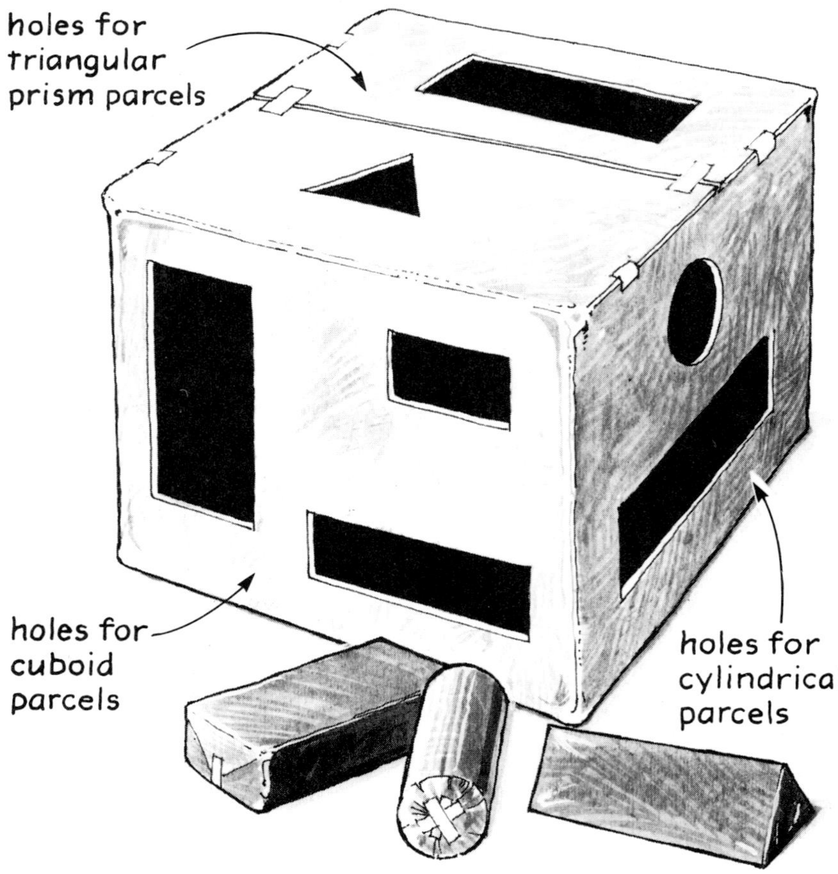

1 Spend a short time playing with the commercially produced posting box. Choose one of the blocks belonging to it and ask the children about its faces. Are they flat or curved? How many are there? Can the children draw a shape like one of its faces? What shape would the posting hole be to fit this block? Will it have straight or curved edges? How many edges? Can the children see a shape like that on the posting box? Let a child find which hole the block does go through. Was the hole the shape they thought it would be?
2 Give the children a cuboid parcel to look at. What shape will the hole need to be to fit this parcel? Is there more than one possible shape for the hole? Produce the large 'posting box' you have made and let the children look at the 'cuboid' holes. Point to one of the holes and ask the children if they can find a face on the parcel which matches this hole. Can the children turn the parcel so that they can post it through this hole? Can they find faces to match the other holes? Can they manipulate the parcel so that it can be posted through the other holes? How many differently-shaped holes can be used?
3 Do the same thing with the triangular prism and the cylinder. The children will discover that there is no face on the cylinder which matches the rectangular hole.

Activity Pt3—Packing

Investigating the packing properties of cuboids, triangular prisms, cylinders, rectangles, triangles and circles

You need:
three shoe boxes; enough small identical cuboids to fill one of the shoe

boxes exactly; enough small triangular prisms to fill the second shoe box, and enough small cylinders to fill the third. (The size of the boxes is not important; use whatever empty containers are available.) Each child needs: a piece of sugar paper with three rectangles drawn on it; a piece with three triangles drawn and another piece with three circles drawn. Mosaic pieces (i.e. small rectangles, triangles, and circles preferably cut from gummed paper) are also needed. (The relative size of these shapes should be such that the patterns shown in sections 3 and 4 can be produced.)

1 If possible let the children help to unpack a delivery box of equipment which has arrived at school. They are sure to notice the loose packing which surrounds the boxes inside. Why is it there? What would happen to the boxes if they didn't fit tightly?
2 Give the children the shoe boxes to pack. Let one child use cuboids, another triangular prisms and a third cylinders to pack the boxes. Can the small shapes be packed neatly so that they won't move? Is there any wasted space? Are there gaps between the 'packages'? Which shapes are best for packing without leaving gaps?
3 Look again at the end shapes of the small 'packages'. There are rectangles, triangles and circles. Ask each child to take the paper with rectangles on it and fill in the shapes with the mosaic pieces: (i) rectangles (ii) triangles (iii) circles.

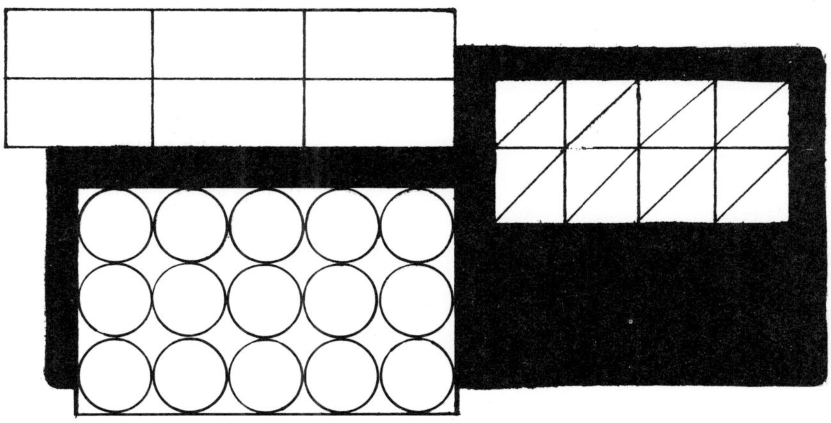

Rectangle mosaics

4 Ask the children to use their mosaic pieces to fill in a triangle and then a circle. Which pieces leave gaps in the triangle? Which leave no gaps in the triangle? Which pieces leave gaps in the circle? Which leave no gaps?

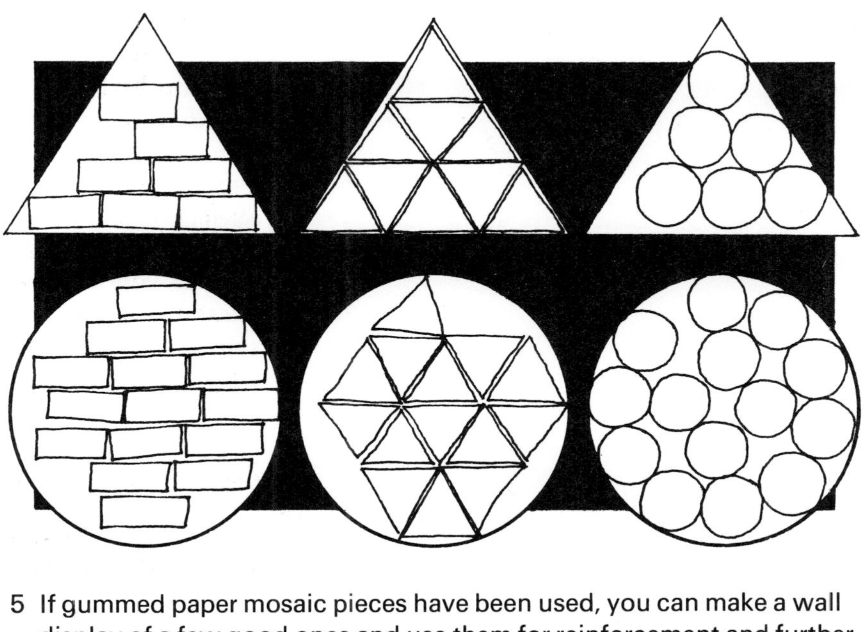

Triangle mosaics and Circle mosaics

5 If gummed paper mosaic pieces have been used, you can make a wall display of a few good ones and use them for reinforcement and further discussion.

Activity Pt4—Heavy or light?

Investigating the non-relationship between size and weight

You need:
five objects of different size and weight (the largest should not be the heaviest and the smallest should not be the lightest); five boxes (matching the objects in size) in which the objects can be packed; five differently-coloured papers for wrapping the boxes; a set of balance scales; some felt markers.

1 Give the children the five objects and the five boxes. Ask them to choose the best box for each object. This should produce some discussion about comparative size. Suggest that the children put the objects in order of size and the boxes in order of size and then match objects and boxes one-to-one.
2 Once the objects are in the boxes, let the children wrap each box with a different colour paper. This is very good for manipulative skills. It draws attention to faces, edges and corners which you can discuss with the children.
3 When the parcels are wrapped ask the children to put them in order of size again. Which is the biggest? (They can identify it by colour.) Which is the smallest? Write the results on a sheet of paper so that the children can read it with you. The colour word should be written in the corresponding colour. For example, The **red** parcel is the biggest. The **green** parcel is the smallest.
4 Now draw the children's attention to the weight of the parcels. Let each child hold each parcel to feel its weight. Which do they think is a heavy parcel? Let a child hold this parcel in one hand and hold each of the other parcels in turn in the other hand. Is the 'heavy' parcel heavier than each of the others? If it is, it is the heaviest. Ask the child to place the 'heavy' parcel on the table. Then the procedure is repeated with the other parcels until the children have the parcels in order of weight. You can use the balance scales to check this order and to explore the relationship between size and weight as you feel appropriate.
5 Questions you might ask are: What colour is the heaviest parcel? What colour is the biggest parcel? Is the biggest parcel the heaviest? What colour is the lightest parcel? What colour is the smallest parcel? Is the smallest parcel the lightest?

Making and doing activities

The problem for the child is:
'Can you make an envelope?'

You need:
a selection of different kinds of paper (of different weights and different colours, some dark, tissue paper and some transparent paper, some paper which is very suitable for making envelopes); some glue; pairs of scissors; sellotape; a collection of commercially-produced envelopes showing different methods of construction and, if possible, magazines or circulars in their sealed plastic envelopes.

1 The problem	Can you make an envelope?
2 Exploring the problem	What is an envelope for? What does it have to do? When do we use envelopes?
3 Ideas for solving the problem	How can you make an envelope from a sheet of paper? The children will need to experiment. Let the children carefully undo a few envelopes to see how the paper has been folded and stuck together.

4 Making

When they have decided how they are going to make their envelopes, provide them with a selection of papers of different strengths, colours etc. and let them choose which to use. Encourage them to talk about the properties of the different papers. They may like to test tear-strength and opaqueness. Will a written address be visible to the postman/woman? Let them make their envelopes and encourage them to do it as neatly as possible.

5 Evaluating

Do the envelopes work? Would the postman/woman like them? You can have a display of envelopes – both those made by the children and your collection.

Further activities

Some suggestions

1 Ask the postman/woman to come to school to talk about his/her job.
2 Make a collection and display of materials used in packing to fill gaps in boxes. Common ones are paper scraps, corrugated card, polystyrene pieces, bubble plastic, moulded polystyrene. Chocolate boxes are interesting with their moulded trays.
3 How can we estimate how big a piece of paper is needed to wrap a parcel? Let the children experiment.
4 We have pretty wrapping paper for special presents. Can the children make a piece of wrapping paper that would be nice for a present for a baby or a Christmas present?
5 Find out how goods that arrive at a supermarket are packed. What are the advantages of cuboid packs in cuboid boxes? Why are cans and bottles usually cylindrical and not cuboid?
6 How are seeds 'packed' e.g. peas in pods, sweet corn, tomatoes, broad beans, etc.?

Language

Mathematics

Physical education

Creative arts

Science

People and their jobs and occupations

Starter Book page 18

Science activities

Making and doing

Teachers' Book page 54

Further activities

Teachers' Book page 55

Introduction

Science activities

'Jobs in the kitchen' illustrates how many kitchen activities have a science-related perspective. Again we have an example of cooking which emphasises that cooking is based on chemistry. When making scones we investigate what difference the absence or presence of baking powder makes to the result. It is a simple investigation but a good example of a cause and effect relationship.

In children's investigation and comparison of different ways of cleaning, we must take care not to press the investigation too far. They will be able to discover which ways work reasonably well and they will probably be able to make some comment about which they think is best. But since it is unlikely that they will make any attempt to recognise or control variables at this stage, the recorded results will probably be a statement as to whether a particular method was successful or not accompanied by any comments which the children want to make.

There are many different ways for the children to record their results, for example by using a simple key as in activity 4.

Making and doing activities

The problem for the child is:

'Can you make something which will stop ice cream melting?'

When Anna's family find the refrigerator full it poses a problem as to how to keep their ice cream until later. The children are invited to help them to solve the problem. They do not necessarily realise that what keeps things warm (insulation) will also keep them cool and they will learn a great deal from this activity.

Jobs in the kitchen Science activities

Activity K1—Scones

Investigating the effect of using baking powder when making scones

You need:

mixing bowls; teaspoons; a pastry board; a rolling pin; kitchen paper; a set of balance scales; two knives; two greased baking trays; an oven. These are the quantities needed to make scones; a quarter of a 250g block of margarine, four times the weight of margarine in plain flour, four level teaspoonfuls of baking powder, one teaspoonful of salt, and milk to mix. *Two* lots of scones are made, so twice the above amounts will be needed for this activity, except for the baking powder (only four teaspoonfuls are needed).

1. Ask the children to wash their hands.
2. Get out all the ingredients *except the baking powder* and tell the children you are going to make some scones for tea.
3. Put some kitchen paper in each pan of the balance scales. Discuss whether the pans are level. What does it mean if they are level? Cut a quarter of the block of margarine and place it on one of the balance pans. What happens? Why?
4. Tell the children that you need four times as much flour as the quarter-block of margarine. How can the piece of margarine be used to do this? Weigh out one portion of flour and talk about the movement of the pans and how they know that the weights are equal. Put this portion of flour on a piece of kitchen paper and then weigh the other three portions out separately so that you can count the four portions with the children.

Put all the flour into the mixing bowl, add a teaspoonful of salt and stir this into the flour. Take the margarine and add it to the flour. Show the children the piece of kitchen paper and ask what has produced the translucent mark? Remind them that when you have handled fats and oil before they have left marks like this. Does the mark go away as the mark from a patch of water would?

5 Chop up the margarine into the flour and divide the mixture into a few portions so that a number of children can help to rub the fat into the flour. (Consult a cookery book if necessary.) Encourage the children to talk about what happens and how the mixture becomes crumbly.

6 Collect all the mixture together into your bowl and add milk to produce a soft non-sticky mixture.

7 Divide the mixture into a number of equal portions and let the children form the pieces into rounds about 2 cm thick. (They should all be the same size.) Make a couple of scones yourself and put one of yours and the children's on the greased baking tray. (Keep one of your scones 'raw' so that you can compare the cooked ones with it.) Whilst you are starting to tidy up 'discover' that you have forgotten the baking powder.

8 Point out to the children that the scone mixture only requires four teaspoonfuls of baking powder and show them how little this is. Tell the children that you had better make another lot of scones properly, using the baking powder.

9 Make a second batch of scones including the baking powder this time. Let the children tell you how to do it so that you do not forget anything. Suggest that they could construct a flow chart that would make it easier not to forget. Help them to do this.

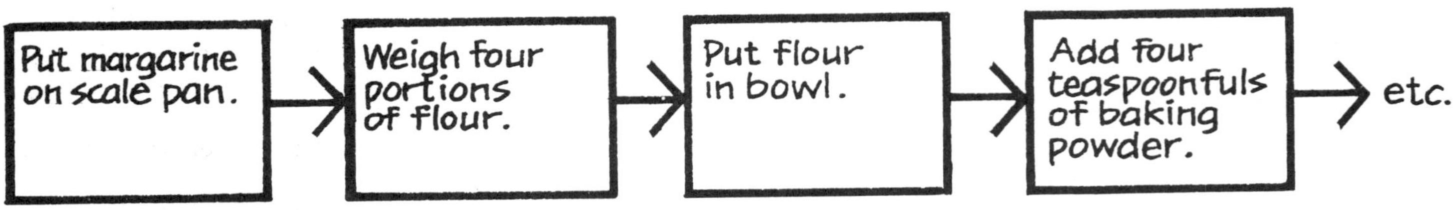

As before keep one raw scone for comparison and put these scones on the other baking tray. Put both batches of scones in the oven (240°C) and leave them to cook for 10–15 minutes.

Comparing scones

10 When the scones are cooked discuss the changes which have occurred in cooking. Compare the cooked scones with the raw ones. Let the children tell you how the cooked scones are different from the uncooked ones. Are they the same in any way? They will be able to make various observations and encourage them to use all their senses.

11 Discuss the differences and similarities between the scones on the two trays. How do they look different? How do they look the same? What was different about the way they were cooked? Can the children understand that the absence of baking powder was the only difference in the making and this caused the difference between the scones (provided that your oven cooked them evenly)?

12 Fresh warm scones taste good even if the absence of baking powder produces a biscuit-like result. The children will notice the difference in thickness of the scones and the difference in texture. They probably will not notice any difference in taste. Any scones which are not eaten at this stage can be kept until the following day and another judgement made on the comparative tastes.

Activity K2—Baking powder

Investigating the differences and similarities between salt, caster sugar and baking powder

You need:
salt; caster sugar; baking powder; teaspoons; jam-jars; magnifying glasses; warm water; yoghurt cartons.

1 Remind the children how adding the baking powder made such a difference to the scones and suggest that they might be able to find out what is special about baking powder. (Tell them immediately that they must not taste the substances. They must just look at them and find out how they behave. Baking powder tastes unpleasant – but is, of course, harmless.)

2 Let the children observe the substances by: looking with the naked eye; looking with a magnifying glass; watching how the substances flow when they are poured; rubbing them between finger and thumb. Encourage the children to describe differences and similarities.

3 Provide the children with jam-jars and ask them to put a yoghurt-cartonful of cold water into each of three jars. Tell them to put one teaspoonful of salt in one of the jars and stir well; put one teaspoonful

Dissolving experiment

of sugar into the second; and one teaspoonful of baking powder into the third jar. What happens? How do they behave differently? How do they behave the same? (They should notice particularly that the baking powder produces small bubbles.) You can discuss the process of dissolving with the children in a manner similar to that used in discussing dissolving in 'The supermarket', Science activity 6, section 3, on page 18.

4 What happens if warm water is used instead of cold water? (The children may notice that the substances dissolve more quickly and that the baking powder produces bubbles faster.)

5 Can anyone suggest why baking powder does make a difference to scones?

Activity K3—Greasy plates

Investigating which is the best cleanser for greasy plates

You need:
three washing-up bowls of comfortably warm water; a bar of toilet or kitchen soap; washing-up liquid; washing powder; six small plates greased with hard margarine or butter; three small dishes; four jam-jars with water-tight tops; a strainer; a magnifying glass; yoghurt cartons; hard margarine; hot water; teaspoons.

1 Ask the children to find out if they can clean the plates by holding them under the cold water tap? What happens? Does the grease change? (It may become harder.)

2 Tell them that they had better try to wash the plates with some hot water. Put the three bowls of comfortably hot water on a table with the toilet (or kitchen) soap, the washing-up liquid and the washing powder. Tell them that you want them to find out which is best for getting grease off plates. Suggest that first of all they find out whether hot water by itself is any use. What happens when they put hot water on a greasy plate? What happens to the plate? What happens to the water? Can the children explain it? Do they remember what happened in 'The cook' activity when they ran water over their greasy hands (*Teachers' Book A*, page 70)?

3 When they have explored the effect of water alone suggest that they investigate the effectiveness of the three cleansers. Pour a little washing-up liquid into one dish; some washing powder into another; and put the tablet of soap in the third. Can the children tell you the differences? Which is solid? Which is liquid? What about the powder? Let the children use the magnifying glass to see the tiny solid particles and again emphasise the ways in which it is different from a liquid.

4 Suggest that the children use a different cleanser in each washing-up bowl and try to wash one of the untreated greasy plates. Talk to them about how much of the cleanser they need to use and how convenient each of them is. Let them carry out their investigations and come to their conclusions, giving their reasons. (Interpret 'best' here as most effective or most convenient. Do not worry about uncontrolled variables – control of variables can come later.)

5 Ask the children where they think the grease might have gone. Suggest it might be possible to find out if you 'wash up' in a jam-jar. Get the four jam-jars and put a level teaspoonful of margarine into each of them. Is it a liquid or a solid? What does it not do which it would do if it was a liquid? What does it do which tells them that it is a solid? Now let the children put a yoghurt-cartonful of hot water into each jar. What happens? What happens to the margarine? (Does it melt? float?) Now put the top on one of the jars and shake it? What happens? Put it on one side and watch it whilst continuing with the rest of the investigation.

6 Add the washing up liquid to one of the jars. Put the top on and shake it. What happens? Put it on one side and watch it.

7 Ask the children to add a bit of toilet soap to one of the other jars and washing powder to the third. Let a child shake them and leave them to stand.
8 Let the children observe the jars as the water cools until it is quite cold. What happens? How are the jars the same and how are they different? What happens to the margarine in each of the jars? Can they still see it? Is it still a solid? Where is it? (Where there is some floating on the top the children may need to strain off the bits to realise that the bits are solid and that they are margarine.)

Activity K4—Red marks

Investigating which cleaning agent is required to remove different red marks

You need:
a tomato; tomato sauce; red powder paint; red felt-tip pen; red crayon; red food colouring; red jam; beetroot; blackcurrant juice; lipstick; teaspoons; a knife; six small bowls; scrubbing brush; a small piece of cotton cloth for each child; washing powder; soap.

1 Put out all the red things and ask the children how they are the same. How are they different? Draw their attention to the different shades of red – some will be deeper and some paler. Help the children to understand that there are many shades of red which we describe with names like: pinkish red, brownish red, orangey red or crimson. But these shades all belong to the set 'red'.
2 Now let them smell each item and ask them to describe the smells. Which has the strongest smell? Which has no smell?
3 Give each child a small piece of cloth. Let the child choose one of the items with which to make a mark on his/her piece of cloth. When they have done this, ask them how they did it. They may answer: "I poured it" or "I spread it" or "I squeezed it", etc.
4 Now ask the children to remember which are their own pieces of cloth and place all the pieces in the centre of the table.
5 Suggest now that they each choose a piece of cloth which is not their own and ask them to identify the mark by matching its colour and smell with the appropriate item.
6 Tell the children to dry the pieces of cloth for a few minutes. Ask them to make labels for the marks e.g. jam, paint, etc.
7 Suggest now that they should try to find out which is the easiest way to wash out the marks. Discuss with them what would be the first thing to try. Encourage them to suggest cold water. Let the children try to wash out the marks with cold water either from the tap or in the bowls. Did the mark wash out? You can record results in a table.

	tomato	tomato sauce	jam	paint	felt pen	lipstick	etc.
Cold water removes							
Warm water removes							
Rubbing with soap removes							

Or you can construct a mark removal flow diagram.

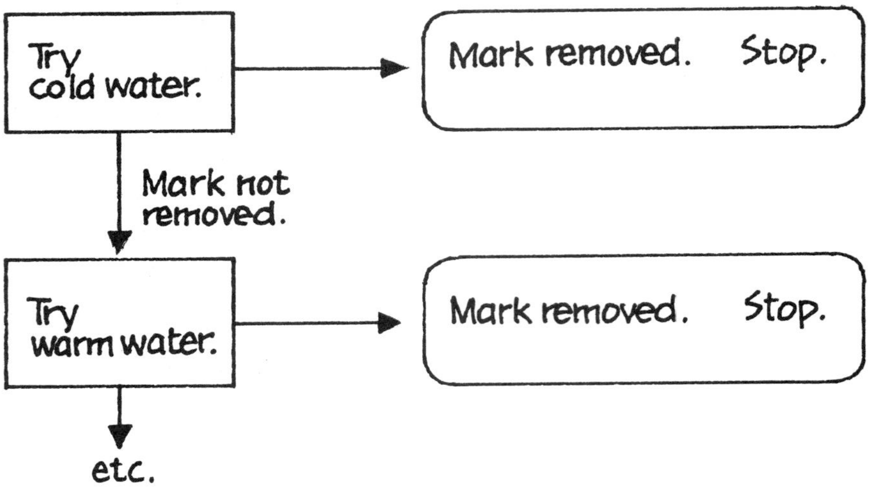

8 Ask the children for suggestions of other means of removing the marks. Follow the suggestions as far as possible. One suggestion might be soaking and this is easy to try. Ask them to put equal quantities of warm water in the bowls and add a teaspoonful of washing powder to each bowl. Let them stir the washing powder in with their fingers. Can the children tell you that the powder is dissolving?

9 Put each of the marked pieces of cloth into one of the bowls and leave them until the end of the day. Remind the children to put the labels near the bowls.

10 Discuss the results of soaking and let the children put the pieces of cloth in order of cleanness. Ask them which marks are easy to remove and which are difficult?

11 The children could record their results with crayon drawings of the marks at each stage, to show the mark gradually fading.

Activity K5—Tea-leaves

Observing that something from tea-leaves dissolves in water but most of the tea-leaf does not dissolve

You need:
a glass pan; a heat source; tea bags; two heat-resistant glasses or glass tea-cups; teaspoons; a sieve; a tea-strainer; a tea-pot; a cup and saucer for each child; milk; sugar; instant tea; a magnifying glass.

1 Ask the children what is needed to make a cup of tea. Put out the items as the children suggest them.

2 Put the glass pan of water on to boil. Ask the children how they will know when it is boiling. Can they tell you that the water will bubble a lot and produce steam? Emphasise the dangers of boiling water and of steam which you may not be able to see.

3 Whilst the water is heating, show the children a tea-bag and ask them what they think it is made of. Can they see inside the bag? Can they see through the bag? Let them take the tea out of the bag and open the bag to make a single layer. Let them hold this up to the light and use a magnifying glass to see the tiny holes (not always visible).

4 Now ask them to describe the tea.

Let them use the magnifying glass. Draw their attention to the tiny bits which are different shapes and different shades of brown. Can they tell you why the tea didn't come through the holes in the tea bag? Let them rub the tea between their fingers and thumbs and ask them how it feels. Encourage them to say that it is dry and crunchy. Do tea-leaves smell?

5 Put the tea-leaves from a tea-bag in one glass and a tea-bag in the other glass.

(Point out that this is special glass and that they must never try this with an ordinary glass. Emphasise also that they must never try to use boiling water themselves. Talk to them about making sure that pan handles do not stick out and generally take the opportunity to discuss safety matters.)

Pour some boiling water into each glass and ask the children to notice what happens in each case. Make sure that they are aware that the water which you are pouring in is colourless. How does the water change when it is poured on to the tea?

6 Wait until the tea-leaves and the tea-bag have sunk and then ask the children what they think has happened. They may say that the tea-leaves have dissolved. Let a child use a teaspoon to find out if the tea-leaves and the tea-bag are still there.

7 Ask the children which is easier to get out of the glass, the tea-leaves or the tea-bag? Let one of them lift the tea-bag out with a teaspoon and then ask the children how you can get the tea-leaves out. They may suggest pouring from one glass to another or they may suggest using a sieve or tea-strainer. Try any reasonable suggestions but finally remove the tea-leaves with a sieve. Let the children feel the tea-leaves again and ask if and how the tea-leaves now feel different. Can they tell you that the leaves are wet, warm, shiny and stuck together? (Save the tea-leaves until later.)

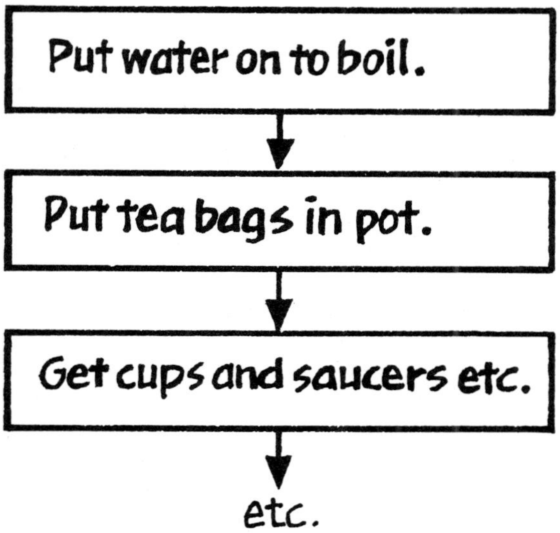

8 For the next part of the activity you could help the children to record what is done by using a flow chart.

Boil some more water and make a pot of tea using two tea-bags. Whilst you are waiting for it to brew, the children can put out the cups and saucers (one-to-one correspondence). Let them put the milk and sugar in the cups and encourage them to feel the sugar in the bottom of the cups with their teaspoons. Ask the children what they can feel and what they think will happen to the sugar. They should be able to tell you that the sugar will dissolve.

9 Pour a cup of tea for each child and let the children drink it when they are ready. How does the tea they are drinking look different from tea without milk?

10 Save the used tea-leaves and let them dry. Ask the children to compare these with the unused tea-leaves. Encourage them to notice that the used tea-leaves are softer and a lighter brown. Ask them which has the stronger smell – unused tea-leaves or used tea-leaves. Can the children tell you what has happened to cause the colour to change and why the smell has faded?

11 Put the teaspoonful of 'instant' tea into a glass and let the children watch what happens when you pour boiling water on it. What colour is it? What does it look like? Does it look like tea? If you put milk and sugar in it, does it taste like 'tea-leaf' tea? Are there any tea-leaves? Can the children guess/suggest what 'instant' tea is? (The stuff from tea leaves which dissolves.)

Activity K6—Kitchen walls

Investigating which kitchen wall surfaces are easy to clean

You need:
a variety of kitchen wall 'soilers' based on children's suggestions (grease, jam, tomato sauce, dirty finger-marks, pencil, ball-point ink, felt-pen ink, powder paint, etc.); samples of materials which might be used for kitchen walls (wallpaper of various kinds, plastic materials, surfaces coated with different kinds of paint); toilet soap; kitchen soap; washing powder; scouring powder; mild kitchen cleaner; washing-up liquid; cleaning cloths; a nylon pan scourer.

N.B. Ideally the wall covering samples should be stuck on to small pieces of board to make the investigation easier for the children.

1 Let the children discuss in general terms why we cover walls in the house with paper or paint them. What kind of paper do we put in different rooms? Do we put paper in all rooms? What are the problems with paper? What do you think might be good for a kitchen?

2 Ask the children what kinds of marks they might need to wipe off the kitchen walls. Help them to think of things like grease, jam, tomato sauce, pencil scribble, ball-point marks, felt-pen marks, powder-paint marks, etc.
3 Produce your samples of wall surfaces and let the children mark each sample with the 'soilers' they have decided to investigate.
4 Suggest they leave the samples for a while to dry because that is probably what would happen on a real kitchen wall.
5 Now tell the children that you are going to try to find out if it is possible to clean kitchen walls when they get dirty. Produce the variety of cleaning materials and let the children find out which surfaces they can clean without spoiling them. When they have discovered that paper is very difficult to clean let them concentrate on finding out how effective the cleaners are on the more durable surfaces. Can they pick out one that is better than the others? They could record their results in a table similar to that used in Activity 4, page 51.

Activity K7—Paper towels

Investigating how well paper towels absorb water

You need:
three different kinds of paper towels (try to get one very thick and one very thin); jam-jars; teaspoons; plates; magnifying glasses.

1 Put the three kinds of paper towels on the table and give each child a piece of each kind. Let them examine the pieces and describe them, noting differences and similarities. Ask them to use a magnifying glass to see the structure of the paper. Is the piece made up of more than one layer?
2 Now point out to the children that in the starter picture Jenny's grandmother was trying to decide which towel would be best for mopping up the drink that Jenny had spilt. How can they find out which is the best 'mopper-up'? Let the children make suggestions and try out any workable ideas.

   Possible methods are:

   Put the piece of towel on a plate and find out how many teaspoonfuls of water can be put on the towel and spread right across it without producing a puddle.

   Take three jam-jars and put the same amount of water in each. Find out (visually) how much water one of the towels will soak up from one of the jars. Use the other jars to test the other towels. Which towel soaked up most?

Making and doing activities

The problem for the child is:
'Can you make something which will stop ice cream melting?'

You need:
ice-cream cubes (frozen milk) or ice-cubes could be substituted; various kinds of paper including newspaper; pieces of cloth of various kinds; pieces of plastic; polythene bags; various packing materials (wood shavings, shredded paper, polystyrene pieces); junk (cartons, yoghurt cartons etc.); a thermos flask (preferably wide-necked); a selection of 'cold' bags and containers e.g. a freezer bag, a 'cold' bag, an ice-box, polystyrene cup, double sided cup, etc.; scissors; sellotape; glue.

1 The problem	Can you make something which will stop ice cream melting?
2 Exploring the problem	Why does ice cream melt? What can you do to stop it getting warm?

3 Ideas for solving the problem

Put it in a pottery dish/a glass dish? Wrap it up in something – paper/cloth? How much paper/cloth? What kind of paper/cloth? Put it in a box and fill the box with something?

There are many ideas to explore. In this problem it will probably be appropriate to keep the commercial solutions until the children have produced their own solutions but if they are lacking ideas they could examine a freezer bag and decide what is special about it.

4 Making

The difficulties will depend on what they are trying to do. Just wrapping something in lots of newspaper is very effective. It is important to put the material used for heat insulation all the way round (including the lid).

5 Evaluating

When the children have made their 'cold' bags or boxes or decided what to do, they can put their ice-cream in and see how long it stays solid. (Reinforce liquid – solid). They can discover which method works best. You can also use the commercial solutions you have collected and try these.

Further activities

Some suggestions

1 Provide the children with a collection of cans and packets of various categories of food. Let the children decide how they would sort them to put them away in the kitchen.
2 How does an egg-beater work? What makes it go round?
3 Make meringue. Why does it have holes in it? What is in the holes?
4 What are handles made of e.g. knife handles, forks, spoons, kitchen utensils, tea pots, pan lids, pans, casserole dishes? Why? What materials are good for pan handles? (i.e. They do not get hot.)
5 Tell the story of the Gingerbread Boy. Make some gingerbread biscuits. Grow some root ginger. (Plant root ginger as bought in the shop – it grows quite easily.) Find out how ginger is used in cooking.
6 Make a collection of spices for matching smells.

LEVEL 2: TOPICS

INTRODUCTION TO LEVEL 2

The overall development of basic skills will enable children to employ increasingly sophisticated and refined techniques for recording and communicating. This will be particularly marked as they gain confidence in oral work and are more able to put their observations and thoughts in writing. Their growing ability to manipulate numbers and to undertake measuring activities opens up further possibilities.

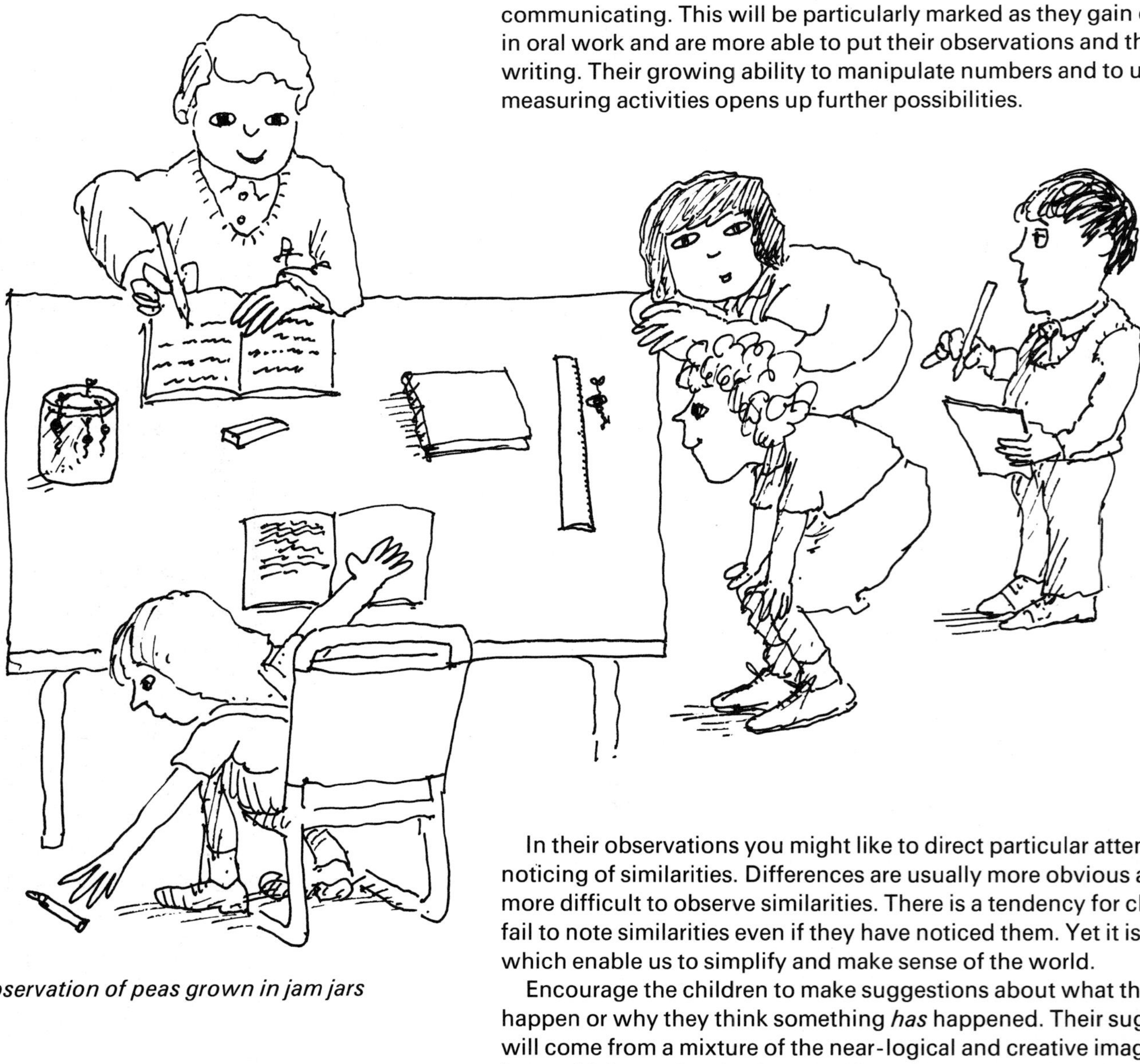

Observation of peas grown in jam jars

In their observations you might like to direct particular attention to the noticing of similarities. Differences are usually more obvious and it is more difficult to observe similarities. There is a tendency for children to fail to note similarities even if they have noticed them. Yet it is similarities which enable us to simplify and make sense of the world.

Encourage the children to make suggestions about what they think *will* happen or why they think something *has* happened. Their suggestions will come from a mixture of the near-logical and creative imagination – a base which can develop into the kind of base a creative scientist needs! There will be many small instances where the children's suggestions can be profitably explored and sometimes used.

You will also find opportunities to refer to the small facets of science which people use in their jobs, hobbies and occupations. For example, gardeners need to know the right conditions for germinating seeds and growing young seedlings; the police need to be able to observe carefully and record their observations. The children will be able to see that these activities are close to the activities which they themselves are undertaking.

Language

Mathematics

Physical education

Creative arts

Science

People and their jobs and occupations

Starter Book page 20

Science activities

Making and doing

Teachers' Book page 68

Further activities

Teachers' Book page 69

Introduction

Science activities

This topic coincides with Spring when, in general, seeds germinate readily and the seedlings which emerge can be grown on either in plant-pots or outdoors, at home or at school. Children take great delight in the study of living things and will enjoy having personal responsibility for plants. One of the snags in work with seeds and seedlings is that nothing happens immediately. Careful organisation is necessary to sustain interest and maintain continuity.

The topic provides opportunities to use a variety of means of recording results – drawings or descriptions, or tape-recordings if you feel that this is appropriate. It also provides a number of instances where children can be asked to describe both differences and similarities using several of the senses. The observing and recording of similarities is a particularly useful exercise which is easy to undervalue.

Making and doing activities

The problem for the child is:

'Can you make something to keep the birds away?'

You can explain to the children that many birds eat seeds as their main food and seeds sown by gardeners are a good meal for them. The problem is to make something to keep the birds away from the seeds. It can be solved in a number of ways (only some of which are open to the children). By not posing the problem in the form, 'Can you make something to *scare* birds away?', more options are left open for the children to explore.

Easter Science activities

Activity E1 — Yellow flowers

Observing a set of yellow flowers; investigating the effect of temperature on the life of cut flowers

You need:
eight yellow daffodils of the same variety and eight yellow tulips of the same variety (they should be in tight bud and, if possible, one variety should be short and one should be tall); other yellow flowers if available (including small ones such as primroses and pansies); eight jam-jars; labels; a flower vase; a magnifying glass.

1 Put the various flowers on the table and let the children sort them into the different kinds. Tell the children what the flowers are called. Write these names on labels and label the sets of flowers.
2 Direct the children's attention to the stems and leaves (if the flowers have any). Let the children use a magnifying glass to observe detail and ask them to make comments and comparisons about stems and leaves e.g. length of stem, colour of stem, structure of stem – is it hollow or solid? Do the stems smell different? Could they distinguish between them just by smell?
3 Choose eight 'identical' daffodils in tight bud and eight 'identical' tulips. Make sure that the daffodils have stems of the same length and that the tulip stems are the same length. Put the rest of the yellow flowers in the vase and label the vase 'set of yellow flowers'.
4 Take the eight jam-jars and tell the children that you want them to put the same amount of water into each jar and let them decide how to do this. Tell them then to put two of the tulips into each of four jars and two of the daffodils into each of the others.
5 Now ask the children where they think the flowers should be put to last for the longest time. They can discuss this amongst themselves. Try to use their suggestions. Possible places are – near a radiator, on your table, in a cold place. You might like to lead them towards putting the flowers in the refrigerator.
6 Write the days of the week on a chart beginning with the present day and use this to mark off the days and record what happens.

Place / Day	Near radiator	On table	In corridor	In a refrigerator
Wednesday	Flowers in bud	Flowers in bud	Flowers in bud	Flowers in bud
Thursday	Flowers open	Flowers nearly open	Flowers still closed	Flowers still closed
etc.	etc.	etc.	etc.	etc.

7 For the record for the starting day, ask the children to draw and colour a picture of how the flowers look at this stage. (Some parts of the flowers may still be green and the structure of the flower will not be visible.)
8 The children will probably not be able to record the gradual day-to-day changes for all the flowers but, when there is a change which they can record, encourage them to do so. In any case once the flowers have opened sufficiently for their structure to be seen let the children observe them in detail.
9 What can they tell you about the flowers? How many petals? How are they arranged? Are they the same colour all over? Are they dull or shiny? Do the flowers smell? What can the children see inside the flower? Can they find the stamens and the pistil? What happens if they touch the stamens with their fingers? What comes off? (pollen) What does it feel like? What does it look like? (Let them use a magnifying glass.) Can they compare two kinds of flowers? Are all the flowers of the same kind exactly the same?
10 Keep the flowers and record what happens to them in the different locations (different temperatures). Where do flowers last longest? (Where it is cool.) What is a good way of making flowers last a long time at home? (Take them out of a warm room and put them somewhere cool – if there is nobody about to enjoy looking at them.)

Activity E2—Easter eggs

Investigating hollow shapes

You need:
two hen's eggs (one blown – make a pin hole at each end of the egg and blow hard; make the hole bigger if necessary); wallpaper-paste powder; a large container for the paste; a round balloon for each child; a large supply of newspaper; string; felt-tip pens; round-ended scissors; a large mirror; a bowl of water.

1 Show the children the two eggs and ask them to find out how they are different – weight, sound when gently tapped. What happens if the two eggs are put in a bowl of water? Can the children tell you that one of the eggs has been emptied? Do they know the word 'hollow'? Why do they think the hollow egg floats?
2 Tell the children that they are going to make a hollow Easter egg to hold a surprise present for Easter. Start off by letting the children help you to make the paste. Ask them to tell you what the paste looks like as a powder and what happens to it when it is mixed with the water. What does it feel like as they stir it? Do they notice that it gets stiffer? Is it a liquid or a solid?
3 Give the children a balloon each and let them talk about what it feels like, what colour it is, what it smells like, how big it is and how the thin rubber looks.
4 Start to blow up the balloons with the help of any of the children who can assist. What happens to the balloons? What changes? What stays the same? (Make the balloons about the size of a small melon and provide one for each child.) Can the children tell you that the balloons change from being flat shapes to spheres?
5 Let them press their fingers into the balloons and notice how they feel. Do they notice how the thin rubber has become thinner and paler in colour? Let them tap the balloons gently and see what happens and then throw them up gently and catch them. Can the children tell you that the balloons are light and they bounce?

Covering balloons with papier mâché

6 Show the children how to cover their balloons with pasted newspaper. Ask them how the newspaper changes when it is pasted and it is wet. Do they notice that it tears more easily? (The balloon will need at least four layers of newspaper so you may prefer to do this in two sessions.)
7 When there are sufficient layers on the balloons ask the children how they feel different. The balloons can now be put to dry. They may take three or four days.
8 When the balloons have dried, ask the children again how the balloons have changed. Will they bounce? What do they sound like if tapped using a pencil?
9 Tell the children that you are going to cut the spheres in half. Give them each a piece of string and ask them to put the string round their balloons to show you where you will have to cut to produce two halves. Help them to draw along this line with a felt-tip pen and then cut along the line using the round-ended scissors.
10 What has happened to the balloon? Does it look any different?
11 Put the large mirror on the table and ask the children what they will see if a half of one of the spheres is put on the mirror. Let them try this and discuss how the reflection is upside down and it makes the half look like a whole.
12 Tell the children to line the 'eggs' with kitchen paper before decorating them. When the 'eggs' are finished, the children can put a few sweets inside and tie the two halves together with a ribbon.

Activity E3—Seed potatoes

Observing the growth of potatoes over a period of four months

You need:
four seed potatoes with sprouts; a potato without sprouts; large spoons; four clear polythene bags (minimum 20×30 cm); a large black polythene bag (dustbin liner); soil; kitchen paper; magnifying glass; a jug of water.

1 Show the children the five potatoes and ask them which one is different. (Four have sprouted and one has not.) Let the children feel the potatoes. Do they feel different? How do the seed potatoes feel? What do their skins look like? (Let the children use a magnifying glass.)
2 Now suggest that the children use the magnifying glass to look at the sprouts. Can they see many tiny sprouts and fine white hairs? What are the sprouts and hairs?
3 Ask the children what you will need to plant the potatoes. They will probably be able to tell you that you need soil and a container. How do potatoes grow? Do the children know?
4 Give the children the polythene bags, the soil, the seed potatoes and the spoons. Let the children half-fill the bags with soil. They then put in the potatoes (one in each bag) and cover them with soil without completely filling the bags. Can the children suggest anything else which the potatoes might need? (Water.) Let them pour a little into each bag. Fasten each of the bags and put them carefully into the dustbin bag. Tie this so that no light will get in and place it in a cool but accessible place.
5 Remember to water the potatoes when necessary and each month take out one of the potatoes. You might like, for example, to do this on the first day of every month and to record this on a chart.
6 When you remove the potato in its bag, carefully slit open the plastic bag so that you do not disturb the growth and let the children make observations of as much detail as they can. They can record their observations by making drawings each month showing the development. You can put the potato in a pot to go on growing but you are unlikely to produce potatoes indoors.
7 If you can find an odd corner outdoors, you could grow some potatoes to produce a real crop.

Activity E4—Seed peas

Observing and investigating the direction in which shoots and roots grow

You need:
paper towels (use a 'good' kind as found in 'Jobs in the kitchen', Activity 7); a margarine carton with lid; several saucers; large sticky labels; a packet of seed peas; a jam-jar for each child.
N.B. Seed peas can be bought by the pint. A quarter-pint will give you approximately 350 peas. In this activity 'wrinkled' peas are used. Germination takes 7–10 days.

1 Put 30–40 peas in the margarine carton and put its lid on. Pass it round for the children to decide what is inside. They cannot look inside. Which sense(s) can they use to help them? (hearing) Can the children describe what is inside? Is it one thing or many? Light or heavy? Small or big? Rough or smooth? Sliding or rolling? Which senses are they not able to use whilst the lid is on?

Listening – what is inside?

2 Remove the lid and ask the children which sense they can use now to tell you what the peas look like. Let them describe what they can see. What can they feel?
3 Now tell the children that they are going to grow some peas. Give them each a jam-jar and some paper towels to crumple up and push into the jars. Let each of the children take four peas and push these down between the paper towels and the sides of the jars. (Set up one for yourself at the same time.)
4 Ask the children what you must give the peas so they will grow. (Why do seeds not grow while they are in their packets?) Make sure that the children add just enough water to moisten the paper towels. Do they know why you have chosen this kind of paper towel. (It is the kind which they found mopped up most water when they did 'Jobs in the kitchen', Activity 7, page 54.)
5 Give each child a sticky label big enough for the child's name and a space for marking off the days. Let them stick their labels on their jars and mark off the days until germination. Remind them to keep the paper towels moist but not too wet.
   They can record, for example, "My first pea started to grow on day 10, etc." They can also make drawings to show how growth progresses.
6 Once growth has started ask the children what is happening. Can they tell you which part of the pea plant is growing up and which is growing down? Which are leaves and which is the root?

7 When the shoot and roots in your own jar are about 3 cm long turn the jar upside down on a saucer. Which way are the roots going now? Which way are the leaves going? What do the children suggest could happen if you leave the jar that way up? Leave the jar where the children can follow progress and encourage them to watch what happens. Be careful in the conclusion you come to from this activity. All we can say is that the pea roots started off by going down and the leaves started off by going up. (Did all the children observe that their pea plants behaved in this way?) When your pea plant was turned upside down its root turned itself round and went down and the shoot turned itself round and went up. If you want to say more, you need to try turning more pea plants upside down and also trying this investigation with different seeds.)

8 After about three weeks you could let the children plant their pea plants in soil, preferably outdoors. They might like to take them home to do this.

Activity E5—Tomato and pepper seeds

Investigating whether tomato and pepper seeds from a packet behave like the fresh seeds

You need:
two margarine or yoghurt cartons for each child; potting compost; large spoons; cling film or polythene bags; rubber bands; sticky labels; magnifying glass; a hammer and large nails; tomatoes; peppers; a large mirror; four plates; a good supply of yoghurt cartons; a piece of wood as a hammer board; a knife; packets of tomato and pepper seeds.

1 Cut a tomato in half through its stalk and put one half on the mirror. What do you see in the mirror?
2 Now do the same thing with the pepper. What do you see in the mirror this time?
3 Now take the halves of the tomato and scrape the seeds on to a plate. Let the children look at the seeds and feel them. They will see that the seeds are in little sacs of liquid. Now put the seeds from the packet on another plate and ask how they are different. The children will notice that the seeds are dry and furry. They feel soft and silky. If the children use a magnifying glass they will be able to see tiny white hairs on the seeds.

4 Take the pepper and remove the seeds from it and put these on a plate and put some pepper seeds from the packet on another plate. Ask the children to tell you all they can about the seeds. How are they the same? How are they different? Make sure that they look at the seeds through the magnifying glass. What sticks out of the sides of the seeds?

5 Ask the children to decide whether they would like to grow peppers or tomatoes and tell them you want to find out whether fresh seeds or seeds out of packets grow best. They will each need to prepare two planting cartons.

6 Give each child two cartons and see if they can remember that they must start by making drainage holes in the bottom of the cartons. Let them use the hammer and a nail to make the holes. Whilst they are waiting for the hammer and nail, ask them how the compost is different from the soil they used when they planted the potatoes. (You could provide them with a sample of soil so that they can compare the compost and the soil directly if you wish.) They each need to fill two cartons with compost and write two labels.

Planting packet seeds and fresh seeds

7 When the children are ready to plant their seeds, tell them to water the compost and watch until the water drains through. Into one pot put five seeds from the packet and in the other put the five fresh seeds and sprinkle a little compost on the top. Cover the cartons with cling film or plastic bags and put the cartons in a warm place until the seeds germinate.

8 The children can keep a record in a similar way to that used when they were investigating peas. Ask the children to compare what happens to the seeds in their pairs of cartons. What happens in the same way? What happens differently? Does one lot of seeds start to grow before the other or do they both start to grow at more or less the same time? Does one lot grow faster than the other? Is it possible to say whether seeds from the packet are better than fresh seeds or the other way round? Is it impossible to decide which are best?

9 When the seedlings grow their first pairs of leaves, let the children very gently ease them out with an old fork and transplant them singly into yoghurt cartons of compost. (Remember the drainage holes.) Put the cartons in a light place and let the children care for them and watch them start to grow. They can eventually take the plants home. Both pepper plants and tomato plants will flourish on a window-sill and produce fruit if properly cared for. Refer to a gardening book or local garden shop for advice if you wish to cultivate the plants to maturity.

Activity E6—Sweet corn

Investigating the effect of temperature on the germination of sweet corn

You need:
a packet of sweet corn seeds; a yoghurt carton full of compost for each child (plus one for you); cling film; pencil; ruler; access to refrigerator.

1 Show the children the picture on the seed packet so that they will be able to see what they are trying to grow. Tip the seeds out and let the children examine them carefully and describe them in terms of size, colour, texture and sound when shaken. (You could produce some of the peas which you investigated in Activity 4 and let the children compare the peas with the sweet corn. How are peas and sweet corn the same? How are they different?)

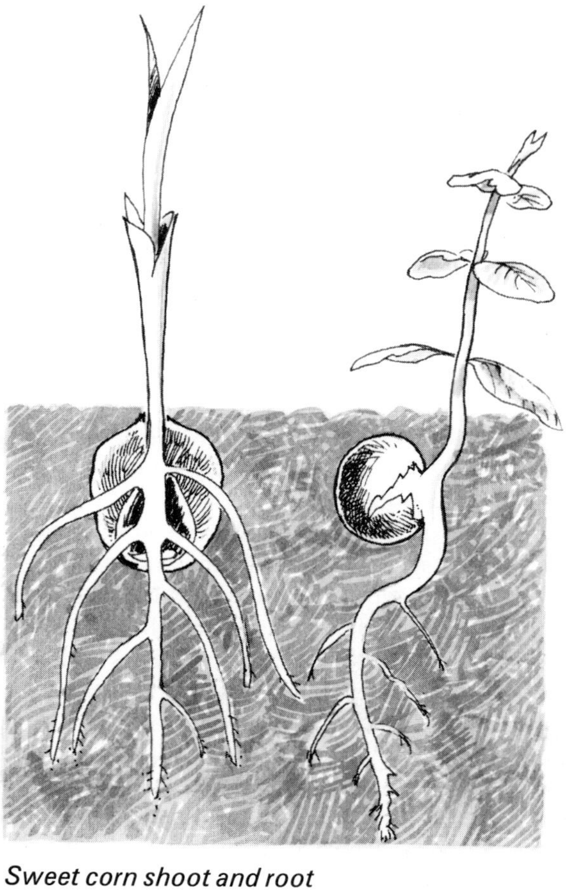

Sweet corn shoot and root
Pea shoot and root

2 Tell the children that you want them to plant two sweet corn seeds in each of their cartons. They must be planted 3 cm deep. Get the children to count off 3 cm on a ruler and measure this far on a pencil and mark it carefully. They should then use the pencil to make two holes in the compost and drop the seeds in and cover them with compost. You need to set up a carton as well. Make sure that the compost is moist and cover all the cartons with cling film.
3 Tell the children that you want to find out what is the best place to put the seeds to start them growing. Do the children think that a warm place or a cold place will be best? Suggest that you could try different places to find out. Say that you will put yours in the refrigerator to find out if the seeds like to be cold and suggest that some of the children put theirs in a very warm place and some in a place that is not quite so warm. Let the children suggest appropriate places or help them to think of places and put the cartons there.
4 When the seeds start to grow take off the cling film covers. Which seeds start to grow first? Is it the seeds in the very warm place or the seeds in the cold place or the seeds in the not so warm place? Let the children watch their own and the other children's seeds and see which ones appear first.
5 When the seedlings are a few days old tell the children that there will be only room for one in the carton so they must pull one out. Tell them to decide which is the weakest and pull that one out very gently. They can now examine the seedling and its root. Can they describe it? Can they tell you how the shoot and the root come out of the seed? Can they remember how the pea shoot and root came out of the pea? Can they put the seedling on a ruler and tell you how long the shoot is and how long the root is?

Activity E7—Cucumbers

Investigating the effect of light on plant growth

You need:
a packet of cucumber seeds; a carton of compost for each child (and one for you); cling film.

1 Let the children look at and handle the seeds. Ask the children to describe them in terms of colour, size, shape, texture and sound when shaken.
2 The seeds need to be planted 2 cm deep. Tell the children to count 2 cm along on their rulers and to measure this distance on their pencils. They can then make holes in the compost.
3 Tell the children that cucumber seeds need to lie on their sides to germinate well. Let the children carefully plant their seeds, cover them with compost and make sure that the compost is moist. Then cover the cartons with cling film. Set up a similar carton for yourself.
4 Put all the pots in a warm place and remove the cling film once the seeds have germinated. Make sure that the seedlings have adequate light and water them regularly.
5 Ask the children what they think would happen if the plants had to grow in the dark during the day as well as at night. Suggest that you put your plant in a dark place and leave it there to find out what happens. Do this when the plant has a few leaves and leave it in the dark for about a week. Either put it in a dark cupboard or in a lightproof box or plastic bag.
6 After about a week show your plant to the children and ask them how your plant looks different from theirs. What has happened to your plant which has not happened to theirs? What did their plants have which yours lacked?

Making and doing activities

The problem for the child is:
'Can you make something to keep the birds away?'

You need:
milk-bottle tops; foil; silver paper; tissue paper; tissues; polythene sheet (shop bags to cut up); polystyrene pieces; a variety of paper and card; junk materials of all kinds (to make a scarecrow?); string; thread; scissors; sticks; twigs; a large blunt needle.

1 The problem	Can you make something to keep the birds away?
2 Exploring the problem	Why do you need to keep the birds away from seeds? How do the birds get to the seeds? How can you stop them? How long will whatever you make have to last? What sort of conditions will it have to stand up to?
3 Ideas for solving the problem	Could you put something over the ground to protect the seeds? Could you make something which would frighten the birds? What materials have you that could be used? Which materials will stand up to the weather conditions and to the birds? (If the children have not yet used any of the materials they may need to set up an investigation to find out if the materials will withstand the weather.)
4 Making	The problems encountered here will depend very much on what the children decide to make. If they lack ideas you could encourage them towards threading milk bottle tops and bits of

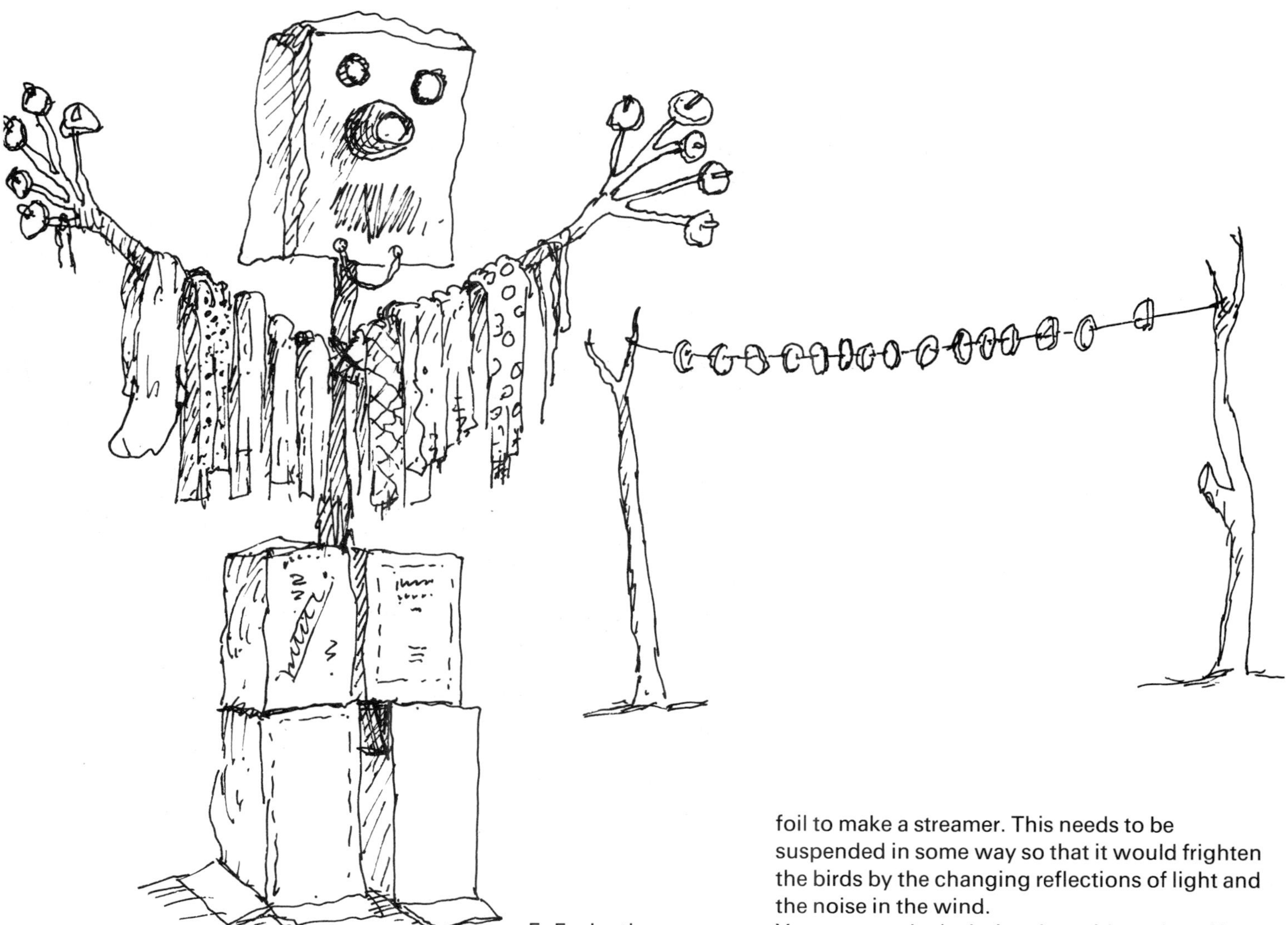

Scarecrow made from junk and threaded milk bottle tops

foil to make a streamer. This needs to be suspended in some way so that it would frighten the birds by the changing reflections of light and the noise in the wind.

5 Evaluating

You can put the 'solutions' outside and see if they do keep the birds away and stand up to the weather.

How do farmers keep the birds away?

Further activities

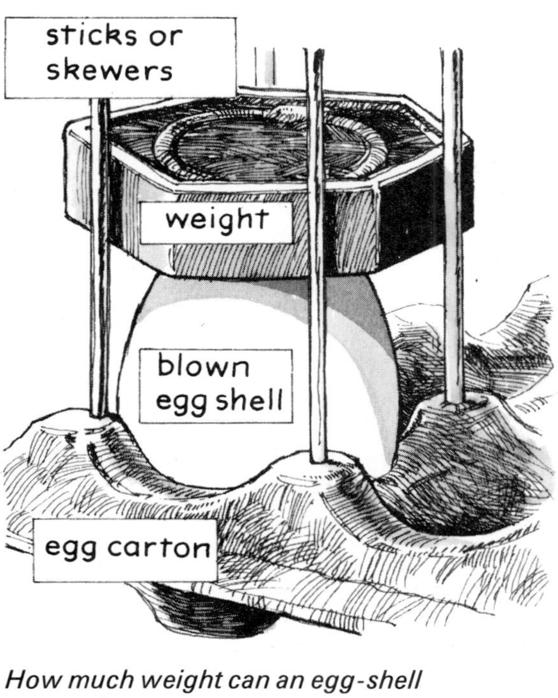

How much weight can an egg-shell support?

Some suggestions

1 Half-fill identical jam-jars with water and add one measure of wallpaper-paste powder to the first jar; two measures to the second jar; three to the third, and so on.

Stir the mixtures well and leave the jars to stand for 15–20 minutes. Use a pea-timer (page 80) to discover how long it takes to empty the paste from each of the first three jars. You can record your results on a table. Do the children think that the fourth jar will take a longer or shorter time than the third jar?

2 Test the effectiveness of different paste mixtures by using them to stick small identical boxes to a vertical surface. Whilst the paste is still wet, small weights can be put in the boxes and you can investigate what weight each paste mixture can support.

3 Can the children find flowers that can be put into these sets?
Sometimes yellow   Always yellow   Never yellow

4 Hens are quite big birds and they sit on their eggs. How much weight can an egg-shell stand before it breaks? Blow several eggs carefully and use the egg shells. Support them in an egg tray or similar and arrange weights on top.

5 Use your library to find out what various birds' eggs look like. Find out where the birds build their nests.

6 Find out how chocolate Easter eggs are made.

Language

Mathematics

Physical education

Creative arts

Science

People and their jobs and occupations

Starter Book page 22

Science activities

Making and doing

Teachers' Book page 76

Further activities

Teachers' Book page 77

Introduction

Science activities

The activities in this topic develop further the processes of observing and classifying and provide opportunities for recording using set nomenclature and simple sorting keys. These are constructed by children actually handling objects and physically putting them in place. The recording is a pictorial representation of what was produced. In Activity 4, 'Torches', the children explore the components which are needed to make the torch produce light. They work with a simple circuit which provides them with more experience of what metals do and other materials do not do. Do not push the children too quickly towards generalisations. It is more important that they gain experience.

Making and doing activities

The problem for the child is:
'Can you pick up things without touching them with your fingers?'
This activity does not involve making anything but is a problem-solving exercise which the children will enjoy tackling.

The police Science activities

Activity Po1 — Lost property

Classifying, using two or three attributes

You need:
a pencil; scissors; an iron nail; a zinc nail; an iron screw; an aluminium screw; a brass screw; a plastic fork; a stainless steel fork; a strong magnet; a piece of tissue paper; a flat balloon; a thin plastic drink cup; a sealed empty metal can; a stoppered plastic bottle; a thin plastic bag; wooden blocks (large and small).

1 Put all the objects on the table and let the children examine them and make their own comments about them.
2 Tell the children that you are thinking of one of the objects which is on the table and that you will tell them two things about it. Then say, for example, "It is pointed and attracted by a magnet." The children can then pick out the set of pointed things (pencil, scissors, nails and screws, forks). Ask them now to find out which of these are attracted by a magnet and let them test the set of pointed objects which they have picked out. They can record their results like this.

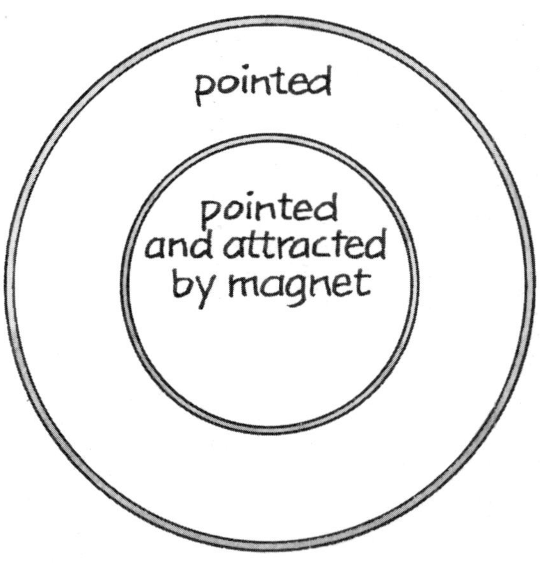

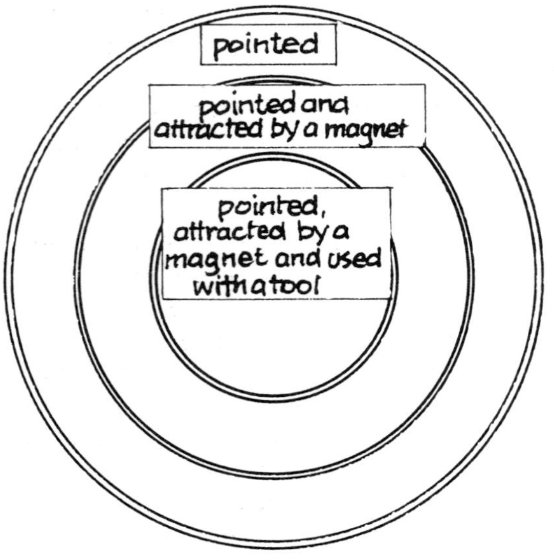

Sorting into sets

Tell the children that you will tell them something else about the object you're thinking of: "It is pointed, attracted by a magnet *and it is used with a tool*." The children should then be able to select the iron nail. You can provide the labels for the sets and sets within sets. The children can draw their own records.

3 Put the objects together again and say, "The object of which I am thinking is very thin and it is flexible." (Make sure that they do understand the word 'flexible'.) The children will have to decide which objects are very thin e.g. tissue paper, plastic bag, etc. Make sure that the deflated balloon is included. Next the children should decide which of these is flexible.

Finally you can tell them that the object is very thin, flexible and it will *stretch*. They should now be able to pick out the balloon.

You could help the children to draw a flow chart on a large piece of card or on the floor or a table.

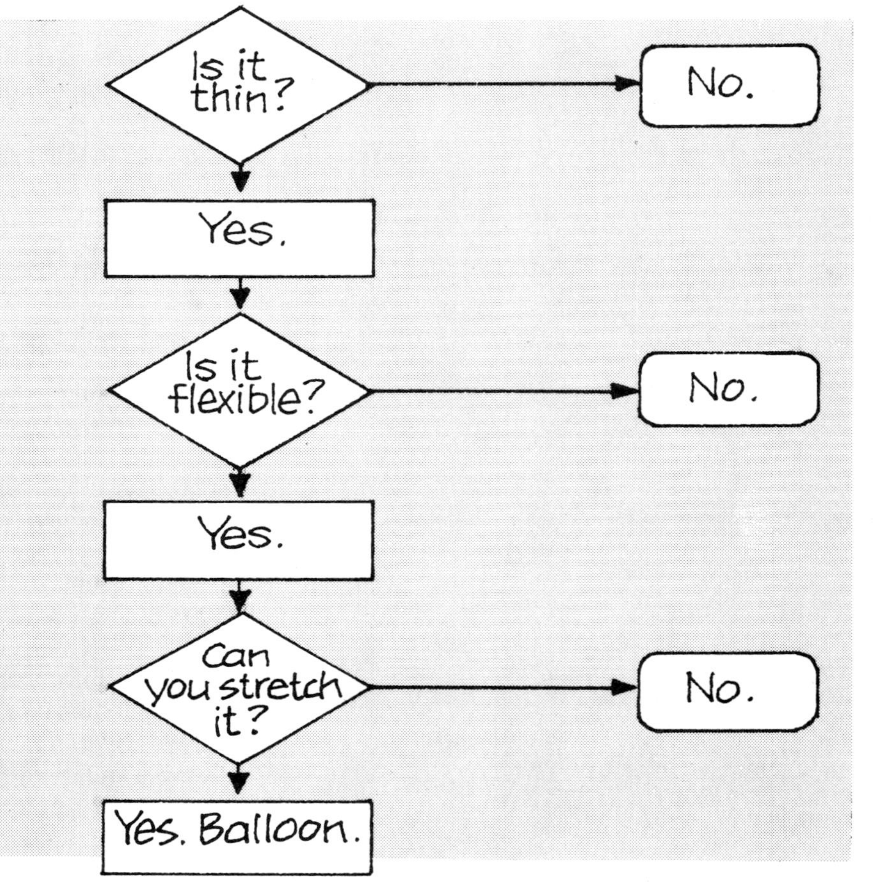

4 Do this activity several times with the children until they are ready to choose an object and suggest attributes themselves. Tell them to think of an object and say three things about it. The first thing should be about what it is like e.g. colour, shape, texture, smell and the second thing should be about what it does e.g. floats/sinks, bends, rolls, spins, lets light through, pours, dissolves, melts, etc. (You can use any random collection of items for this activity.) The third thing should be a special distinctive characteristic of the particular object.

Activity Po2—Lost persons

Observing the features of an individual and communicating the observations to a second person

You need:
several large sheets of sugar paper; sellotape; felt-tip pens; paint and brushes; a scarf.

1 Begin by asking two boys in the group to stand side by side. Ask the rest of the group how these two children are the same (not clothes).

The children should be able to tell you that they are both boys, they each have one head, two eyes, two ears, one nose, one mouth, hair, two legs, two feet, two arms, two hands and one body.

2 Now ask how the two children are different. Tell the children to look at the shape of the body. Is one boy fatter than the other? Does one have longer legs than the other? Does one have bigger feet? Encourage them to consider how the hair is different e.g. straight/curly, fair/dark, coarse/fine, longer/shorter. Look at the eyes. Are they blue, brown, grey, green? Does one have a fairer or a darker skin? Do either of them have any marked features e.g. freckles?

3 Repeat this with two girls and then with a girl and a boy.

4 Blindfold one of the children in the group and ask another of them to stand in front. Ask the blindfolded child to identify the other by touching. What can the blindfolded child tell you about the hair of the other child? What cannot be discovered by touching?

5 Now tell the children that you are going to describe someone in the class so that the other children can identify him. Say, for example, "He is tall with short brown hair and brown eyes." Let the children first choose the 'tall' set, then the 'short brown hair' sub-set and then the sub-set within this of 'brown eyes'. If there are several members of this sub-set, you will have to give more attributes.

6 When the children are ready let them take turns at describing someone with the rest of the class helping to choose the members of the sets and sub-sets as they are described.

7 Explain to the children that you are going to have an 'identification parade'. Suggest that they work in pairs. One child of the pair should lie down on a large sheet of paper so that the other one of the pair can draw round his/her body. The children should then change places so that each of them has a turn.

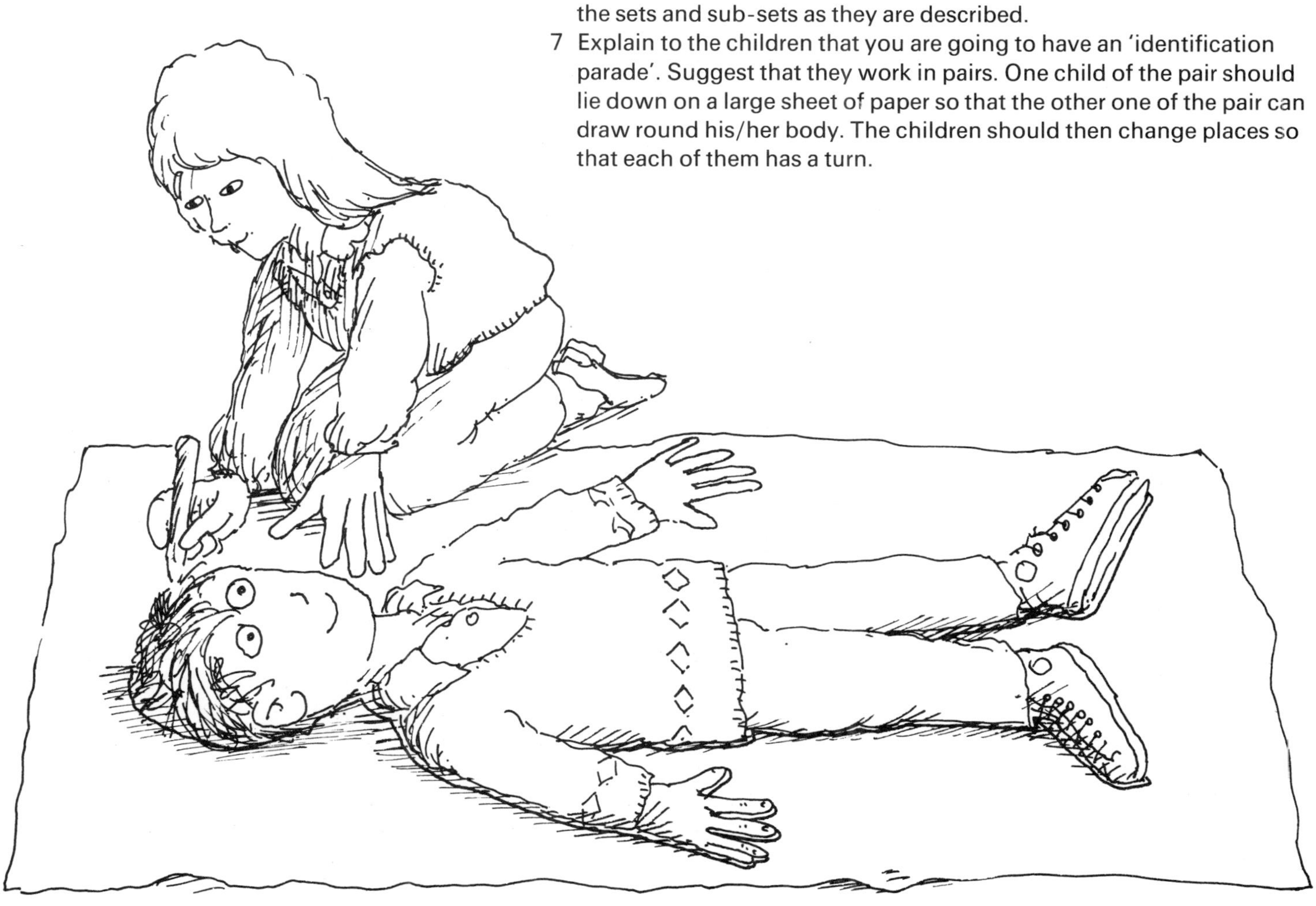

8 Suggest that the children now paint in their partner's features. They will have to look very carefully so that they get the details correct. They can complete their pictures by painting in the clothes.

9 When they have finished they should write the name on the back of the drawing. You can make a display of them and the children can try to identify them.

10 When this is completed there is plenty of visual material for the children to use for sets and for block graphs e.g. hair colour, eye colour, height, etc.

Activity Po3—Fingerprints

Observing and investigating hands

You need:
a large mirror; several sheets of white paper; one or two ink pads; scissors; pencils; magnifying glasses; kitchen paper.

1 Begin by telling the children to look carefully at their hands. How many fingers have they on each hand? How many thumbs? Do they know which are the palms of their hands? Do they know which are their knuckles/wrists? Can they match their hands exactly with palms facing inwards/outwards?
2 Let one of the children put his/her hand palm down on the mirror. What is seen in the mirror? Which hand does it look like? What happens if the child holds one hand with his/her thumb against the mirror? Which hand does the reflection look like? Can they make the reflection look like the hand it belongs to? (No. The reflection is the mirror image of the object. One of our hands is the mirror image of the other, ditto our feet. Don't try to explain this to the children. Just let them absorb the experience.)
3 Ask the children which hand they write with. Can they tell you whether it is the left hand or the right hand? Using 'first' for index finger, 'second', 'third', and 'fourth' ask the children which fingers they use to hold a pencil and scissors.
4 Now give the children magnifying glasses and let them examine their hands. How is the palm different from the back? Draw their attention to the joints on the back of the hand and then to their finger tips. Ask them to describe what they see. Do both hands look exactly the same? Has one hand got features that the other hasn't?
5 They should now work in pairs and stand facing each other. Let them match their hands to their partners. Can they tell you which hands are touching – left or right? Ask them if their hands are bigger/smaller than their partners' hands. Suggest now that they shake hands. Which hands are touching now? What happens if they put their right hands together palms facing? (There is a lot of exploring to do here. All the discoveries are the result of the mirror image relationship between our hands.)

Left hands together

6 Let one child sit at the table with his/her hands on a piece of paper. Let another child stand behind and draw round the hands. Discuss which is the left hand and which is the right hand and then label them.
7 Now tell the children that they are going to make fingerprints. Suggest that they begin with the fourth finger on the left hand. Let them practise getting a good print by pressing the finger on to the ink pad and then pressing several times on to a piece of white kitchen paper. When they are satisfied tell them to print their finger in the appropriate place on their drawn hands and to continue until they have a full set.
8 When they have washed their hands let them look at their fingerprints using a magnifying glass. Do all the prints look the same? How are they different? Are they different from those of the other children? How are they different?
9 You can cut out the drawn hands, label them on the backs and then mix them up and see if the children can find their own 'hands'.

Activity Po4—Torches

Investigating which materials would make a 'switch' for a torch

You need
a variety of torches; two or three spare torch bulbs; a clear light bulb; a magnifying glass; a collection of small pieces of a variety of materials (polystyrene, strips of different kinds of plastic, strips of aluminium foil, strips of metal bottle tops including wine bottle tops, strips of silver paper, pieces of wood, rubber, cloth); a variety of small objects made of plastic, wood and metal (including coins and a small metal spoon); a circuit as shown on the left. (See also pages 149–151.)

A circuit

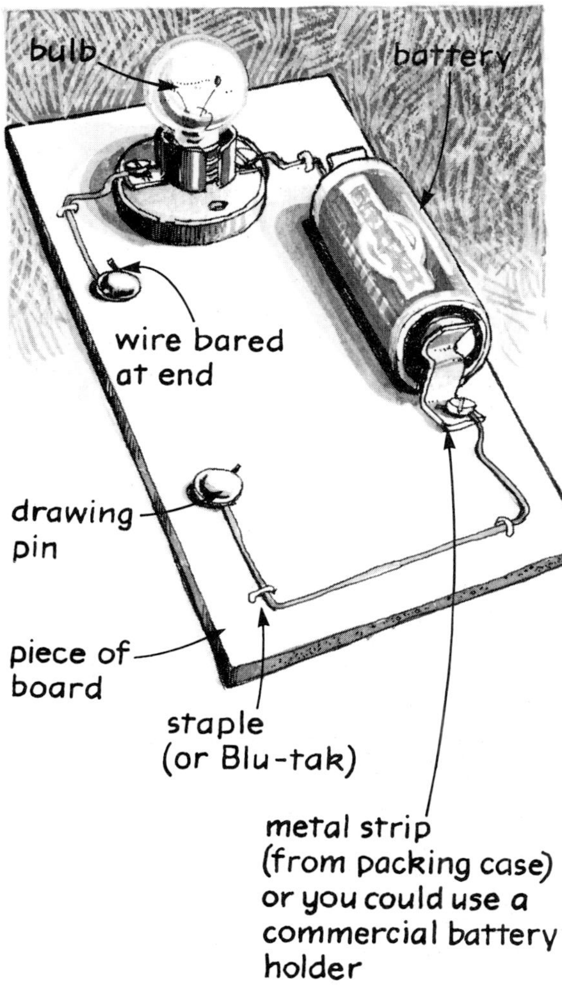

1 Let the children handle the torches and make their own comments about them. Can they switch them on? Which gives the brightest light? How are the torches the same? How are they different? Can the children find different ways of sorting them into sets (shape, colour, material, type of switch, bulb arrangement)? Can they use their developing 'science' vocabulary in their descriptions?
2 Ask the children what they think is inside each torch. What do they need to do to get the torches apart (pull/screw)?

Let each child take a torch apart whilst the rest of the group watch. Ask them how many batteries are inside and what shape they are. Let them screw the holder back on without the batteries. How does it feel different (lighter)? Does it work? Does it matter which way round the batteries go? Let them try to put the batteries back in so that the torches work. Can they tell you how the batteries should be arranged? Can they draw a picture to help someone who doesn't know?
3 When the torches are put together again draw the children's attention to the lens end of the torch and encourage them to describe its shape. Which part of the torch lights up? Give them the spare torch bulbs to look at. What are they made of? What is inside? Let them use a magnifying glass to find out. (The bigger electric light bulb is easier to see.) What can they see round the bulb in the torch? Are all the torches silvery round the bulb? If the children had any problem before in telling you how torches are all the same you could ask them again now.
4 Now show them the circuit and tell them that this is like a torch opened out and without its case. Indicate the bulb and the battery and the gap. Point out that the light is not on. If this was a real torch what would they have to do to make the light come on? (Switch it on.) Explain that you don't have a switch but if you could put something across the gap you think you could make the light come on. Show them that a small metal spoon and a line of coins firmly touching each other work.

Say that you would like them to find out which of the things in your collection would act as a switch and suggest that they put the things across the gap one by one. What will happen if the pieces do work as switches? What will happen if they don't? Give the children two sorting circles. Label one "Does work as a switch." and the other "Does not work as a switch."

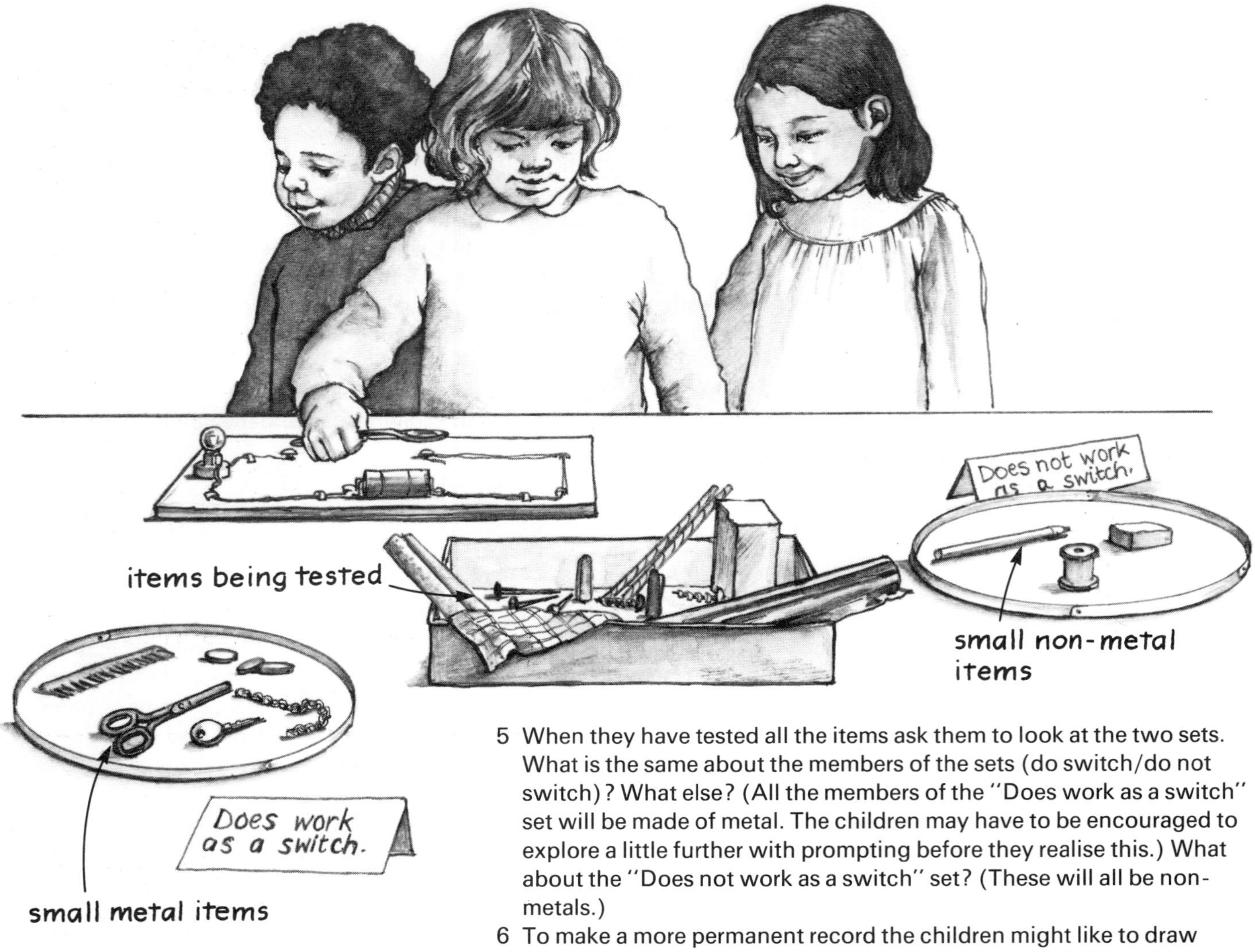

5 When they have tested all the items ask them to look at the two sets. What is the same about the members of the sets (do switch/do not switch)? What else? (All the members of the "Does work as a switch" set will be made of metal. The children may have to be encouraged to explore a little further with prompting before they realise this.) What about the "Does not work as a switch" set? (These will all be non-metals.)
6 To make a more permanent record the children might like to draw round each object or material; colour it; cut it out and then stick it in the correct circle. If you like you can also let the children label each of the items they have drawn round.

Making and doing activities

The problem for the child is:
'Can you pick up things without touching them with your fingers?'

You need:
on a non-metal tray, a number of small objects which the children can pick up and transfer to another non-metal tray (several small stainless steel teaspoons, empty fairly wide-necked plastic bottles, plastic cups, something with a small ring which can be hooked up, a saucer containing a small amount of milk, a yoghurt carton, a match box); a saucer on the other tray; for each child to use as a picking-up aid: a length of stiff wire, a balloon (uninflated), a strong magnet, a sponge, two rulers.

1 The problem	Can you pick up things without touching them with your fingers?
2 Exploring the problem 3 Ideas for solving the problem 4 Making	Let the children look at the various items which are to be picked up and at the picking up aids which are provided. The problem is different from previous ones in that there is not really anything to make. The children need to consider how they can best use the aids to pick up a particular item. If they do not think of inflating the balloon or bending the wire to make a hook, ask them which of the aids would be more useful if their shapes were changed.

Picking things up with a magnet, an inflated balloon and wire

5 Evaluating — Did they manage to move the things from one tray to the other without touching them with their fingers?

They might like to record their results like this:

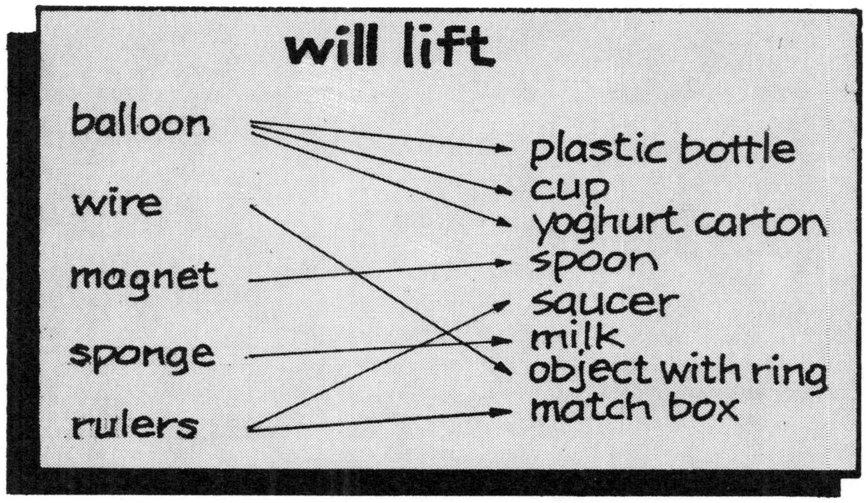

They will discover other connections.

Further activities

Some suggestions

1 Invite your local police officer to talk to the children about his/her work (not just road safety).
2 Look at other media for making fingerprints e.g. cooking oil, talcum powder, paint, charcoal, carbon paper.
3 Play Kim's game. (Put out a collection of objects and let the children look at them. Then remove one without the children seeing. Let them look again and decide which object is missing. There are a number of variations of this game.)
4 Make an identikit picture using iron filings and a magnet. Place the magnet underneath the paper drawing of a face and put the iron filings on top. The children can move the magnet so that the iron filings form 'hair', a 'moustache' and a 'beard'. The picture can be 'fixed' with hair spray.
5 The children can draw a self portrait using a mirror or draw a portrait of a friend sitting opposite.
6 The children could act out a story about being lost.

Language

Mathematics

Physical education

Creative arts

Science

People and their jobs and occupations

Starter Book page 24

Science activities

Making and doing

Teachers' Book page 84

Further activities

Teachers' Book page 84

Introduction

Science activities

One of the features of this topic is the use of a 'pea timer' to enable children to investigate how long it takes them to carry out various actions and to compare the times. In particular they start to investigate the relationship between distance and time taken. For your own class you may be able to provide evidence that there is a direct relationship between the distance you have to go (in following possible fire escape routes) and the time taken, but the children may not yet be ready to appreciate this.

The investigation of breathing will add to the children's understanding of themselves and how their bodies work.

Making and doing activities

The problem for the child is:
'Can you decide where to put the fire station in a model village?'

This is a different kind of problem. The solution requires a decision as to where the fire station should be so that the houses can be reached as quickly as possible.

The firefighter Science activities

Activity F1—Charred wood

Observing some properties of wood and the changes caused by burning

You need:
several small branches about 1.5–2 cm thick pruned from trees or shrubs (some should be burned to produce ash and charred wood); a piece of drawing charcoal for each child; wax crayons.

1 Give the children some pieces of the branches. Ask them to observe them closely. What can they tell you about the pieces? Help them to notice that the bark is like a skin. What colour is it? How many different colours can they find in the bark? Do the colours make patterns? Are there light patches and dark patches?
2 What does the bark feel like? Is it smooth or rough? Are there any patterns in the texture? Let the children make a rubbing of the bark using wax crayons. Do all the rubbings look the same/different? Why are they the same/different? Let the children pull some bark off the branches. What is it like? Is it the same colour all the way through? What colours can they see? What does it feel like? Is it rigid or flexible? Is it dry or damp?
3 Now ask the children to look at the wood inside. What colour is it? Can they see any lines? What patterns do they see on the cut ends of the branches? Is it easy to break bits off or to snap the branch in two?
4 Ask the children to check that their hands are clean. Give them a charred branch. What has happened to it? How has the burning changed the branch? How does it look different? What colours can they see? Can they see any other differences – pieces missing, cracks, etc.?
5 How does it feel different? Can they peel a piece of bark off? What happens? Is it still flexible? What happens to their hands? Can they break the branch where it is charred? Can they see any of the patterns that they saw in the new wood?
6 If the charred wood makes a mark on their hands will it make a mark on paper? Let the children find out whether it will. Give them a piece of drawing charcoal each. Can they tell you how it has been made? What is it? Let them use the charcoal to draw a branch of a tree or some of the patterns they have seen. Draw their attention to how the charcoal smudges.

Activity F2—Speed and movement

Investigating ways of moving and their relative speed

You need:
two small boxes or tins; about twenty dried peas or wooden beads.

1 Take the children into the school hall or outside. Tell them there are two points to move between e.g. the wall and the window. Ask them to find different ways of moving from one to the other. How many ways can they find with just their feet coming into contact with the ground e.g. walking, hopping, skipping, running, jumping? Which do the children think are quite fast ways of moving? Which do they think are quite slow?

2 Can the children think of a way of checking which is the fastest way of moving and which is the slowest? They may suggest two or three children racing against each other using different ways of moving. Try this. Why do they all have to start and finish in the same place? Was it a good test? Will someone running always go faster than someone jumping?

3 What happens if children race over a short distance and over a long distance? How big is the gap between the winner and the second over the short distance? How big is the gap over a long distance? Why do they think the gap is different? The children will probably say that racing makes them very tired or out of breath if they have to do it for very long. All the ideas that emerge will make good discussion points.

Using a pea-timer

4 Is there anyone who is very fast at hopping? Can that child hop faster than he or she can run? How could the children find out? An easy way of timing is to use two open boxes and some dried peas or wooden beads. A child moves the peas from one box to the other, one at a time. The number of peas moved can be counted. The children can find out their own fastest and slowest ways of moving with a friend operating the pea-timer.

This can be recorded. For example,
When I ran my friend moved 5 peas.
When I hopped my friend moved 8 peas.
I can run faster than I can hop.
I hop more slowly than I can run.

Activity F3—Clothes and speed

Investigating the speed of dressing using different fasteners

You need:
shoes with laces and buckles; jackets and coats with buttons and zips; hats; a pea-timer (page 80).

1 Look at the children's shoes. Discuss the different types of fastening. Which are easy to fasten? Which are hard to fasten? Which are quick to fasten? Which are slow? Do the children think it is quicker to fasten laces or buckles? How can they find out? You may arrange a race between children with buckles on shoes and the children with laces on shoes. Did all the 'laces' beat all the 'buckles' or vice versa? Or did some 'laces' beat some 'buckles'? How many 'laces' were there in the first five to finish?
2 Are some children quicker at fastening laces than buckles and are others quicker at fastening buckles than laces? Use the pea-timer to check. Why do you think that is? Can the children suggest that practice improves performance or that some buckles are stiffer than others?
3 The children could use their model shoe-lacing cards which they made (page 7) to find out if practising helps to speed up performance. Working in pairs they could use a pea-timer to find each other's times for tieing laces. They could then both practice for an agreed length of time or number of 'ties' and then repeat the timing process to see if they have improved their performance.
4 Now look at coats or jackets comparing zips and buttons. What do they have to do to make comparison of buttons 'fair'? Are zips always faster than buttons? How much faster is the fastest 'zip' than the slowest 'buttons'? Use the pea-timer.
5 Give the children a selection of shoes, jackets and hats. Can they choose a pair of shoes, a jacket and a hat that they would be very quick to put on? They should give reasons for their choice. Can they choose a pair of shoes, a jacket and a hat that they would be very slow to put on? Again ask for reasons. Try out their suggestions using a pea-timer and find out if they were right.

Activity F4—Breathing

Investigating breathing

You need:
things which the children can blow along (feathers, tissue paper pieces); small boats; string; strips of paper; scissors; jam jars; milk straws; water tray or access to a sink; a washing-up bowl of water; paper bags.

1 Let the children explore what happens when they blow out. They can blow along pieces of tissue paper, feathers, etc. They can blow boats across water. They can blow on their hands and blow through straws into water. What comes out when they blow out or breathe out? Can we see it? What colour is it? How do they know something comes out?
2 Where does the air go in and out when they breathe? Can they breathe with their mouths shut? Where does the air go in? Can they breathe with both their noses and their mouths shut? (Beware of too much deep breathing. Punctuate the breathing questions with plenty of discussion.)
3 Where does the air go when they breathe in? Which part of the body moves? How does it move? Tell them to put their hands on the sides of their chests. Breathe in and out. What can they feel? Do their chests get bigger or smaller when they breathe in?
How could we measure the chest? Try out the children's suggestions. Strips of paper or string cut where they meet round the chest provide a simple solution. Each child should have two pieces – one to measure round the chest on the out-breath and one to measure the chest when it is expanded. A friend should wrap the paper or string

round and mark it before cutting it the right length. In this way the two measures can be compared. The strips of paper can be stuck on a sheet of paper to show the results of this investigation.

How big is your chest when you breathe in and out?

4 How much air comes out when they breathe out? Could the air be caught in something? You could let the children try blowing into bags. Remind them of the bubbles that go into the water when they blow under water through a straw. Is there any way that they could catch the bubbles? Use a jam-jar and turn it upside down in a bowl of water. Does the water go into the jar (No)? What is in the jar (air)? How can they get it out? Fill the jar with water and invert it under the water surface. What happens if they lift up the jar but keep the mouth of the jar below the surface? Is there any air in the jar? Can they blow through the straw so that air goes into the jar?

5 Can they fill the jar with air with one blow? How many blows does it take? They can record the results graphically.

Activity F5—Moving water

Investigating a siphon

You need:
a water tray; a bowl or bucket; a block to support this; a transparent plastic tube; various objects to make 'hills' over which the siphon tube can pass.

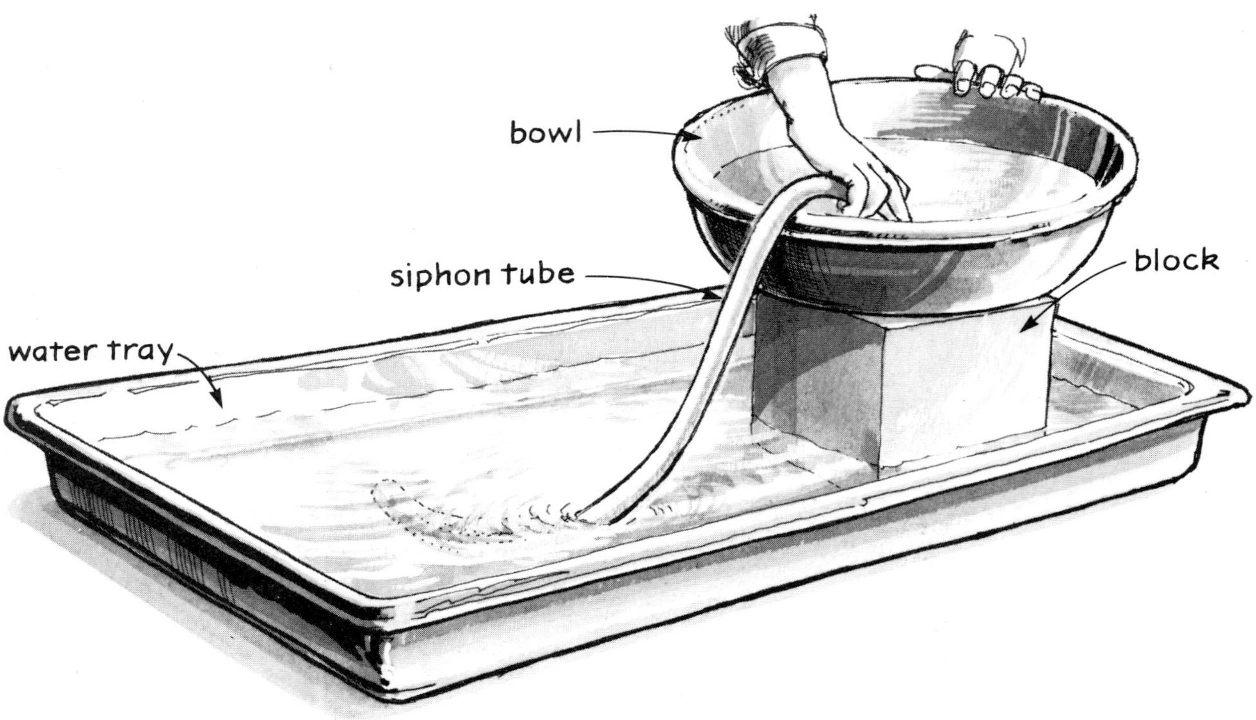

1 Put the bowl or bucket full of water on a block in the water tray.

Show the children how to fill the tube with water. Let two children work together. The first child should hold the end of the full tube firmly and hold its end beneath the surface of the water in the bowl or bucket. At the same time the second child keeps tight hold of the other end of the tube and holds it in the tray. When both ends are in position the first child can let go and then the second child. What happens?

2 Let the children use the various objects to make 'hills'. How high a hill can they make the water go over? Can the children tell you? Can the children show you? Can they explain what they have discovered?

Water going over 'hills'

Activity F6—Fire drill

Investigating escape times and distances; is the shortest route the quickest?

You need:
suitable objects to use as arbitrary measures e.g. unmarked metre sticks, a pea-timer (page 80). Note: If the times to be measured go beyond 'twenty peas', it may be necessary to collect in multiples of ten peas.

This may be a difficult activity if the escape route is long or complicated by stairs, etc.

1 What must the children do if the fire bell goes? Which way must they all go out? How far is it from their classroom to the door where they go out? What could be used to measure the distance? The children may choose to count strides or feet or use a stick to measure. Is there any other door to the outside which is nearer to their classroom? Try measuring to other doors. If there is one nearer why do they not use it for fire drill? Find out how long it takes for your class to get outside by the different routes using the pea-timer. Which is the shortest route? Which is the quickest route? They can record their results in a table.

2 Do all the classes have the same distance to go to an outside door? Which class has the furthest distance to go? Which has the shortest distance?

3 Which class would they expect to get outside most quickly? Why do they think that? You could arrange a fire drill and let them use pea-timers to time other classes.

Making and doing activities

The problem for the child is:
'Can you decide where to put the fire station in a model village?'

You need:
for each group – a plan of the village; materials for making model houses, traffic lights, pelican crossings, etc. which each child can put in place on his/her village plan. The plan should be drawn on a large piece of card. Make it fairly complex.

For example:

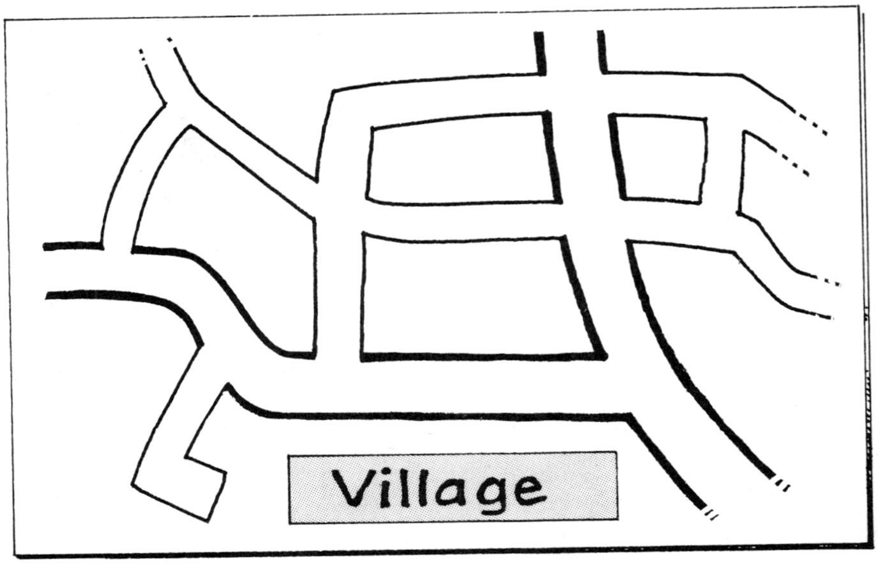

The children can then decide where to put the houses, the school, the church, etc. and make models of these and put them in place.

1 The problem	Can you decide where to put the fire station?
2 Exploring the problem	If there is a fire, the fire engine needs to get there as fast as possible. Which route will be the fastest? Where should the fire station be so that it can get quickly to all the houses? Is distance the only important thing? What about traffic lights, etc.?
3 Ideas for solving the problem	The children might like to try putting the fire station at different points and estimating whether this is more or less a central position.
4 Making 5 Evaluating	When they have decided where to put their fire stations, ask them to measure the distance to the furthest house in each of their villages and make a note of any 'hold-ups' the fire engine might encounter on the way.

Further activities

Some suggestions

1 Visit a fire station or arrange for the fire engine to visit your school. Let the children check what kind of fasteners are on firefighters' clothes. What kind of special clothes do they have? Why?
2 Investigate the use of colour and sound as danger warnings.
3 Look at quick escapes – chutes, ladders, slippery poles, etc. Why are they quick?
4 Find out what other jobs firefighters do apart from putting out fires.
5 Look for fire hydrants and talk to the children about why they are needed. How far apart are they? How can we measure the distance?
6 Ask them to write a story about a fire.

Language

Mathematics

Physical education

Creative arts

Science

People and their jobs and occupations

Starter Book page 26

Science activities

Starting points	*Starter Book* page	26
Activities	*Teachers' Book*	86
M1 Drinking straw Investigating using a straw		86
M2 Sterilised or pasteurised? Investigating milk		87
M3 Cottage cheese Investigating what happens to milk when vinegar is added		88
M4 Bottles and glasses Investigating what happens when you look through bottles and glasses which are empty and then filled with water		89

Making and doing

Teachers' Book page 90

Further activities

Teachers' Book page 91

Introduction

Science activities

This topic provides an opportunity to explore a number of interesting areas. Milk is a remarkable substance which undergoes many changes. The cream can be processed to produce butter. Cheese can be produced and so can yoghurt and junket. Even if milk is just left alone it will rapidly undergo change and become sour.

We have picked out the changes in souring and in producing cheese as processes which children can observe and investigate. The production of cheese is surprising. We start with a liquid. We add something and a solid appears. We have a cause and an effect.

Observing mould growth on bread can be the beginning of an on-going study of moulds. There are a wide variety of moulds which will grow on different foods particularly fruits and vegetables. You can even establish a mould garden in a covered aquarium tank or you can grow your moulds in plastic bags. (Do not be tempted to grow bacteria from breath, fingers, etc. as is sometimes suggested in science books. This is not acceptable classroom activity.)

Activity 4 involves very careful (and puzzling) observation which the children will enjoy. Because it is puzzling they may find it quite difficult to record what they see. They may need reassurance that they are indeed seeing what they think though they cannot understand why!

Making and doing activities

The problem for the child is:

'Can you make a game (or toy) in which you have to blow through a straw?'

This is a very open-ended problem which may produce a variety of solutions.

Milk Science activities

Activity M1—Drinking straw

Investigating using a straw

You need:
a glass half-full of milk for each child; ordinary drinking straws; 'bendy' straws; 'fun' straws; yoghurt cartons.

1 Give the children their glasses of milk and give each of them an ordinary drinking straw. Ask the children about the straw's colour and its shape. Can they recognise that it is a cylinder? Suggest that they try just sucking through the straw. What happens? What do they feel in their mouths (air)? Ask them what happens if the end of the straw is covered with a finger before sucking?
2 What happens if the children blow down their straws? What can they hear? What can they feel if they put their hands near the end of the straw? How far can the children move their hands away from the ends of the straws and still feel the air? Suggest that they put their fingers over the ends of the straws and try to blow again. Why is it hard to blow? Can they tell you that the air cannot get out?
3 Let the children have a drink of milk through their straws. Suggest that when they are sucking they put their tongues over the ends of the straws and carefully lift the straws out of the milk. What happens? Now tell them to move their tongues. What happens to the milk in the straws now? They can try the same thing with the 'bendy' straws and the 'fun' straws. Did the shape of the straw make any difference? Let them finish drinking their milk.

4 Ask them to put some drinking water in their glasses, after they have been washed. Ask the children if they can transfer the water from the glass to the yoghurt carton without touching the glass or the carton. Some children may continue to use their tongues, others will realise that it is easier to use a finger to cover the straw.

Activity M2—Sterilised or pasteurised?

Investigating milk

You need:
a pint (or half-litre) bottle of sterilised milk; a pint (or half-litre) bottle of pasteurised milk; a bottle opener; several clean yoghurt cartons; a funnel; sticky labels; a ruler.

1 Put both bottles of milk on the table and ask the children how they are different. Can they tell you that the sterilised bottle is thinner than the pasteurised? Can they tell you that it has a narrower neck and a smaller base? Draw their attention to the fact that the sterilised bottle has a bigger space at the top. Can they see through the milk? Can they see through the space? Introduce the word 'transparent'.
2 Ask the children if they think the bottles will sound the same when tapped. Try this and see if the children can identify the bottles by sound alone.
3 Get the children to look at and feel the tops of the bottles. What are they made of? Which is the harder material and which the softer? Which do they think will be easier to remove? Let a child try to remove the tops by pressing the centres. What happens? How can we take the top off the sterilised bottle? Show them a bottle opener and ask the children to tell you how the bottle opener is doing its job. Which bit of it is pressing down? Which bit is pulling up? What is your hand doing?

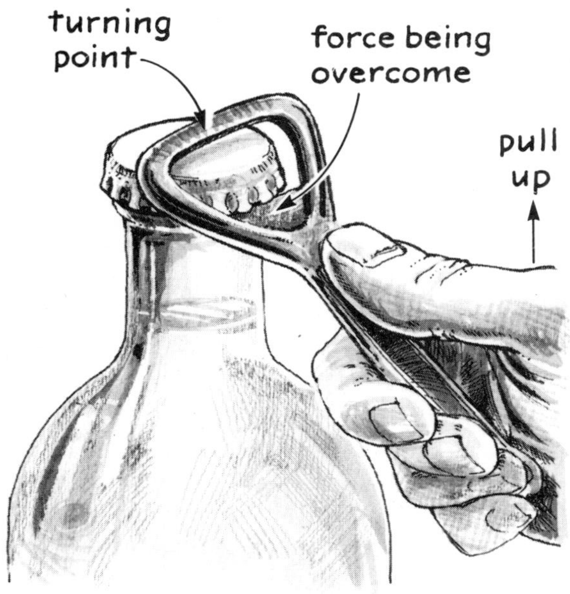

Bottle opener

4 Now ask the children which bottle has more milk in it. How can they find out? They will probably suggest finding out how many yoghurt cartons can be filled from each bottle. Take your collection of yoghurt cartons and let one child find out how many can be filled from the sterilised bottle. Let another child pour the milk from the pasteurised bottle. The children can then count the cartons and tell you that both bottles must hold the same. Is it what they expected? If they look at the bottles again can they tell you why they made a wrong guess?
5 Tell the children that you need the milk back in the bottles. Ask them which bottle will be difficult to pour into. Why is this? What could they use to make it easier? Remind them of a funnel if they have forgotten this. Let them use a funnel to return the milk to the appropriate bottle.
6 Give each of the children two yoghurt cartons and two labels and tell them to write their names on both labels and put an S on one and a P (S sterilised and P pasteurised) on the other. Now pour a small amount of milk into each of the appropriate cartons. Give the children a small drink of the two kinds of milk. Suggest that the children smell the milk. How are they different?
7 Now ask the children what they think will happen to the milk if it is left overnight. Leave the milk in a warm place (so that it will go sour).
8 Next day ask the children to look at the milk again. How has it changed? How does it look different? How does it smell different? Has the same thing happened to both kinds of milk? What happens if you tip the pasteurised milk to one side? What is left on the side of the carton? What has formed on the surface of the milk? Tell the children that the pasteurised milk has turned sour. Has the sterilised milk done the same thing?
9 Ask the children if they can think of a way of stopping pasteurised milk going sour. They may suggest putting it in a cool place or putting it in the refrigerator.

10 Try the children's suggestions and help them to draw their own conclusions about which kind of milk keeps better and where milk should be kept to keep it fresh. Get them to understand that sterilised milk keeps longer than pasteurised milk and that warm conditions make the milk go sour faster.

Activity M3—Cottage cheese

Investigating what happens to milk when vinegar is added

You need:
one pint (half-litre) pasteurised milk; two glass pans; vinegar; a tablespoon; sieve; slices of bread; butter/margarine; a perforated spoon; kitchen roll; cheese cloth/muslin; a colander; samples of cheese; small plastic bags; funnel; heat source; a plate and knife for each child; two yoghurt cartons and labels for each child.

Warning

This activity involves tasting.
You must emphasise to the children that we only taste things that we know are food. We never taste anything else. They must never taste anything in the classroom unless you tell them to do so. Make sure that this activity is carried out under hygienic conditions – wash hands, use a tablecloth, etc.

1 Give each child a piece of bread, a plate and a knife. Put the butter/margarine on the table along with the milk. Tell the children that they can butter their bread and whilst they are doing this ask them why it would be difficult to spread the milk with the knife. Can they tell you that milk is a liquid and butter is a solid?
2 What happens to the butter/margarine on the bread? (It stays where it is spread.) What happens if milk is put on bread? Let the children dip a small piece of bread into the milk and then tell you that the milk soaks into the bread because it is a liquid.
3 Tell the children that you are going to make the milk go solid. You are going to change it. Put the milk into the saucepan. Do not more than half fill it. Put the milk on to heat and let the children tell you what they see happening. (You can also put a pan of water on to heat at the same time so that the children can compare the water and the milk.)
4 Remove the milk from the heat when it boils and let the children watch as it starts to cool and settle in the pan. Now add one tablespoonful of vinegar and let the children take turns to stir the mixture. What happens? Encourage the children to say that some solid bits have been formed but there is also some liquid. What has been done to the milk to make it change? What has caused the change? (Heat and adding vinegar.)
5 Tell the children that the solid bits are called curds and ask if they can think of a way to separate the curds from the liquid (the whey). Try out their suggestions and let them try other ideas e.g. a perforated spoon, a colander, kitchen roll, a sieve, cheese cloth. Which works best and why?
6 When the curds have been removed encourage the children to look at the remaining liquid. How has it changed? How is the smell different? How is the taste different? How is the colour different?
7 Show the children the curds and suggest that they put some on their bread and taste it. Point out that you have made the milk change so that a solid has been produced as well as a liquid even though you started with one liquid (milk) and added another liquid (vinegar) to it. Do they know what the curds are? Do they know that they have made cottage cheese?
8 Let the children put the pieces of bread which were soaked in milk in the plastic bags. Leave these in a warm place for some days and let the children observe what happens. Do they all grow the same sort of mould or are they different? (Do not open the bags – the moulds may occasionally have a 'hay fever' effect on certain individuals.)

9 Put samples of the cottage cheese and other cheeses in plastic bags and leave these in a warm place. What happens to them? Mould growth provides opportunities for the children to devise various ways of recording their results. You can encourage them to describe, draw or keep a 'diary' according to their abilities and interests.

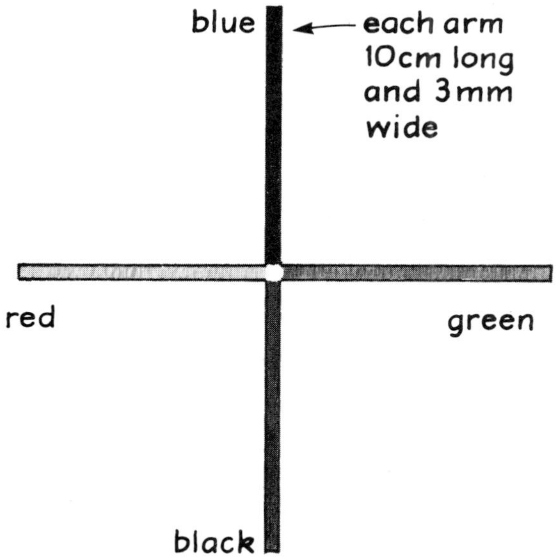

Activity M4—Bottles and glasses

Investigating what happens when you look through bottles and glasses which are empty and then filled with water

You need:
a variety of clear glass or plastic bottles with smooth sides (some should be cylindrical of varying diameters including milk bottles, some should have flat parallel faces) and jam-jars (all these bottles and jars should be stoppered); various clear plastic and glass glasses (tumblers, smaller glasses, wine glasses); an unrinsed milk bottle; a drawing of a cross as shown on the left.

1 Show the children the milk bottle. Remind them how milk goes sour and discuss why we rinse milk bottles before returning them to the milkman/woman. Show them how difficult it is to clean a milk bottle which has been left unrinsed.

2 Tell the children that they are going to find out what the little boy in the starter picture could see through the bottle. Let the children first of all look at all the bottles and encourage them to use their expanding 'science' vocabulary to describe the bottles as accurately as they can. Tell them to find a small object to look at and to remember what it looks like and how big it is.

Then suggest that they look at the object through the empty bottles. They can try turning the bottles in various ways. How does the object look through the bottles? What is different? What is the same? (There will probably be very little difference apart from distortions produced by the uneven glass.)

3 Now tell the children to fill the bottles and jars with water to the very top. (Try to get rid of the air bubble. If you have one, discuss with the children what it is.) They should then put the stoppers or lids on tightly. Let them now look at their objects again. They can put the bottles near their objects and stand away or they can put their eyes close to the bottle and go very near to the object. They should try the bottles upright (vertical) and on their sides (horizontal).

Looking at objects through bottles of water

4 What happens now? What is the same? What is different? (A cylindrical bottle will act like a lens. When close it will magnify and the children should notice this. It only acts in one direction so that if it is vertical, objects look wider but not taller. Objects close to will be the right way up and the right way round. Objects further away will be the wrong way up and the wrong way round.)

5 Get the children to put their bottles on their sides and go close to their objects so that they see them the right way up and magnified and then let them find out what happens as they go away from the object.

(If the positioning is right the children should see their object change from being the right way up to being upside down or vice-versa. It seems incredible to them when they first see this. You can let them look at the cross you have drawn. The colours will change place vertically. A vase of flowers also provides fun.)

6 Now try with the bottles vertical. In this case the children will see the colours of the cross change sides.

7 Let the children find out what happens with flat sided bottles and jars.

8 Ask the children to put water into glasses of various kinds. Let them look through the sides and from above. What happens? What do they see? How is what they see different from what is really there? (Convex curved bottles or glass bases magnify when close to. Concave bases, which many glasses have, diminish what is seen.) Can the children find a glass that makes things look smaller? Can they suggest why it makes things look smaller whilst the other glasses make things look bigger?

Making and doing activities

The problem for the child is:

'Can you make a game (or toy) in which you have to blow through a straw?'

You need:
straws (straight, bendy and crazy varieties); ping pong balls; pith balls would be useful; cotton wool; tissue and other papers; card; glue; scissors; a variety of junk; a water tray; a stapler; nails; hammer; thread.

1 The problem — Can you make a game (or toy) in which you have to blow through a straw?

2 Exploring the problem — What can air blown from a straw do? (Move something e.g. pieces of tissue paper, bits of cotton wool, pith balls, ping pong balls, floating things, hanging things?)

3 Ideas for solving the problem — Blow football, blow crazy-golf, a blow obstacle course, a blow boat race, blowing a windmill round?

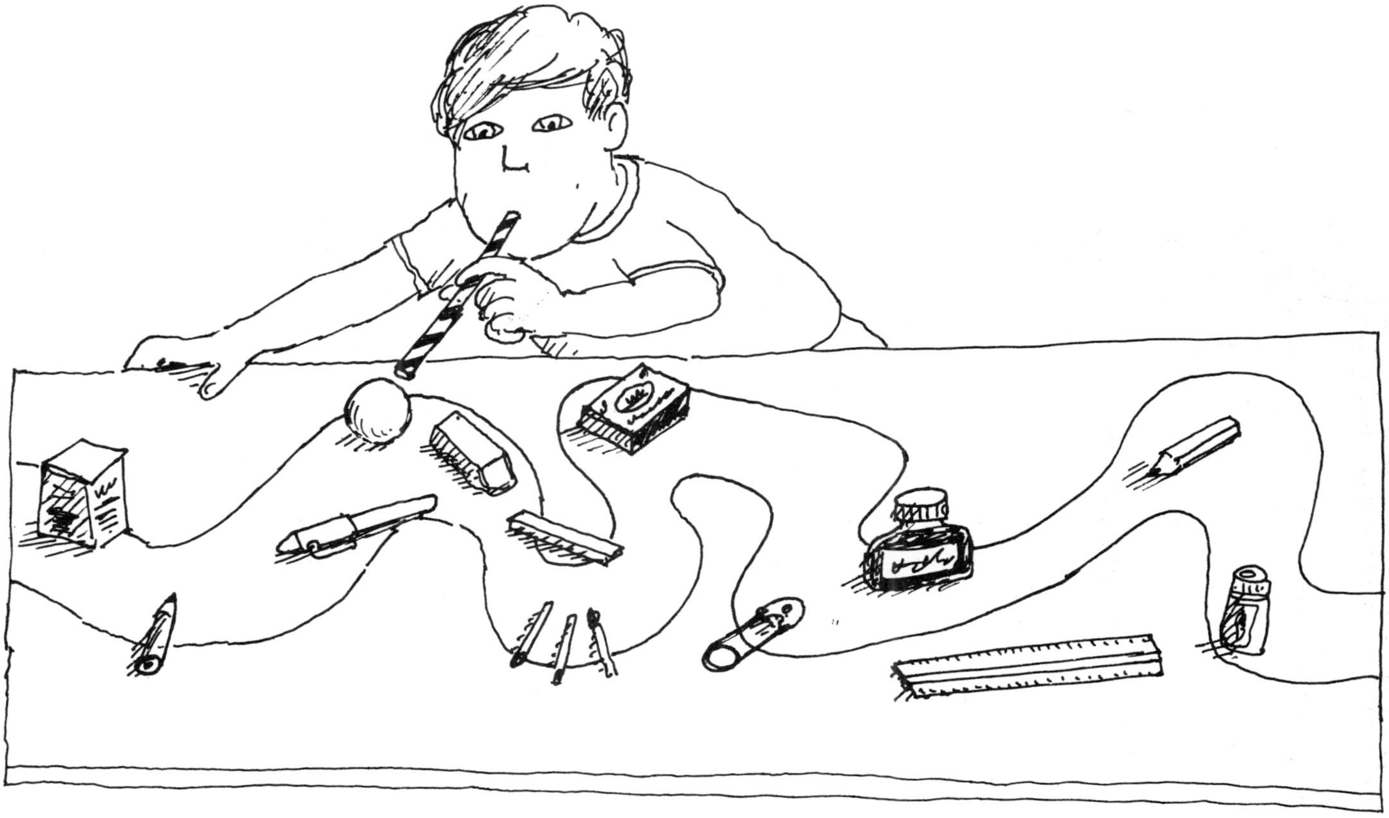

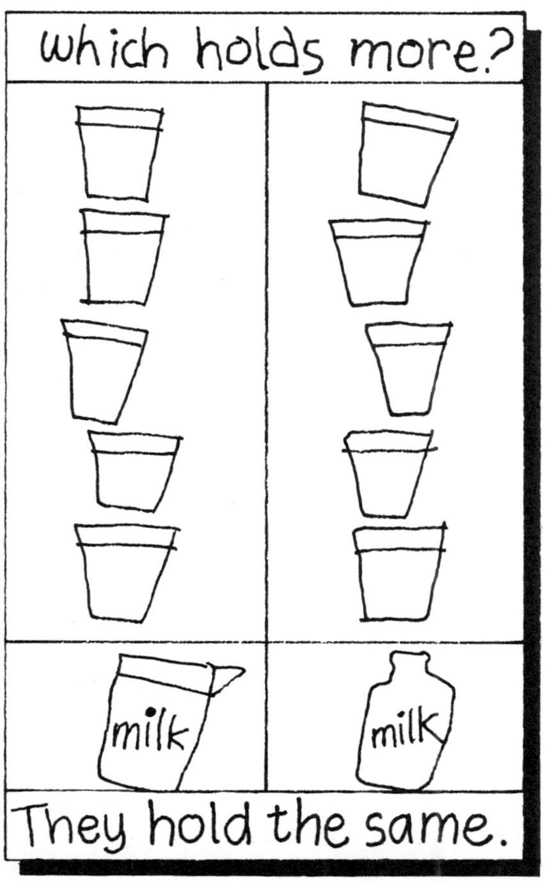

4 Making — Encourage the children to produce a solution which is as attractive as they can make it. Some of them might like to try a second version to improve on the first attempt.

5 Evaluation — The children will enjoy using each other's attempts and you might be able to arrange to let children from another group try the games and toys.

Further activities

Some suggestions

1 How are card milk containers made waterproof? Let the children examine the card and see if they can find an answer.
2 Get a pint bottle of milk and a squat pint carton. Ask the children which they think contains more. Let them find out by filling yoghurt cartons and counting them. They could record their results as shown on the left.
3 Let the children investigate the sounds made when bottles containing different amounts of water are tapped.
4 Act out the nursery rhyme 'Little Miss Muffet'.
5 Make a red milk jelly. What does it look like? What happens to the milk? What does it taste like? (Compare it with an ordinary jelly.)
6 Make bubble pictures. Add washing-up liquid to a saucer of paint and blow through a straw to make bubbles. Place a sheet of paper over the saucer to get the bubble effect.

Language

Mathematics

Physical education

Creative arts

Science

People and their jobs and occupations

Starter Book page 28

Science activities

Making and doing

Teachers' Book page 99

Further activities

Teachers' Book page 100

Introduction

Science activities

The activities in this topic cover a wide range of concepts and provide children with the setting for them to carry out a variety of investigations. Friction is, perhaps, not one of the most obvious concepts for consideration by young children but it is a very important one and one which in practical terms (in terms of easily provided experiences) is readily understandable. Without friction, walking would be impossible as would be a great many other things we take for granted.

Another activity which could be singled out is activity 7, 'Fountain'. Here children are able to experience the transfer of their energy used in squeezing a squeezy bottle to produce a jet of water. They are able to see immediately that the harder they push the stronger and more powerful is the jet. It is another small step in the development of understanding.

It is this amassing of experience of all kinds which is so important at this stage in learning to work scientifically. All the explanations (and the worrying about explanations) can come later.

Making and doing activities

The problem for the child is:

'Can you make a model slide and a stairway or ladder up to it?'

The park Science activities

Activity Pa1 —The slide

Investigating friction

You need:
a large stiff triangle (a plastic or wooden one from your shapes box); plasticine; powdered chalk; talcum powder; fine sand; washing-up liquid; cooking oil; floor polish; several wooden blocks of a size children can hold in one hand; different kinds of shoes and plimsolls.

1 Ask the children to think about the slide in the park. Hold your triangle so that it is resting on one edge. Check that the children can name the shape. Along one of the sloping edges press some plasticine to represent steps.

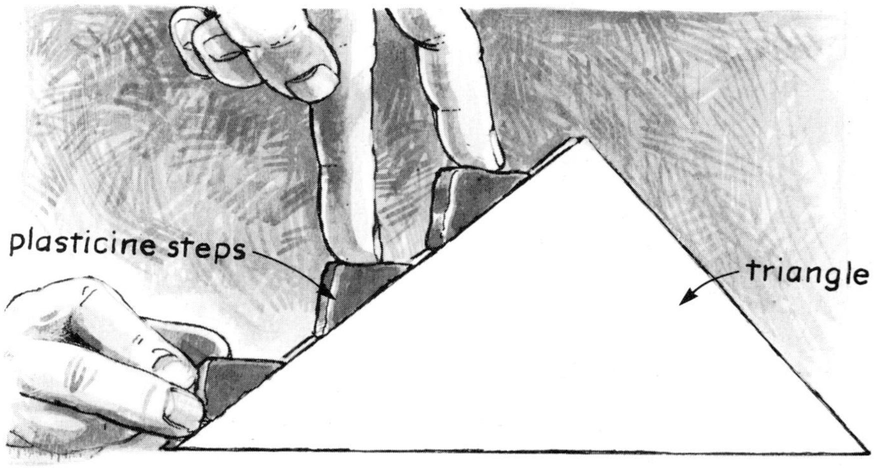

2 Tell the children that this represents the slide and the steps up to it. Walk your fingers up the steps and ask the children in which direction your fingers are going. Now slide your fingers down the other side. Ask again in which direction your fingers are going. Can the children tell you which is easier – going up or coming down? Which is quicker? Why?

3 Ask them to think what would happen if they tried to go up the slide side. What would be the best kind of footwear to stop them from sliding down again?
4 Take the children to an area where there is a smooth-tiled floor surface or something similar. Ask each child to take off one shoe and sock. Tell them to push their bare feet along the floor. How does it feel? They will probably say that it is cold. Encourage them to think about how it feels to move a foot along on the surface. Tell them to put their socks back on again and tell you how it feels now. How does it feel different? Which moves more easily, the bare foot or the foot with the sock? Can they decide which would be the best for sliding? Do the same kind of investigation with different kinds of shoes and plimsolls and let the children draw their own conclusions. Why would it be difficult to do P.E. wearing socks?
5 Now discuss with the children which substances cause us to slip if they are accidentally spilled on the floor. Tell the children they are going to find out what happens if some things are spilled on the floor. Have ready some powdered chalk, talcum powder, fine sand, floor polish, washing-up liquid and cooking oil. Work again in an area where the floor is smooth-tiled or similar and at widely-spaced points spill a small amount of each substance on the floor. Leave the container alongside so that the children can see what has been spilled.
6 Get the wooden blocks. Show the children how to press on them and push them along to find out how slippery the surface is. Let them test each 'spill' using a different face of the block.
7 When they have finished ask them which 'spill' made the floor most slippery. Did any of the materials make the floor less slippery? (If they don't notice that the chalk does this, chalk a fresh area of floor and let them try again.)
8 Can the children suggest why the 'spill' which made the floor most slippery did so? Which things do they have to be very careful not to spill? What should they do if they do spill them? Where do they have to take great care not to slip?

Activity Pa2—The roundabout

Investigating circular motion

You need:
a hoop or quoit; a round cheese box or lid for each child; pins; crayons; spent matches; pencil stubs; a record turntable; old magazines and catalogues for pictures of wheels, etc.

1 Talk to the children about roundabouts. Why are they called 'roundabouts'? Discuss the idea that they go round and round and that the centre stays in the same place.
2 Ask the children if they can make themselves go round and round. They will probably spin round on their feet. Can they spin round in other ways – on their heels, toes or seats? What do they have to do to make themselves go round and round – (push against something with some part of their bodies).
3 Give one child a hoop (or a quoit if you are short of space) and ask the child what shape it is. Ask him or her to make it go round and round. (The child will probably roll it.) Ask the child what the hoop is doing and what he or she did to make it move. How can he or she make the hoop go more quickly or more slowly? Let other children try making it move quickly or slowly. Encourage them to realise that making it move quickly needs a big push and making it move slowly requires a small push.
4 How is the way the hoop goes round different from how the roundabout goes round? (The hoop is vertical and the roundabout is horizontal. The centre of the roundabout stays in one place and the centre of the hoop goes forward parallel to the ground.)
5 How can they make the hoop go in a different direction when it is rolling along? You can show the children that they must give it a push in the appropriate direction to make it change its path.

6 Give each of the children a round cheese box or lid. Ask them what the shape is called. Can they make their cheese boxes roll quickly and slowly? How must they push them? Who can make a cheese box roll furthest?
7 Now ask the children to think about the roundabout again. Can they make their cheese boxes go round and round like the roundabout? Give them pins, crayons, spent matches and pencil stubs and see if they can think of a way to make their boxes spin in a horizontal plane. You could show them a record turntable to help them.
8 Ask them where they need to make the hole in the cheese box. Let them try to fix 'spindles' of some sort in their cheese boxes. How can they make their cheese boxes spin? They may try to twist the spindle. Show them that they can also make the cheese box turn by holding the 'spindle' in a vertical position and pushing the edge of the box. The 'twist' and the 'push' produce the same effect.

9 Give the children some old magazines and catalogues and ask them to cut out pictures of things which go round and round e.g. bicycle wheels, car wheels, steering wheels, gear wheels. Ask them to put their pictures in two sets "Things which go round and round like a roundabout" and "Things which go round and round like a hoop." How are these two sets different? (See 4 on page 94.)

Activity Pa3—Swings

Investigating the relationship between time of swing and length of string for a pretend swing

You need:
thin string or thread; scissors; large wooden beads all the same size.

1 Cut three pieces of string approximately 50 cm, 100 cm, and 200 cm long. Show the children the string and discuss 'longer than', 'shorter than', 'longest', 'shortest'.
2 Give the pieces of string to the children and tell them to thread a bead on each string and to place the bead in the middle of each string. When they have done this ask them how they can be sure that the bead is in the middle of the string. Help them to see that the length of string on each side of the bead needs to be the same. Use the word 'equal' in describing this. Let them compare the lengths.
3 Knot the ends of each of the strings to form loops and attach them to conveniently placed horizontal sticks so that the beads can swing freely. Now ask the children to make the beads swing like the swings in the park.

4 Whilst they are doing this talk to them about grandfather clocks or wall clocks with pendulums which go 'tick-tock'.
5 Now get the children to look at the longest pendulum and help them to say 'tick-tock' in time with the swings. Do this a few times and then turn their attention to the shortest pendulum and let them follow the rhythm of this. Do this a few times until they notice that they are saying 'tick-tock' more quickly for the short pendulum than they were for the long one.
6 Let them experiment with the long pendulum and the short one and discover that it doesn't make any difference if they try to 'push' the pendulum to make it go faster. (The time of swing depends only on the length.)
7 Ask them to guess/suggest what will happen for the middle pendulum and then let them try that one. You might like to let three children each move their arms in time with one of the pendulums so that the other children can see how differently the 'swings' are moving.

Activity Pa4—Seesaw

Investigating a pretend seesaw

You need:
a number of pretend seesaws made by sticking match-box trays to the ends of rulers and balancing them either on a match-box or Toblerone packet (double-sided Sellotape is useful for holding the match-boxes in place and the ruler in the balance position);
a variety of small objects which will fit in the match-box trays e.g. beads, counters, cubes, weights, paper clips, Lego blocks, marbles etc.; straws; small labels ('will balance'); a stiff 2 m plank of wood; a brick (or block of similar size). The plank is to form a seesaw across the brick. For extra safety small blocks of wood can be nailed to its underside so that the ends do not hit the floor and trap small misguided feet!

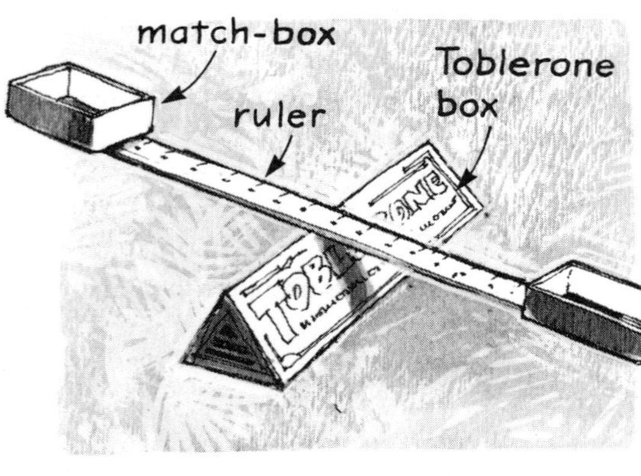

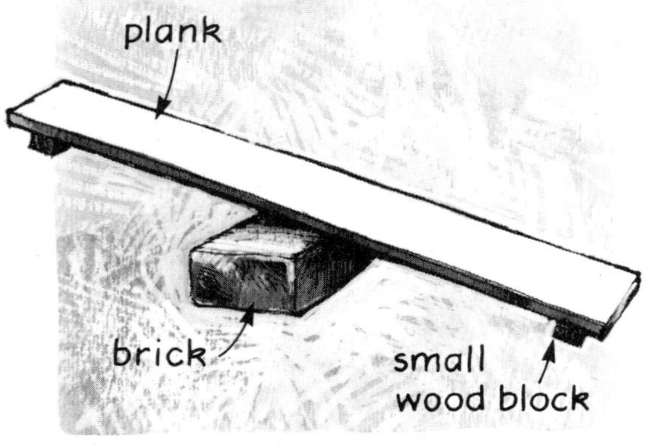

Making a seesaw

1 Give the children the pretend seesaws which you have made and ask the children to place the ruler so that it is level. Where is the ruler balanced? (It should be at its centre.) Make sure that they understand the words 'level' and 'balanced'.
2 Now suggest to the children that they gently push one end of the ruler down. What happens to the other end? What happens to the other end if they gently lift one end up?
3 Put out your collection of small objects and suggest that the children put one of the objects in one of their match-box trays. What happens? Now ask the children to remove the object and put it into the other match-box tray. What happens now? Ask them next to find an object to put into the empty tray which will make the ruler balance again. The most obvious solution is to use an exactly similar object. Help them

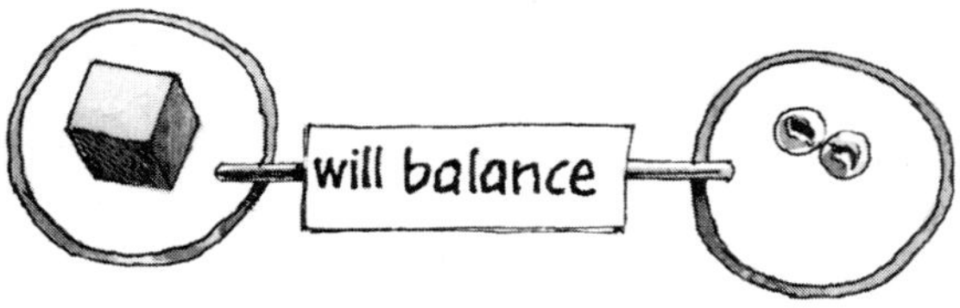

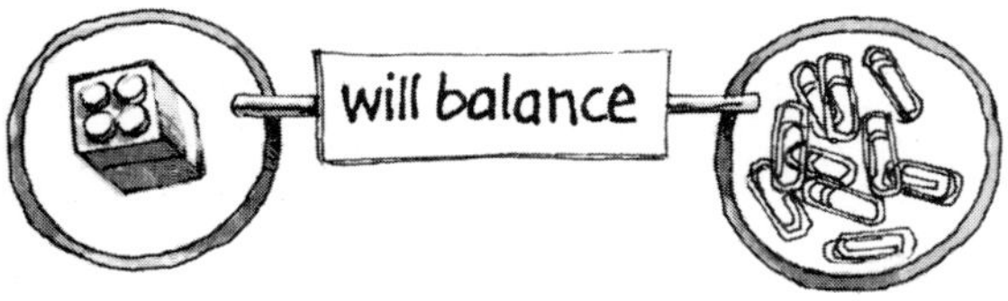

towards this solution (amongst others). Encourage them also towards solutions which require a number of objects at one end to balance a single object at the other end. Let them record their results by providing a number of straws with 'will balance' labels attached to them which can be used for joining objects or collections of objects that balance.

Try to ensure that every child has at least one balance in which a number of 'light' objects are balancing one 'heavy' object.

4 Bring into the classroom a plank about 2 m long. Balance it across a brick. Stand on one end of it. Now invite the children to suggest how they might make it level again. Let them explore the possibilities. They may start to grasp the idea that if the load on both ends is equal the seesaw will balance. Discuss their experiences with them and help them towards understanding.

Activity Pa5—Picnic

Investigating the properties of paper (dishes and plates)

You need:
plastic teaspoon and cup; paper dish; paper plate; paper serviette; metal teaspoon; cotton serviette; pottery cup; dish and plate; washing-up bowl; washing-up liquid; warm water.

1 Put on the table the picnic items i.e. plastic teaspoon and cup, paper dish, plate and serviette, the metal teaspoon, the pottery cup, dish and plate and the cotton serviette. Let the children count the items. (There should be ten.) Ask how many have circles in them and how many have not. How many are soft to touch and how many are not? You can continue to devise simple sums and observation exercises until their attention wanes.
2 Suggest now that they put the items in pairs e.g. two teaspoons, two dishes. Perhaps they could count in twos to ten. Encourage the children to talk about how the two members of a pair are different in weight, feel, appearance. Let them, for example, look at the cups. How do they feel different? Which feels colder/heavier? Which one will bend/not bend?
3 Put the items together again and ask the children to give you something which, for example, is round and feels cold; something which is not round and feels soft.
4 Now put the pottery items together and ask the children how they are the same. They may say that they are all hard, round and shiny and made of the same material.
5 Put the paper items together and ask how they are the same and how they are different. Do the children recognise that they are all made of paper?
6 Put the plastic items together in a similar way. Do the children recognise that they are made of plastic?
7 Ask the children to decide which would be the best things for a picnic. Encourage the children to think about the desirable properties of picnicware e.g. light in weight, unbreakable, etc. Which of the items they have been looking at would be best for a picnic?
8 Let the children sort the items into two sets, a 'picnic set' and a 'kitchen set'.
9 Get the bowl of warm water for washing up and suggest to the children that they investigate how the two sets withstand washing up. (This is more effective if the items have been used and need washing.) Let the children start on the 'kitchen set'. Ask them to observe what happens to the things as they are washed. Are there any changes? Can the items be used again?
10 Then let them wash the 'picnic set'. Are there any changes? Can the items be used again? Which items cannot be used? Which items can? Why? Can the children see that pottery, plastic and metal are not changed by washing but paper is? Why are paper plates and dishes used for picnics but not normally in the kitchen?

Activity Pa6—Reflections

Observing and investigating reflections

You need:
a large mirror; plasticine; toy ducks (optional); a variety of objects to place on the mirror – a cup, a small bottle, a small vase of flowers, a variety of metal spoons, paint, paper.

1 Place the mirror flat on the table. Talk to the children about it and ask the children to describe it. Help them to notice that it is smooth, shiny, and feels cold.
2 Now let the children make some plasticine ducks (or use the toy ducks) and put them on the mirror. What can they see in the mirror? Tell the children the ducks they can see in the mirror are 'reflections' of the ducks which are on the mirror. The children might like to draw what they can see or you could give them a drawing of a duck and ask them to draw its reflection.

3 You can try putting other objects on the mirror and discussing with the children the reflections they can see.
4 Encourage the children to explore the classroom to find other things in which they can see reflections e.g. windows, polished wood, silver paper, spoons, etc. A little stage management will extend the possibilities. Ask the children how all these things which produce reflections are the same.
5 Let the children look at themselves in a variety of spoons and encourage them to talk about the reflections they see. What shape of shiny surface produces reflections that are the right way up and what shape produces reflections that are upside down?
6 Let the children make paint-blob patterns by putting a blob of paint on a piece of paper, folding it in half and pressing gently. Let them open up the papers and leave the paint to dry. When it is dry, fold the paper back along the fold line and let the children hold one half of the blob against the mirror. What do they see? What does the reflection look like? Do the children recognise that the reflection is the same as the other half of the paint-blob pattern?

Activity Pa7—Fountain

Investigating some properties of water; investigating force

You need:
waterproof aprons for all the children; a water tray; a good supply of squeezy bottles; access to a tap; small polythene bags; tall empty plastic shampoo bottles or similar which will knock over easily.

1 Give the children the waterproof aprons. Go with them to the sink. Part fill the sink with water and ask one of the children to make the tap drip. Get the other children to beat the rhythm of the drip and ask them where the sound is made by the drip. Encourage them to notice the shape of the drip as it leaves the tap and as it enters the water. Let them feel the drops and catch some in their hands. What happens to the shape of the drops? What does the water look like now? Encourage the children to see that the drops come down one by one and then merge together in their hands.

2 Ask one of the children to make the water trickle. Encourage them to notice that the water is now joined together in a continuous stream. Again let them feel the water as it falls from the tap. How does it feel different from the drops? How does it sound different?

3 Now let the children turn the tap full on. Ask them to describe what the water looks like now and what happens when it hits the water in the sink. Let them feel the force of the water. How does it feel different from the trickle? Can they catch some of the water this time?

4 Let the children play with the squeezy bottles in the water tray and ask them to make drips, trickles and forceful jets. How do they squeeze to make drips (gently) and to make jets (hard)? Can they make the water go up?

5 For the rest of the activities, the water tray will, with careful supervision, be adequate but a day pleasant enough for outdoor activity would be a bonus!

Organise a competition to see who can make a jet of water go furthest. Let them explore what they can do to improve the performance. For example, is it better to have the bottle full to start with? Does it matter at what angle the bottle is held? What is the best way of getting a good strong squeeze?

6 Another activity which will help children to understand the connection between how hard you push (the energy exerted) and how forceful the jet is (how much energy it has) is to let the children use their squeezy bottle jets to knock over tall plastic bottles (or other unstable objects). How far away can they put the tall bottles and still knock them over?

7 Give the children the small polythene bags and let them make two or three pin holes near the bottom and two or three near the middle. Let them fill the bags with water and screw the top round to keep the water in. By squeezing the bags they can make the jets vary in strength and direction.

Making and doing activities

The problem for the child is:

'Can you make a model slide and stairway or ladder up to it?'

You need:

a shoe box for each child; card; paper; glue; scissors; plasticine; sellotape; foil; plastic bags; spent match sticks; pieces of straws; cocktail sticks; thin garden canes or sticks.

1 The problem	Can you make a model slide and a stairway or ladder up to it?
2 Exploring the problem	What must a slide be like (sloping at an angle and slippery)? How can you make a ladder or a stairway?
3 Ideas for solving the problem	Suggest the children use a shoe box or similar for the platform at the top. What can you use for the slide which is smooth and slippery – plastic, card covered with foil? How can you make steps – a paper or card concertina; sticks with match sticks across for steps?

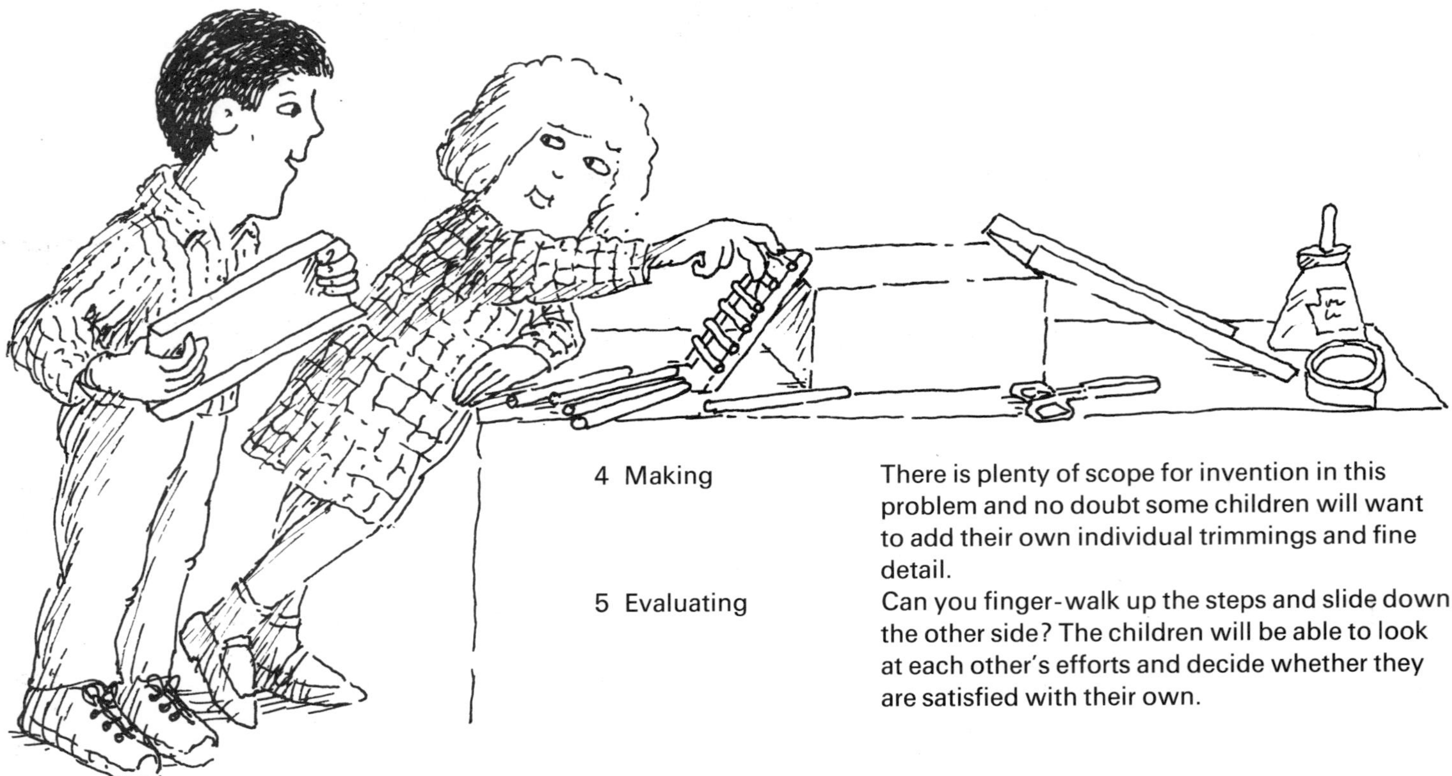

Making a model slide

4 Making	There is plenty of scope for invention in this problem and no doubt some children will want to add their own individual trimmings and fine detail.
5 Evaluating	Can you finger-walk up the steps and slide down the other side? The children will be able to look at each other's efforts and decide whether they are satisfied with their own.

Further activities

Some suggestions

1 Set up a 'swing' by fixing a sawn off squeezy bottle to a string. Leave the fine jet hole in place and make sure that the bottle is clean and dry. Hang it so that it can swing freely and fill it with salt. Let it swing over dark-coloured sugar paper.

It will produce intriguing patterns. The salt can be mixed with dry powder paint for more colourful effects.

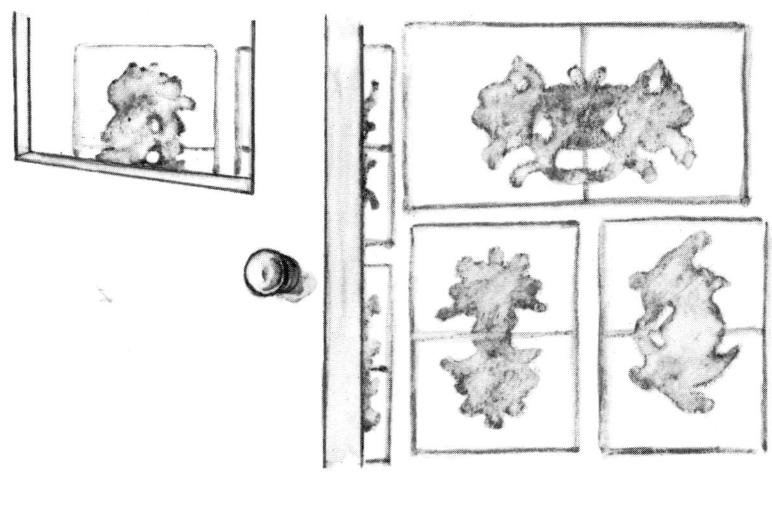

2 In P.E. use 'round and round' and 'up and down' for your themes.

3 Put pieces of very light-weight materials on the record turntable and spin it slowly. What happens? Now spin it quickly. What happens? Have any of the children had to hold on very tight on a roundabout because they felt that they would be spun off?

4 Swings are often hung on chains. What is a chain? Why is a chain used? What are chains made of? Collect examples of different kinds of chains. Can the children make paper chains?

5 Take the children to the park and let them make observational drawings of trees, flowers, ducks etc.

6 Let the children use the school camera to take photographs in the park at different times in the year. Can the children later identify the seasons and put the photographs in order?

EXTENSIONS

Introduction

In the very early stages of developing *Longman Scienceworld*, it was recognised that there were areas of concern to which particular attention should be given. As a result of this, a series of guiding principles was drawn up, and this is set out below.

Principles

About science

1 Science is a way of looking at the world which is unique and therefore different from the view of the world provided by other disciplines.
2 Being able to look at the world scientifically requires the development of particular skills, abilities and attitudes.
3 By looking at the world in this way, a body of scientific knowledge has been produced.
4 Science is a major contributor to technological development.
5 Science is used in society in all sorts of ways. People use it in their work and hobbies. Everyone is confronted with it in everyday life.

About science for young children

6 Science for young children is an active process, which requires the development of those skills, abilities and attitudes which will enable them to explore their surroundings in a scientific way.
7 The scheme concerns itself with ideas and information – with scientific knowledge – because the children themselves will acquire ideas and information, as a consequence of their own active exploration of their surroundings. This information and these ideas will be relevant to the children since they will be the children's own.
8 It is probable that the information and ideas will be concerned with the immediate environment because that will be the context of most of the children's active exploration. Equally, if we are concerned to develop children's ability to work scientifically, it is likely that things and actions in the close environment will be most effective in arousing children's interest and encouraging their active involvement.
9 A particular scientific idea can be introduced in a wide variety of contexts. Scientific investigation and activity can be concerned with a wide range of subjects. It is, therefore, necessary to establish criteria for selecting contexts. The contexts chosen here reflect the following concerns:
   - interest for the children;
   - compatibility with the whole curriculum – the contexts must fit the normal curriculum pattern;
   - potential for the development of scientific skills;
   - provision of a wide range of experiences across the sciences;
   - provision of experiences of some major areas of understanding, e.g. life processes, energy conversion, etc;
   - potential for showing how a scientific perspective is useful and is relevant in a variety of circumstances – in everyday life, in jobs and in hobbies.
10 It is very important that children should develop an understanding of the relationship between science and technology. They should be provided with opportunities to engage in simple problem-solving activities. Working towards the solution of a problem is valuable in its own right; at the same time, it provides many opportunities for scientific investigation, and enables children to bring together their developing skills and abilities not only in science but also in other disciplines.
11 Evidence furnished by Piaget and others suggests that there is to some extent a developmental pattern which most children follow. This should be taken into account, but the scientific activities proposed should encourage development rather than just provide a passive response to this developmental pattern.

About teachers and science

12 The form of *Longman Scienceworld* and its classroom approach should be compatible with the normal patterns of organisation used by teachers in primary schools.

13 Many teachers feel that they have had little experience of science in their own education and believe that they do not have a solid enough basis from which to teach it. This science scheme should help these teachers to overcome their doubts and provide the information and encouragement necessary to give them the confidence to introduce science into the curriculum.

14 Teaching science involves careful attention to classroom organisation. The materials should provide the teacher with adequate guidance and advice.

15 Science has great potential for providing opportunities and stimuli for the development of language and the application of mathematics. These opportunities should be exploited.

16 Following children's progress in acquiring scientific skills and abilities is an important aspect of ensuring that children are given systematic help in developing their skills and abilities. Particular attention should be paid, therefore, to recording progress.

Some of these principles have been expanded to present a more detailed framework. They follow in the form of Extensions A–J.

Extension A Scientific skills

Science for children in the primary school is essentially about observing, investigating and making sense of the world. The intention of *Longman Scienceworld* is to provide children with opportunities to carry out these investigations and to foster the development of the necessary skills, abilities and attitudes.

First, it must be made clear that 'investigating' is not the same as 'experimenting' as conventionally used in describing scientific activity. Our investigating differs from experimenting in a way which is best made clear diagramatically. In essence, conventional science works like this:

Diagram 1

Observing → Classifying → Recognising and stating patterns

↓

Making predictions based on these stated patterns

↓

Designing experiments to test these predictions

↓

Carrying out the experiments

↓

Analysing the results, recognising the significance of these results

(Controlling variables → Designing experiments to test these predictions; Controlling variables → Carrying out the experiments)

Opinions differ about the order of the early stages of this sequence but it remains that experimenting is about careful planned testing of a formally stated prediction based on a formally stated recognition of a pattern. The sequence involves a high level of understanding and the ability to manipulate and communicate ideas. In the planning of experiments, it is necessary to be able to recognise and plan the control of a range of variables. Again, this involves thinking in a highly sophisticated way.

Manipulation of ideas at this level is inappropriate for most children of primary school age (and indeed for many older children). It is probably the complexity of thinking which is implied in this approach to science that has led to the non-acceptance of a number of primary science curriculum developments.

What then is meant by 'investigating'? Firstly, some investigations are an extension of observing. Instead of just observing what is, the child carries out some action and finds out what happens when . . . , or what happens if . . . . Observing the sound when an object is tapped, planting seeds, or adding water to salt are investigations at this simple level. An event is provoked and what happens is observed. No prediction is being tested but observation is being directed towards looking for some change. (Simple observation is concerned with observing what is there. No change is provoked although a change may be observed, e.g. changes in nature.)

At this simple level of investigation, no attempt may be made to recognise or control variables. The investigation is concerned with what happens on a particular occasion. The investigation requires planning; the results are observed, communicated and recorded. Measurement may be involved and there will be discussion of what is observed. It is the nature of this discussion which will probably determine what happens next. Children may be content with the information they have acquired or, with encouragement, they may begin to frame questions of the sort, 'If that was what happened when we did that, I wonder what would happen if we did this?' It is this kind of thinking which leads to a more refined pattern of investigation, which can best be described diagramatically.

Diagram 2

This differs significantly from the statement about experimenting in Diagram 1. Children are not expected to be able to make formal statements of patterns, or recognise and control a range of variables. Expectations are pitched lower and chances of success are greater. Progress to the more formal sequence of experimenting may develop over the years. The objective is to help children to develop the skills needed at a pace which is possible for them. It must be realised that being able to recognise and state a pattern of behaviour or being able to recognise and plan the control of a range of variables is a complex task. Some children of primary school age will possess the required degree of maturity but many will need a good deal of help. Nevertheless, many children will, on occasion, show an understanding which is apparently out of phase with their general level of development. This should be noted with pleasure but great care should be exercised in assessing its significance. *Longman Scienceworld* helps children to develop the skills required to carry out investigations. The sophistication of the methods they use will increase as their skills mature.

In the early part of the scheme, the prime concern is to develop the skills of observing and communicating information about what is observed. Measuring is introduced as a refinement of both observing and communicating. Recording and classifying are other skills which are introduced at an early stage. Recognising and describing patterns is recognised as a high level skill which will be developed gradually from the simple standpoint described in Diagram 2. Again, the skill of predicting will be developed by starting with the idea of good suggestions – although for the sake of simplicity and lack of a more appropriate word, the word 'predicting' will be used for 'making a good suggestion'. Controlling variables is another skill to be developed within the limits described, concentrating largely on the idea of making investigations fair.

Development of the skills needed to carry out scientific investigations is brought about in two distinct ways. In some of the suggested activities, one or two particular skills are considered in isolation, e.g. observing or sorting. In other activities, an investigation is suggested that requires a range of skills to be used and developed.

Table 1 overleaf describes the development of skills in the primary years in *Longman Scienceworld*.

Table 1 Development of the science skills

	Children starting the scheme	Children at the end of the infant years	Children at the end of the junior years
Observing	The children can observe using the senses individually as suggested by the teacher. They can compare simple objects.	The children can observe using the senses in combination, aided by a range of measures and magnifiers and over a period of time (change, behaviour, etc.). The most appropriate observations to make are determined by the children prompted by the teacher. The children can, in retrospect, identify the most appropriate observations.	The children can observe using the senses in combination aided by a range of measures and magnifiers used with skill and over a period of time (change, behaviour, etc.). The children can decide which will be the most appropriate observations to make.
Communicating	The children can communicate in simple oral statements assisted by the teacher's prompts.	The children can communicate in detail using a range of methods. In retrospect, they are able to choose the most appropriate from a number of possible methods tried.	The children can communicate in detail using a refined range of methods and can choose for themselves the most appropriate method to use.
Measuring	The children can compare two objects placed side by side.	The children can measure using a range of equipment including some standard measures. They can exercise judgement about the level of accuracy/ approximation which is appropriate. They can measure with precision.	The children can measure using a range of equipment. They can use their own judgement about what should be measured and how accurately the measurement should be made.
Recording	Some children can record by simple picture or mathematical representation.	The children can record using a wide range of methods including mathematical representation. With prompting they can choose retrospectively, from a number of methods tried, the most appropriate for a particular purpose.	The children can record using a wide range of methods including mathematical representation. They can choose in advance the most appropriate method for a particular purpose.
Classifying	The children can classify according to one characteristic suggested by the teacher.	The children can classify into sets and subsets using complex criteria if prompted by the teacher.	The children can classify into sets and subsets using complex criteria selected by themselves. They can use and construct simple keys.
Recognising patterns	The concept is not appreciated.	When making observations, the children may seek patterns if prompted by the teacher. They can recognise common factors in the information obtained by observing a number of instances. They are not able to describe the pattern formally. They may or may not be able to identify other instances which fit the pattern.	When making observations, the children seek patterns in the information obtained. They recognise common factors in the information obtained by observing a number of instances. They are able to recognise other instances which fit the pattern.
Predicting	The children make suggestions, guesses or predictions based indiscriminately on experience and fantasy.	The children make reasonable suggestions based on observations which may be carried out over a period of time. Some causal relationships are recognised.	The children base their suggestions on firm evidence including recognised patterns. There is increasing recognition of causal as distinct from casual relationships. They use known concepts in making suggestions.
Controlling variables	There is little appreciation of the existence of variables, and minimal recognition of causal relationships.	The children start to identify one or two obvious variables. These may or may not be relevant. The children are able to find out whether or not they are relevant. When a variable is identified, the children are able to find a way of controlling it if prompted by the teacher.	The children are aware of a wide range of variables and can, on most occasions, identify and control those which are relevant.
Investigating	With clear directions from the teacher, the children can carry out and understand simple investigations.	The children may suggest what they would like to investigate or test. They can design and carry out simple investigations with only minimal help with practicalities. They start to notice the more obvious variables and can suggest ways of testing whether they are relevant. With some help, the children can control one or two of the variables they have identified.	The children can design and carry out simple investigations with confidence. They can identify and control most relevant variables. They can review their investigations critically and check results by repetition.

Each of these skills will be developed in a structured way through the scheme. This step by step progression is set out in Table 2 which follows. The table not only indicates the stage of development of the skills in the work at the different levels, but it also provides a guide as to what the children should be able to do when they have completed the work of a particular level. It should be noted that in going from one level to the next, the skills are cumulative and the skills taught at each level build on those acquired earlier.

The *Record Sheets* for *Longman Scienceworld* which are available separately are based on this table of skill development.

Table 2 is in two parts. Table 2(i) covers the infant years and Table 2(ii) covers the junior years. Both parts are included here so that teachers of infants may see the progression through the junior years of those skills which are being developed in the infant years.

EXTENSION A

Table 2(i) The infant years

	Year 1		Year 2	
	Level 1	**Level 2**	**Level 1**	**Level 2**
Observing	The children can observe differences and similarities using the senses individually as specified by the teacher. One attribute at a time is observed and direct comparisons are made.	The children can observe using more than one sense and can cope with more than one attribute. Observations are still immediate and teacher prompted.	The children choose appropriate senses to observe changes, behaviour and movement. Arbitrary measures are used to refine observation.	The children can observe movement in relation to time. They are able to select increasingly appropriate arbitrary measures and start to see some need for standard measures.
Communicating	The children can make simple oral statements describing and naming in terms of one property. They can use pictorial representation suggested by the teacher. They ask questions.	The children use more accurate oral descriptions for more than one property. Sets can be described pictorially.	The children can include in their oral descriptions the time sequence of events related to change. They can use a very simple block graph as a means of communication.	The children can now extend their oral descriptions to include comments on results. They can make statements and justify these with reasons. They can use block graphs and pictorial representation more freely.
Measuring	The children can describe length and weight orally. They can make direct comparison of unequal lengths and use their hands to compare unequal weights directly. They can describe capacity (non-relative). They can time-sequence in simple fashion.	The children can match objects of the same length or use several objects to make up the length. They can decide whether containers hold more or less by judgement and by counting. Weighing and time sequence are as at level 1.	The children can measure length using repeated units and limb measures. They can use balance scales to balance and order weights. They can compare capacity by emptying or filling. They can compare fast and slow.	Length, weight and capacity are as at level 1. The children are now able to measure time, e.g. with an egg timer.
Recording	The children can make classroom displays of sets by grouping actual objects. They can use simple pictorial representation and show relationships using arrows provided by the teacher.	The children can use simple tallying and pictorial representation. They can match words and sentences to appropriate sets. The recording method is suggested by the teacher.	The children can use simple charts relating to behaviour and movement. They are able to indicate by ticking in appropriate columns. They can use double-ended arrows for balances etc. and simple graphs. They are able to do their own drawings and copy simple sentences. The method of recording is suggested by the teacher.	The children are able to write their own sentences, use greater than and less than signs, and use a simple matrix. They exploit their improved accuracy in drawing and cutting out. If the teacher suggests two methods of recording, the children are able after discussion to choose the more appropriate.
Classifying	The children can sort for one attribute by matching an example provided by the teacher.	The children can sort for two attributes decided by the teacher; if the teacher sorts, the children can identify the criteria being used.	The children are able to suggest more than one way of sorting a given collection and decide their own criteria. Sorting criteria may include purpose, movement and behaviour if these are identified by the teacher.	The children can sort according to the properties of materials using very simple keys. They are able to notice and match several common features of different materials.
Recognising patterns	The children are unlikely to be able to appreciate the idea.		The children are now better able to recognise similarities and describe these.	With prompting, the children can look for patterns in their observations.
Predicting	The children can suggest what will happen next. There is some evidence that the suggestions are based on experience, but reality and fantasy overlap considerably.		The children can make reasonable suggestions about likely outcomes based on the observations made in the course of an activity.	
Controlling variables	The children generally have little appreciation of the variables. The teacher controls the variables by providing restricted sets of materials and guiding investigations.		The children generally have little appreciation of the variables. The teacher controls the variables by providing restricted sets of materials and guiding investigations.	If the teacher suggests that a variable may be affecting the outcome of an investigation, the children may or may not recognise this as significant.
Investigating	The teacher can set a problem of the 'What happens when ...?' type. The teacher provides a restricted set of materials and suggests the method. The children are able to carry out the investigation and make the necessary observations.		The teacher can suggest a problem. The children make suggestions about approaches and solve some of the practical problems. They need support and guidance and practical help. The teacher draws attention to related features but does not refer directly to cause and effect.	In the practical design of the investigation, more than one method may be tried by the children and a comparison made. The children begin to notice related features and some will recognise cause and effect relationships. Investigations include 'Which is best?' as well as 'What happens when ...?'

Year 3

	Level 1	Level 2
Observing	The children can make observations at different times which are related to each other in sequence, so that they are able to observe gradual changes. They can use some standard measures to refine observations.	The children can make judgements about the level of detail and accuracy needed in their observations. They can appreciate to some extent the concept of approximation. They can increase the accuracy of their observations by using standard measures. In retrospect, they can choose which observations are most appropriate for the task.
Communicating	The children can make detailed observations orally and can express their reasons for choices. They can produce simple written accounts including mathematical representation and, orally, they can discuss the appropriateness of the means of communicating which they have used.	Orally, the children are able to give a detailed account of what was done and why, what happened and in what order. They can take part in a discussion of their results and draw some conclusions. Their written communications are increasingly appropriate.
Measuring	The children appreciate the need for a standard measure and can use the metre. They can now weigh, using $\frac{1}{2}$kg and kg. They can balance against gram weights. Capacity and time are as at year 2, level 2.	The children can measure using rods marked in cm and 10 cm. They can measure straight and curved lines. They can weigh using grams, measure capacity in litres and half litres, and can calculate time intervals.
Recording	The children are able to record some measurements by using more detailed graphs. They are able to produce their own representational and observational drawings. They are able to attempt their own written records and can record over a longer period of time, noting and interpreting development. If the teacher suggests methods of recording, the children are able to comment on the usefulness of these and decide which to use.	The children's ability to draw proportions more accurately and to match colours more precisely is used in recording; this reflects their increasingly precise and accurate observational skills. Written accounts are more detailed and orderly, and records can be kept competently over a period of time. The children can suggest different methods of recording and use these. In retrospect, with prompting, they can choose which was the most suitable method and give reasons for their choice.
Classifying	The children can sort into sets and subsets. Sorting criteria may include characteristics of plants and animals.	The children can sort using more complex and less evident criteria. They can use simple keys.
Recognising patterns	The children can now recognise patterns. They will probably not be able to describe the pattern formally. They may or may not be able to identify other examples which fit the pattern.	
Predicting	The children can make reasonable suggestions based on observations over a period of time. They can recognise some causal relationships.	
Controlling variables	If the teacher suggests one variable, the children can discuss its implications and test whether it is or is not affecting the outcome of the investigation.	The children start to identify one or two variables. These will not always be relevant but the children will be able to investigate their relevance. When a relevant variable has been identified, the children should be able to find a way of controlling it.
Investigating	The children make useful suggestions about the design of investigations and carry them out with help. The teacher suggests one variable and the children can find out whether or not it affects the outcome. The children see more cause and effect relationships if the teacher points out related features which the children have not noticed.	The children may suggest what they would like to investigate. They design and carry out investigations with minimal help with practicalities. They start to notice one or two more obvious variables and with help can suggest methods of controlling these. They can carry out an agreed controlled investigation.

EXTENSION A

Table 2 (ii) The junior years

	Year 1		Year 2	
	Level 1	**Level 2**	**Level 1**	**Level 2**
Observing	The children can observe using the senses in combination, aided by a range of measures and magnifiers and over a period of time. They are able to observe change, behaviour, etc. as well as the more obvious features, such as colour. The most appropriate observations are determined by the children, prompted by the teacher. The children can make judgements about the level of detail and accuracy needed in their observations. They can appreciate the concept of approximation to some extent. They can increase the accuracy of their observations by using standard measures. In retrospect, they can choose which observations are most appropriate for the task.	The children are increasingly able to observe detail. Independently, they recognise in advance that some observations may be of more significance than others.	With prompting, the children will seek to observe in detail and will select the appropriate equipment to do this. They are able to suggest in advance that certain observations may be of greater significance than others. With some prompting, they are able to view a sequence of observations as a whole.	Without prompting, the children observe in detail with accuracy. They can select in advance which observations to make and begin to observe for purpose, e.g. they look for similarities and differences in form.
Communicating	The children can communicate in detail using a range of methods, including mathematical ones. In retrospect, they are able to choose the most appropriate from a number of methods tried. Orally, the children are able to give a detailed account of what was done and why, what happened and in what order. They can take part in a discussion of their results and draw some conclusions. Their written communications are increasingly appropriate.	The children can give clearer accounts of their work both orally and in writing. Their oral work is more confident, and after discussion they can choose an appropriate form of written communication. With prompting, they include mathematical communication of various kinds among the methods of communication which they consider.	The children are able to communicate in detail, which parallels the increasing detail they are able to observe. With prompting, they are able to suggest different methods of communication, and after discussion will choose an appropriate method. They include mathematical communication among the methods they consider as a matter of course.	The children's ability to communicate develops in parallel with a more sophisticated approach to observing and investigating. Orally, the children are able to explain the plans and decisions which they make prior to and during observation and investigation. They can state their plan clearly. They can write a clear detailed account of their observations and investigations. They choose mathematical means of communication as appropriate.
Measuring	When directed, the children are able to use an appropriate measuring instrument. Length, Weight, Capacity – comparative, arbitrary, and standard measures where appropriate: metres and half metres, kilograms and half kilograms, litres and half litres. Time – intervals of time using timers and stop clocks Temperature – using a thermometer with easy-to-read scale	The children can measure using the most appropriate measuring instrument for the task within the limits of their conceptual understanding of quantity. Length – metres and centimetres Weight – kilograms and parts of kilogram Capacity – litres and parts of litre	The children can measure using the most appropriate measuring instrument within the limits of their conceptual understanding of quantity and can measure to finer limits. Length – metres and centimetres Weight – kilograms and grams Capacity – millilitres (multiples of 10) Time – minutes and parts of a minute	The children can measure to a finer degree of accuracy using the most appropriate measuring instrument. They can attempt to decide what to measure. Length – metres and centimetres Weight – kilograms and grams Capacity – millilitres (multiples of 10) Time – minutes and seconds
Recording	The children can record using a wide range of methods, including mathematical representation. They are able to draw in more detail and with more accuracy. Written records are more detailed and orderly and can be maintained over a period of time. The children can suggest different methods of recording and use these. In retrospect and with prompting, they can choose which was the most suitable and give reasons for their choice.	The children extend the range of recording methods which they use. They can write short accounts, and suggest the use of tables and block graphs which they construct with help. With prompting, they can consider in retrospect their success in recording.	The children are able to make notes and write a clear account based on these notes. They are able to record a sequence of events. They attempt to choose the most appropriate recording method in advance and for a simple record can proceed independently. They use tables, block graphs and diagrams.	The children begin to consider more carefully in advance the recording method(s) which will be most appropriate for the task in hand. With help, they make a choice and can then proceed.

	Year 3		Year 4	
	Level 1	**Level 2**	**Level 1**	**Level 2**
Observing	The children can identify which observations are likely to be significant and can make these in detail. They make less significant observations in less detail. In embarking on a sequence of observations, they are able to decide which observations are likely to be significant without prompting. They observe for purpose, e.g. they look for similarities and differences in form and behaviour. With prompting, they notice patterns in form and behaviour.	The children are increasingly able to make decisions about what to observe and in what detail to make the observations. They look for similarities and differences in form and behaviour. They look for change and can observe it in detail. With prompting, they observe patterns of behaviour and change.	They are able independently to select which observations are likely to be significant and make these in appropriate detail. They look for similarities and differences in form and behaviour. They look for, and are increasingly able to discern, patterns in their observations of form, behaviour and change.	The children can observe using the senses in combination. They can observe in detail. They can distinguish in advance between more and less significant observations, determine the level of detail which will be appropriate and make their observations accordingly. They look for and observe similarities and differences; with some prompting, they recognise observational patterns of form, behaviour and change, as well as of more obvious qualities such as colour.
Communicating	The children appreciate more clearly that the communications should be suited to the audience for whom they are intended. With help both orally and in writing, they can produce different kinds of communication and, in retrospect, can decide which would be suitable for an identified audience.	With prompting, the children can attempt to match the communication to the identified audience. They are able to describe their investigations and observations clearly and sequentially.	Without prompting, the children attempt to match their communications to the audience. They are able to describe and discuss their observations and the observational patterns they discern. They are increasingly able to convey clear statements about these observational patterns. With help, they can make suggestions connected with these recognised patterns.	The children can communicate in detail, using a refined range of methods, and can choose for themselves the most appropriate method to use.
Measuring	The children can read and record using decimalisation. Length – metres and centimetres, e.g. 1.32 m Weight – kilograms and grams, e.g. 1.250 kg Capacity – litres and millilitres, e.g. 1.625 l They can read scales and dials after selecting the appropriate measuring instrument for the task. They can read different calibrations on a variety of instruments.	The children can select the most appropriate instrument to give an accurate reading, e.g. force meter, spring balance, stopwatch, etc. They can read these instruments competently.	The children can measure, using their own judgement about what should be measured. With guidance, they can decide how accurate the measurement should be.	The children are able to use appropriate standard measures with confidence: (m, cm, mm, cm^2, cm^3, kg, g, l, ml, min, sec, newton). They can record using decimal notation. They can estimate with a reasonable degree of accuracy. They can select the appropriate measuring instrument to suit a particular purpose and read a variety of scales, e.g. thermometer, kitchen scales (both dial and linear), force meter and spring balance.
Recording	The children plan their recording method(s) in advance and include methods such as flow charts, block graphs and tables. They write accurate notes and produce a detailed orderly account. They can consider their efforts critically but may need prompting to act accordingly.	They give increasing consideration to mathematical recording methods and with help use a widening range. They draw and colour more accurately. They begin to consider for whom the record is intended and become aware that different recording methods may be appropriate for different audiences, e.g. self, teacher, other children.	The children plan their recording method(s) in advance, including the recording of a series of events over time. They can keep an observational diary and write an orderly sequenced account from this. They can consider critically the record which they have produced and suggest how it might be improved.	The children can record using a wide range of methods, including mathematical representation. They can choose in advance the most appropriate method for a particular purpose.

Table 2(ii) The junior years (continued)

	Year 1		Year 2	
	Level 1	**Level 2**	**Level 1**	**Level 2**
Classifying	The children can classify into sets and subsets, using complex criteria if prompted by the teacher. They are able independently to sort, using simple criteria. They can use keys for simple criteria and, with help, for more complex criteria.	The children are aware that there are different criteria for sorting which could be used. Using simple criteria they are able to sort in different ways. With help, they extend the range of criteria to include, for example, behaviour and origin. With help, they can construct keys using simple criteria.	The children can confidently sort in different ways, using simple criteria. With help, they can use more complex criteria such as origin, behaviour and change. They use keys more confidently.	In retrospect, they recognise that of a number of methods of sorting used in any particular case one may be more productive and useful than the others.
Recognising patterns	When making observations, the children may seek patterns if prompted by the teacher. They can recognise the common factors in the information obtained by observing a number of instances. They are not able to describe the pattern formally. They may or may not be able to identify other instances which fit the pattern.	When making observations, the children look for patterns and recognise the more obvious patterns in their observations. With help, they describe the patterns orally. They will consider whether a new instance fits the pattern.	The children look for patterns, and with prompting are able to recognise patterns based on more complex observations. The process is assisted if the observations are made concurrently (or nearly so). Their oral description of the pattern improves and with prompting they consider whether new instances fit the pattern.	The children look more systematically for observations which form patterns, and become aware of the wider range of observations which may form patterns. Most patterns which they discern are in static properties, e.g. colour, shape, form, etc. With help, they describe these patterns and consider whether new observations fit the pattern.
Predicting	The children can make reasonable suggestions based on observations over a period of time. They can recognise some causal relationships.	The children make reasonable suggestions based on observations and when causal relationships are recognised they can, with help, make suggestions about effects that the cause will produce. They can suggest immediate and also future changes.	The children can base their suggestions on a number of observations viewed as a whole. They recognise a relationship but may not be able to give a clear oral description.	The suggestions which the children make are increasingly consistent with all the observational evidence. The children become aware that the reliability of their suggestions about future events or changes depends on the reliability of the observations on which they are based.
Controlling variables	The children start to identify one or two obvious variables. These may or may not be relevant. The children are able to find out whether or not they are relevant. When a relevant variable is identified, the children are able to find a way of controlling it if prompted by the teacher.	The children look for variables and notice more possibilities which may or may not be relevant. They can decide whether the more obvious are relevant and, with the help of the teacher, can find means of control.	The children look for variables and begin to draw on their experience in considering whether or not the variables are relevant. They are increasingly able to identify relevant variables and, with help, to find means of control.	The children are concerned to look for variables. They recognise that there cannot be a fair test if the relevant variables are not controlled. They can investigate two or three of the obvious ones and, with help, control those found to be relevant.
Investigating	The children can design and carry out simple investigations with minimal help with practicalities. They notice the more relevant variables and investigate them as part of their overall plan. With help, they suggest ways of controlling the variables and include this control in the design and execution of their investigations.	In designing their investigations, the children become increasingly aware of the possible wide range of variables. With help, they suggest means of identifying and controlling relevant variables and include this in the design and execution of their investigations. In discussion, they will agree that repetition is desirable and with prompting will repeat investigations.	Their range of investigations includes those of the type 'What happens when . . .?', 'What happens if . . .?' and 'Which is best?'. They start to consider investigation of suggestions based on recognised patterns.	They become better at formulating suggestions and questions for investigation. They are more aware of the possible range of variables and this awareness is increasingly reflected in the design and execution of their investigations.

	Year 3		Year 4	
	Level 1	**Level 2**	**Level 1**	**Level 2**
Classifying	The range of sorting criteria which the children can use independently and with confidence becomes wider, to include origin, behaviour and change. The children begin to consider in advance which sorting criteria will be most useful for a particular purpose, and with help they can make an appropriate suggestion. They are increasingly aware of the need to use keys, and with help they can construct them.		They make decisions about which sorting criteria to use with increasing independence, and the methods suggested are increasingly appropriate. In retrospect, the children are able to comment on the appropriateness of their choice. They use simple keys with confidence, and more complex keys with help. They are able to construct simple keys with little help and can attempt more complex keys.	The children can classify into sets and subsets using simple and complex criteria selected appropriately by themselves. They can use and construct simple keys.
Recognising patterns	The children use appropriate observations to seek patterns. They consider not only static properties but also dynamic ones, including, for example, behaviour and change, and they consider observations over a period of time. They recognise these patterns with help and can describe them orally. They can attempt to produce a written statement of simpler patterns and are increasingly able to decide whether new observations fit the pattern.	The children recognise patterns of various kinds and with help can describe them orally and in writing. They are increasingly able to use the patterns as the basis for suggestions about future happenings. They can look for patterns in derived data, particularly mathematical data, and with help can discern patterns in this data.	The children are able more readily to recognise patterns in simple data, and with help to recognise patterns in mathematical data presented in both graphical and tabular form. They are increasingly able to describe the patterns clearly, both orally and in writing. They are able to identify other instances which fit the pattern and to discuss their reasons.	When making observations, the children seek patterns in the information obtained. They recognise common factors in the information obtained by observing a number of instances. They are able to recognise other instances which fit the pattern.
Predicting	With help, the children increasingly make suggestions based on the recognition of an observational pattern. With help, the children can give a clearer oral description of the pattern and consequently, their suggestions become more consistent with the recognised pattern. They use not only observations and derived data but also known concepts.	The children base their suggestions on more complex patterns, including change and behaviour.	Increasingly, the children are able, with help, to make suggestions based on derived data. Their suggestions are more precise and take in all the evidence. They attempt to assess the likely reliability of their suggestions.	The children base their suggestions on firm evidence, including recognised patterns. There is increasing recognition of causal, as distinct from casual, relationships. They use known concepts in making their suggestions.
Controlling variables	The children attempt to identify variables and investigate two or three of the most obvious. With help, they control those that are found to be relevant. They start to consider in retrospect whether they have identified all the relevant variables and whether they have effectively controlled those that have been identified.	The children are increasingly able to identify variables and use their accumulating experience in eliminating non-relevant ones. They can find means of controlling simple variables and with help tackle more complex situations.	As for Year 3 Level 2. In retrospect, the children are increasingly concerned with whether relevant variables have been completely identified and whether they have been effectively controlled.	The children are aware of a wide range of variables and, on most occasions, can identify and control those which are relevant.
Investigating	With help, they start to investigate suggestions based on recognised patterns. They are increasingly concerned with the reliability of their investigations. They appreciate the need for repetition and when prompted repeat observations and measurements.	With help, they can investigate suggestions based on mathematical data. They can work with care and accuracy. They are aware of the need for repetition to check accuracy, and carry out checks without prompting.	The children can investigate simple suggestions and questions with minimal help. They design and carry out simple investigations, paying regard to obvious variables and their control. They consider the level of accuracy required and can use ideas about estimation and approximation.	The children can design and carry out simple investigations with confidence. They can identify and control most relevant variables. They can review their investigations critically and they check their results by repetition.

Extension B Scientific ideas

These are the ideas to which we would like children to be exposed and which we would like them to explore. As stated already, they will meet these ideas in their own environment, and so will be able to experience and explore them in a familiar setting. It is difficult to indicate briefly the depth of understanding which it is hoped children will acquire, but as the ideas arise in the science activities the depth of treatment intended will be clearly explained. Indeed, in most cases, the activities themselves will tell the story.

It will soon become clear to teachers using the materials that it is necessary to return to ideas time and time again, each time probing them more searchingly and using the children's developing skills and abilities to help them towards greater understanding. The role of language in this process is crucial and this aspect is taken up in Extension D, Language in science.

Children's exposure to scientific ideas
The basic ideas are listed below and on page 118. Table 3 overleaf shows at which point in the scheme in the infant years particular scientific ideas are explored. The ideas are presented in a way that will enable children working at a particular level to gain appropriate experience and understanding. In Table 3, the numbering of the scientific ideas corresponds to the numbering used for the statements in the following list. The topic letters and activity reference numbers denote the specific activities in which the ideas are introduced. A key to the topic letters appears on page 118.

Basic ideas

1 Sets – the concept of a set as a group of items sharing a common feature.

2 Colour – primary, secondary, black, white, shades, etc.

3 Shape
- 3.1 2D – square, rectangle, circle, ellipse, triangle.
- 3.2 3D – cube, cuboid, sphere, ellipsoid, cylinder, triangular prism.
- 3.3 Symmetry – mirror images.

4 Concept of quantity

5 Measurement of quantity
- 5.1 Direct comparison.
- 5.2 Arbitrary units.
- 5.3 Standard units.
- 5.4 Approximation, estimation.

6 Spatial relationships and direction, e.g. under, behind, backwards, etc.

Ideas about the physical world

7 The world around us
- 7.1 There is air round the earth.
- 7.2 Air contains water vapour.
- 7.3 Soil is a mixture of things which come from rocks as well as some material which was once living.
- 7.4 The apparent movement of sun, moon and stars follows a regular predictable pattern.
- 7.5 The seasons follow a regular pattern related to the position of the sun.
- 7.6 Water flows to a common level.
- 7.7 Floating and sinking depend on both the kind of material and on the shape.

8 Movement and energy

- 8.1 The (average) speed of an object depends on the distance it travels in a certain time.
- 8.2 Force is needed to move a stationary object or to alter the direction of travel of a moving object.
- 8.3 Objects are pulled towards the earth; weight is a measure of how hard that pull is.
- 8.4 The greater the force, the more energy is required.
- 8.5 Energy can be supplied in many ways: by burning fuel, by eating food, or by doing work and storing the energy, e.g. in an elastic band, in a stretched spring, etc.
- 8.6 The faster an object moves, the more energy it has.
- 8.7 A moving object is stopped or slowed down by energy being removed from it.
- 8.8 This energy may appear as heat (as in braking).
- 8.9 An object moving on a surface must overcome friction.

9 Structure and forces

- 9.1 Forces are needed to change the shape of an object.
- 9.2 The strength of an object or structure depends on its shape and on the material from which it is made.
- 9.3 For a given force, the pressure is greater the smaller the area on which it is exerted.

10 Magnets and electricity

- 10.1 Magnets can attract or repel each other.
- 10.2 Some materials are attracted by a magnet and some are not.
- 10.3 Some materials can be magnetised and some cannot.
- 10.4 Some materials conduct electricity and some do not.
- 10.5 For an electric current to flow, there must be a complete circuit of conducting material.

11 Light and sound

- 11.1 Light travels in straight lines.
- 11.2 Objects can be seen because of the light they give out or reflect.
- 11.3 Sound comes from vibrating objects.

12 Change

- 12.1 Change may be reversible or irreversible.
- 12.2 Change of state is reversible.
- 12.3 Cooking usually produces irreversible changes.
- 12.4 During a change of state, the substance itself does not alter, it merely changes its form.

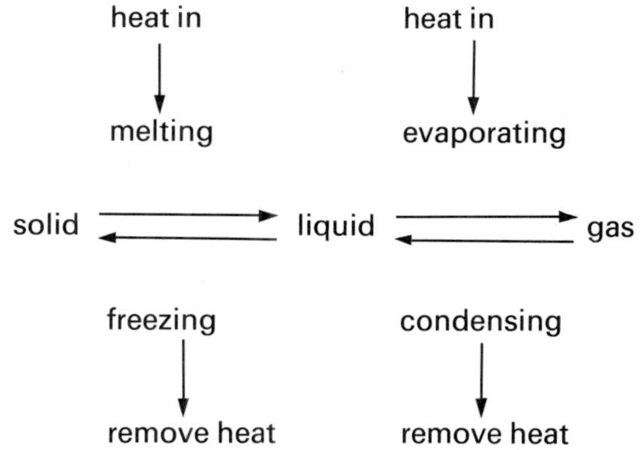

13 Properties of materials

- 13.1 Different materials have different properties.
- 13.2 Materials are used for purposes for which their properties make them appropriate (paper, wood, metals, plastics, wool, cotton, synthetic fibres, glass, brick, stone, rubber).
- 13.3 Materials can be classified by consideration of their properties, e.g. metals, plastics.
- 13.4 Some substances are soluble in water and some are not.
- 13.5 Some substances do not dissolve in water but dissolve in other liquids, e.g. cooking oil. (continued on page 118)

Table 3 Children's exposure to scientific ideas

Basic ideas		Book 1 Level 1	Book 1 Level 2	Book 2 Level 1
Sets	1	H[1,2,7] C[2,3,7] Cl[1,7]	S[6] B[2,3,4,5] Co[2] Ca[1] Sc[3]	Sh[2] Su[1,7] P[4] Sw[1] K[4]
Colour	2	H[1,6] Wh[4] C[1,2,5,6,7] Cl[1] W[2,4]	S[1,2,3,4] B[2,3] Co[1] Sc[1,3,6]	Sh[1] P[2,3] Sw[1,4] Pt[4] K[4,5]
Shape	3.1	H[3] Bo[1,2] Wh[4] C[2,4] Cl[4] W[1,3]	S[1] B[2,4,6] Co[5,6] Sc[4,7]	P[2] Pt[1,2,3]
	3.2	H[3] Bo[1,2] C[2,7] Cl[4] W[3] C[4]	S[1,2] B[2] Co[5,6] Sc[4] Co[3,8]	Su[1,5,7] Pt[1,2,3]
	3.3	Cl[5]		Sh[1] Pt[1]
Concept of quantity	4	H[7] Bo[1,2,3] Wh[1,2,3] C[2,4,6] Cl[1,3,4,5,6] W[1,2,3]	S[3,5,6] B[2,3] Co[2,6] Ca[1] Sc[2,3,6,7]	Su[1,3,5] P[2,3,6] Sw[3,4] Pt[4] K[1,2,7]
Measurement of quantity	5.1	H[7] Bo[1,2,3] Wh[1,2,3] C[2,4,6] Cl[1,3,5,6] W[1,2,3]	S[3,5,6] B[2] Co[2,6] Ca[1] Sc[2,3,6,7]	Sh[3] Su[1] P[2,3,6] Pt[4]
	5.2		Co[4]	Sh[1] Su[5] Sw[3,4] K[1,2,7]
	5.3			
	5.4			
Spatial relationships	6	H[3] Wh[1,4] Cl[5]	S[1] B[3] Sc[8]	P[1,2,3]
The world around us	7.1		Sc[4]	
	7.2	W[4]	B[6] Sc[5]	
	7.3		S[6] Sc[3]	
	7.4			
	7.5	W[1]		
	7.6		Co[8] Sc[8]	Su[3]
	7.7	W[3]	S[6] B[5] Sc[4,6]	P[1] K[3]
Movement and energy	8.1			
	8.2	Wh[1,2]	Ca[1] Sc[7]	
	8.3	H[3] Wh[2]		
	8.4	Wh[1,2]	Ca[4]	
	8.5		S[2] Ca[1] Sc[7] Ca[4]	
	8.6			
	8.7			
	8.8			
	8.9			
Structures and forces	9.1	C[2]	Sc[4]	Su[7]
	9.2			Su[7]
	9.3			Sh[4] P[1]
Magnets and electricity	10.1			
	10.2			
	10.3			
	10.4			
	10.5			
Light and sound	11.1	W[1]		Sw[1]
	11.2			
	11.3	Bo[4] C[3,4]	Co[7]	P[4,5]
Change	12.1	H[6] Bo[3] W[2,3,4]	S[2] B[6] Sc[4,6]	Su[4,5] Sw[4] K[1,3]
	12.2		S[2] B[6] Sc[6]	Su[4]
	12.3	Bo[3] W[4]		Su[5] K[1]
	12.4	Bo[3] W[2,3,4]	S[2] B[6] Sc[5,6]	Su[2,3,4,5]
Properties of materials	13.1	Bo[4] C[4,5] Cl[6,7,8] C[7]	B[4] Co[1,2,3,4,5,6] Ca[1,2,3,4] Sc[1,3,4]	Sh[4] Su[1] P[5] K[1,2,3,4,6,7]
	13.2	C[4,7] Cl[6,7,8]	B[4] Co[5] Ca[2,3,4] Sc[4] Co[6]	Sh[4] Su[1,2,7] K[6]
	13.3		B[5] Co[1,2,4,7]	Su[1] P[5]
	13.4			Su[2,6] Sw[2] K[2,3,4,5]
	13.5			
	13.6		B[2] Co[3,8] Sc[1,6]	Su[3] K[3]
Weather	14.1			
	14.2			
	14.3			
	14.4	W[2,3]		
Living/non-living	15.1	H[8] Wh[1,3,4] C[6]	S[1,3,5] B[1]	Sh[1]
	15.2		S[3] B[1]	
	15.3		S[3]	
	15.4			
Food chains	16.1		S[2]	P[1,3,6]
	16.2		S[2]	
	16.3	H[8]	S[1,5]	
	16.4	H[8]	S[1,5]	
	16.5			
Living together	17.1	H[1,2,3,4,5,6,7,8] C[3,6]	S[1,2,3,5]	P[1,2,3,6]
	17.2			P[1,2,3,6]
	17.3			P[2,3]
	17.4			
Life cycles	18.1			
	18.2			
	18.3	H[8] C[6]	S[5]	
	18.4		S[1,5]	
People	19.1	Wh[1,2,3,4]	B[1,3]	
	19.2	Wh[1,2,3]	B[1,3]	P[3]
	19.3	H[1,2,3,4,5,6,7] Bo[3,4] C[1,2,3,4,5,6,7] Cl[1,2,6] W[4]	S[1,2,3,6] B[2,4] Co[1,3,4,7]	Sh[4] Su[2,3,4,5,6] P[5] Sw[2] Pt[4] K[4,5]
	19.4	Cl[6,7,8]		Sh[4]
	19.5		B[3]	
	19.6			
	19.7			

Basic ideas		Book 2 Level 2	Book 3 Level 1	Book 3 Level 2
Sets	1	E[1] Po[1,2,4] Pa[5]	N[1] G[4] Hn[5] Sg[3]	T[4]
Colour	2	E[1,2] F[1]	G[2,5,6] Ce[2,3,4,5] G[1] N[5]	A[2] Fa[1,4] Fm[2] We[3] A[3] Fa[5]
Shape	3.1	M[1] Pa[1,2]	Hn[1] Hs[2,3] G[1]	T[7]
	3.2	E[2,5]	Hn[1] Sg[2,4] G[4] Ce[1]	T[1,2,3,6]
	3.3	E[2] Po[3]	G[6] Hs[3] Sg[2,6]	A[3]
Concept of quantity	4	E[1,4,6,7] F[2,3,4] Pa[3]		
Measurement of quantity	5.1	E[1] Po[2] Pa[3,4,6]	G[1] Hn[3] Ce[1,3] N[2,5]	
	5.2	E[4] F[2,3,4,6] M[2] Pa[3,6]	G[4] Ce[1] G[5] N[1]	T[7] We[4]
	5.3	E[6,7]	G[3] Hn[1,3] Ce[1,4] Hs[1] N[1,2,3] Sg[1,2,3,4,5,6] G[1,2,4] Hs[2]	T[1,5] A[2,3,5] Fa[2,3] Fm[2,4,5] We[2,3,5,6] A[1]
	5.4		Sg[6]	A[1] Fm[2,5] We[1]
Spatial relationships	6	E[2,4] F[5,6] M[4] Pa[1,2,7]	Hs[1,2,3] Sg[1,2,6] G[2]	T[1,2,3,4,5] We[1,7]
The world around us	7.1	F[4]	G[1,3] Hn[1] Sg[1] G[4] Ce[1,4]	We[3,4,7] Fa[3] Fm[4]
	7.2		G[1] Ce[1,4] Sg[1]	
	7.3			
	7.4			We[1]
	7.5			
	7.6	F[5]		
	7.7	E[2] F[5]	Sg[2] Hn[3]	T[6,7] A[5] Fm[1]
Movement and energy	8.1	Po[1] F[2,3] Pa[3]		T[3,7]
	8.2	F[4] M[2] Pa[1,2,7]	Hs[1] Sg[5] G[3]	T[1,2,3,4,5,6,7] We[7]
	8.3	E[2] Pa[2,4,7]	G[3,4] Hs[2] N[1,2] Sg[3,4] Hs[3]	T[2,5] Fa[2]
	8.4	Pa[1,7]	Hs[1]	T[2,3,5,7] Fa[1]
	8.5		G[3]	T[4,5] Fm[1,3] T[2,3,7] We[7]
	8.6			T[4,5] Fm[1]
	8.7			T[4]
	8.8	Pa[1]		T[4]
	8.9	Pa[1]	N[4]	T[2,3,4] Fa[1]
Structures and forces	9.1	E[2]	Hn[1] Ce[4] Sg[2,3]	T[5,6,7] Fa[2] Fm[3,5]
	9.2		Hn[3] Hs[1,4] N[1,2,3]	Fa[1,2] Fm[3]
	9.3		Hn[3]	
Magnets and electricity	10.1	Po[1]	Hn[5]	
	10.2	Po[1]	Hn[5]	
	10.3		Hn[5]	
	10.4	Po[4]		
	10.5	Po[4]		
Light and sound	11.1	M[4]	Ce[5] Sg[6] Hn[4]	We[1,2]
	11.2		Hn[4]	
	11.3	M[2]	Hs[5]	
Change	12.1	E[2] M[2] Pa[5]	G[6] Hn[1,3] Ce[1,2,3,4] Sg[1] G[1]	T[6,7] A[1,3,4] Fa[3,4,5] Fm[1,2,3,5] We[2,4,6,7]
	12.2		Ce[2]	Fa[3]
	12.3	M[4]	G[6]	Fm[2,5]
	12.4		G[1] Ce[2,4] Sg[1]	A[1] Cs[3,4] Fa[5] Fm[2] We[3,4,5]
Properties of materials	13.1	E[2,4] Po[1,4] M[2,4] Pa[1,5]	Hn[1,2,3,5] Ce[1,2,3,4] Hs[1,4] N[1,2,3,4] Sg[1,3,4]	T[3,4,6] Fa[1,2,3,4] Fm[1,3] We[2,4] Fa[5]
	13.2	Po[4] M[2,4] Pa[1,5]	G[6] Hn[1,2,3] Ce[1,2,3,4] Hs[1,4] N[1,3,4] Sg[1,3,4]	T[3,4,6] Fa[1,2,3,4] Fm[3] Fa[5]
	13.3	Po[1,4] F[1] M[2] Pa[5]	Hn[5] N[4]	T[4] Cs[4]
	13.4		Hn[3]	A[1] Fm[5] We[4]
	13.5			
	13.6	M[3]	Ce[2]	Fm[1]
Weather	14.1		Sg[1]	We[1,2,4]
	14.2			We[5]
	14.3			We[7]
	14.4			
Living/non living	15.1	E[3,4,5,6,7]	G[1,2,3] Hn[4] G[4]	A[1,3,4,5,6] Fm[4] A[2]
	15.2			
	15.3	F[1]		
	15.4			
Food chains	16.1	F[4]	Hn[4]	A[1,2,3,4,5] Fm[4] A[6]
	16.2			A[2,4,5,6]
	16.3	E[3,4,5,6,7]	G[1,2,3]	Fm[4]
	16.4	E[3,4,5,6,7]		Fm[4]
	16.5			
Living together	17.1	E[1,3,4,5,6,7] F[1] M[4]	G[1,2,3,4,5,6] Hn[4]	A[1,2,3,4,5,6] Fm[4]
	17.2		G[3,4] Hn[4]	A[1,2,3,4,5,6]
	17.3	E[3,4,5,6,7]	G[3,4,5] Hn[4] G[1,2]	A[1,2,3,4,5,6] Fm[4]
	17.4			A[2,3,4,5,6]
Life cycles	18.1	E[3,4,5,6,7]	G[3,4]	A[1,3,5] Fm[4]
	18.2	E[3,4,5,6,7]	G[3,4]	A[1,3,5] Fm[4]
	18.3	E[3,4,5,6,7]	G[3,4]	A[1,3,5] Fm[4]
	18.4	E[3,4,5,6,7]	G[3,4]	A[1,3,5] Fm[4]
People	19.1	Po[2,3] F[2,4] M[1]		A[2,4]
	19.2	Po[2,3] F[2,4] M[1]		
	19.3	E[4] Po[1] M[1,4]	Hn[3,4] Hs[4,5]	Fm[2]
	19.4			Fa[3]
	19.5			
	19.6	F[4] M[1]		
	19.7			

13.6 Substances can be classified as liquids, solids or gases according to their properties, e.g. water, cooking oil, washing-up liquid; ice, wood, glass; steam, air.

14 Weather
- 14.1 The sun provides us with warmth.
- 14.2 Rain falls when there are clouds.
- 14.3 Clouds can stop the sun's rays (light and heat) from reaching us.
- 14.4 The type of weather we have is associated with the seasons.

Ideas about the living world

15 Living/non-living
- 15.1 Living things have common properties: growth, respiration, reproduction, nutrition, excretion, and possibly movement.
- 15.2 Non-living things do not have these properties.
- 15.3 Some non-living things were once alive.
- 15.4 Some non-living things occur naturally, e.g. rocks, and some are man-made.

16 Food chains
- 16.1 Living things must eat; they need water and air.
- 16.2 Big animals may eat little animals; eventually down the chain animals eat plants.
- 16.3 Plants need food and water.
- 16.4 Plants get their food from the soil.
- 16.5 The food which plants take from the soil must be replaced.

17 Living together
- 17.1 Plants and animals are very diverse in form.
- 17.2 Their form fits their environment: animals, fish, birds and plants.
- 17.3 Plants and animals are sensitive to their environment and respond to it.
- 17.4 Plants and animals in a particular environment are dependent on each other.

18 Life cycles
- 18.1 All living things have a fixed life cycle.
- 18.2 The life cycle of all members of the same species is the same.
- 18.3 Parents produce offspring of the same kind as themselves.
- 18.4 The life cycles of living things are often linked to seasonal change.

19 People
- 19.1 People are living things. They exhibit variability.
- 19.2 They share the common properties of all living things.
- 19.3 They are able to explore the environment by using their senses.
- 19.4 They are able to protect themselves from the environment.
- 19.5 Children must spend many years learning to care for themselves; this contrasts with other animals.
- 19.6 The different life processes take place in different defined parts of the body.
- 19.7 Apart from the sex organs and those functions which are sexually controlled, the bodies of all people are the same and function in the same way.

Key to Table 3 on pages 116 and 117.

Topics

Year 1: Harvest H, Bonfire night Bo, What can I do? Wh, Christmas C, Clothes Cl, Winter W, Spring S, The bathroom B, The cook Co, The caretaker Ca, School holidays Sc.

Year 2: The shoe shop Sh, The supermarket Su, Pets P, The sweet shop Sw, The post Pt, Jobs in the kitchen K, Easter E, The police Po, The firefighter F, Milk M, The park Pa.

Year 3: In the garden G, Hallowe'en Hn, Celebrations Ce, Jobs in the house Hs, The newsagent N, Spots and games Sg, Transport T, Animals A, Fabrics Fa, The farm Fm, Weather We.

Extension C Summary of the experiences provided by the activities in Science through Infant Topics, Teachers' Books A, B and C

This summary identifies the main ideas which are explored in each activity in *Teachers' Books A, B* and *C*. As the scheme progresses, teachers will need to check the children's record sheets to see which activities individual children have carried out; of course, the extent to which children retain the ideas they have encountered will vary. Teachers should always be prepared to adjust the level of discussion as the children reveal their thinking through the comments they make and the ideas they express.

In Table 3, Extension B, page 116, the activities which contribute towards the development of children's understanding of particular concepts are identified.

Teachers' Book A: Level 1

Harvest

H1 Fruits are different colours. They can be sorted by colour. Certain colours are associated with particular ripe fruits.

H2 Fruits have different surface textures. They can be sorted by texture. Certain textures are associated with particular fruits.

H3 Fruits have different shapes. The shape of an object (e.g. a fruit) determines whether it will roll and how it will roll.

H4 Different fruits have different smells. Some fruits have a peel which may smell different from the fruit inside. Certain smells are associated with particular fruits.

H5 Some things taste sweet and some taste sour. For example, some varieties of apples taste sweet, and some sour. Oranges taste sweeter than lemons. Lemons taste sour.

H6 When an apple is cut and exposed to the air it turns brown. Different varieties of apples turn brown at different rates.

H7 Fruits contain pips, stones or seeds which vary in size, shape, colour, and texture.

H8 Pips, stones and seeds will germinate and grow if planted. Some germinate before others and some grow more quickly than others. The taste of bean sprouts changes as they grow.

Bonfire night

Bo1 Cylinders have curved and flat surfaces. The end of a cylinder forms a circle. A cylinder is the same width (diameter) at any point along its length. Several small cylinders of the same width (diameter) can be put together to form one longer cylinder.

Bo2 Cones have curved and flat surfaces. One end of a cone is wider than the other. A cone can be cut into a series of discs.

Bo3 When potatoes are cooked in their skins, changes take place. Margarine melts on hot potato. Potatoes cooked in their skins will cool at different rates if left with skins intact, skins removed or cut in half.

Bo4 Percussion instruments make different sounds. They can be used to make loud or soft sounds. Sounds can be made by tapping other objects. Some materials make louder noises than others.

What can I do?

Wh1 When we jump, both feet are in the air at once. Some children can jump higher than others, and some further. High or long jumps are harder work than low or short jumps.

Wh2 In equal volumes, some materials feel heavier than others when we lift and carry them. It is harder work carrying a heavy weight than a light weight. We can lift with different parts of our body, e.g. feet.

Wh3 We have the same number of fingers (plus thumbs) as toes. We can achieve a wider range of movement with our fingers than with our toes. We can pick up things more easily with our fingers than with our toes. We can align thumb and index finger. Some animals do not have fingers like ours and they may use their mouths to pick things up.

Wh4 We have particular features on our faces. We can move parts of our faces in various ways. The way we move and hold our faces can show the way we feel.

Christmas

C1 Objects can be matched one to one by colour (e.g. fairy lights and beads).

C2 The texture and shape of a balloon change when it is inflated (rubber stretches; the 2D shape becomes a 3D shape).

C3 Nuts have various shapes, sizes, colours, and textures. All the nuts of one kind are different but they also have recognisable similarities. A nut contains a kernel which can be seen when the shell is cracked open.

C4 Bells of different types have some differences and some similarities. They are made from different metals but these metals have similar properties.

C5 A fine powder (e.g. icing sugar) will pour like a liquid.

C6 Holly has leaves, stems and berries. The top surface of a leaf is different from the underside. The leaves have sharp points which vary in number. The berries contain a seed which can be planted and will produce a holly tree.

C7 Objects (e.g. shiny Christmas tree baubles and glittered ping pong balls) look shiny (reflect light) in different ways.

Clothes

Cl1 A collection of objects (e.g. buttons) can be sorted in a variety of ways.

Cl2 Materials have different textures. The texture is identified by touch alone. The material can be identified by touch.

Cl3 Objects (e.g. sets of clothes and dolls) can be ordered and matched by size.

Cl4 The body has a particular shape. Clothes are made in shapes to match the parts of the body they fit.

Cl5 Some pairs (e.g. gloves) are mirror images. Some pairs (e.g. socks) are identical. Our two feet and two hands are mirror image pairs.

Cl6 Different materials have different heat retaining properties. Gloves are made from many different kinds of material. A glove will reduce the heat loss from the object it covers (e.g. a small hot water bottle).

Cl7 A collection of objects (e.g. hats) can be sorted by purpose.

Cl8 Some fabrics will allow water to run through them, and some will soak up water. Others will not: these are termed 'waterproof'.

Winter

W1 If an object is held vertically and at right angles to the sunlight it may cast a sharp shadow longer but not noticeably wider than itself.

W2 Fresh snow is cold, white and soft. When we walk on it, we leave footprints. It melts on our hands. A full jar of snow taken indoors will melt and the resulting water will not fill the jar.

W3 Ice is hard, cold and brittle. Pieces of ice always float in water, no matter what size or shape the pieces are. Ice melts on our hands or when warmed by being taken indoors.

W4 Bread changes in size, colour, texture and temperature when it is toasted. We heat it to toast it. Moisture comes from the bread. Margarine melts on the hot toast. Bread shrinks as it dries (it loses moisture).

Teachers' Book A: Level 2

Spring

S1 A hyacinth has roots, bulb, stem, flower and leaves. The leaves have a particular shape, colour and texture pattern. The bulb has layers, and feels wet inside. The roots, leaves and stem arise from a particular part of the bulb.

S2 Solid lard does not move or change shape when tilted in a pan. When heated, the lard melts and will then move and change shape when the pan is tilted. When left to cool, the lard becomes solid again. Birds like to eat a variety of food including fruit, seeds, cake and lard.

S3 A living thing (e.g. a real flower) and a non-living thing (e.g. its artificial replica) have some differences and some similarities. The real flower eventually wilts and dies. It lasts longer in water. The artificial flower stays the same and water is not needed.

S4 The colour green can be seen in many living and non-living things. Many shades and tints are all considered green.

S5 Flower seeds can have many different sizes, shapes and colours. The seeds of one type of flower all have certain attributes in common. Different types of seeds can all be planted. They will germinate and grow at different rates and produce plants of their own kind.

S6 Potting compost is made up of an assortment of bits of different shapes and sizes. Some (sticks and leaf material) will float. Some (pebbles, grit, etc.) will sink.

The bathroom

B1 Living things (e.g. babies) have needs which non-living things (e.g. dolls) do not have. Water has certain properties which categorise it as a liquid (e.g. it will pour and splash). Water is clear and colourless. Steam rises from hot water but not from cold.

B2 Soap helps water to remove dirt. Soaps can have various sizes, shapes, colours and smells. Soap can be liquid or solid.

B3 We clean our teeth because food left on them can be harmful. Front teeth are a different shape from back teeth.

B4 Different types of fabric have some similarities and some differences. Some will absorb water better than others.

B5 Bath toys can be made from a variety of materials with different properties. Materials can be identified by their properties. Some toys sink and some float in water.

B6 The steam from hot water will condense as moisture on some surfaces. These then appear to be steamed up.

The cook

Co1 Sugar has various forms. It is made up of bits, which vary in size and colour depending on the type of sugar.

Co2 Spoons can be made from various materials. The material, shape and size are matched to the purpose of the spoon.

Co3 Fats can be liquid or solid and they differ in taste and appearance. They all repel water.

Co4 Sugar and salt can be distinguished by observing the size of the grains and other properties. Granulated sugar, salt and flour pour like liquids.

Co5 The properties of a cylinder make it a suitable shape for a rolling pin. The properties of wood make it a good material for a rolling pin.

Co6 The properties of a cone are utilised in a funnel.

Co7 In some cases, smell alone can be used to identify a substance (e.g. some items of food). Some items can be identified by the sound made when they are shaken in a container.

Co8 Utensils and vessels for food are shaped in particular ways because they are intended for use with solid or liquid food. The shapes relate to the properties of solids and liquids.

The caretaker

Ca1 The shape and structure of nails and screws determine how they are put into wood. The size and shape of the tools used must be appropriate.

Ca2 Some surfaces in buildings are shiny. Some are dull. Some materials can be polished to make them shine. When metal is polished, the polishing rag becomes black.

Ca3 Some substances which are used in school will mark a Formica surface. Some of these substances are easier to remove than others.

Ca4 Scissors and knives are used for different types of cutting. Scissors will cut some things and not others. Some scissors cut better than others.

School holidays

Sc1 Sand behaves in some ways like a liquid, but a stone will not sink in it; it does not find its own level; it will not soak into a tissue.

Sc2 Dry sand behaves differently from wet sand.

Sc3 Pebbles and stones can vary widely in size, colour, shape and texture. Water drains through pebbles, sand and soil at different rates.

Sc4 Arm bands change shape (2D to 3D) when inflated. When deflated they can sink, and when inflated they float. Air is blown (pushed) into them to inflate them; it escapes as bubbles if released under water. Other objects, e.g. bottles, will float when they contain air.

Sc5 Water dries from the hands into the air. If a wet paper towel is exposed to the air and another is kept in an airtight container, the former will dry while the latter will remain wet.

Sc6 Both water and orange concentrate are liquids and can be seen to have the properties of liquids. When they are cooled in a freezer, they change to solids. When brought into a warm room, they change back to liquids.

Sc7 Wheels are circular. The larger the circle, the greater the distance travelled in one revolution.

Sc8 A ball will roll down a slope; water will run down a slope; the surface of water in a container remains level when the container is tilted. All these observations can be used to test whether an object is level or sloping.

Teachers' Book B: Level 1

The shoe shop

Sh1 Some pairs (e.g. shoes) are mirror images. Foot size varies from one person to another. Foot size may be related to height.

Sh2 Sets can be used to determine the order of popularity (e.g. of shoe fastenings).

Sh3 We walk on certain parts of our feet. Footprints made using talcum powder show this. Walking and tiptoe prints look different. Our shoes must be of appropriate size.

Sh4 Shoe uppers and soles can be made from various materials. The materials used and the structure of the shoe are suited to the purpose of the shoe.

The supermarket

Su1 Containers (e.g. in supermarkets) have various 3D shapes. They can be made from various materials, e.g. metal, glass or plastic, each of which has particular useful properties. A matrix can be used to sort a collection of containers.

Su2 Peas are preserved in many different ways, and the processes change the way they look and feel. Water will boil if heated; we can tell when it is boiling by observing its behaviour. The peas change when cooked and have different colours, tastes and textures. When frozen peas are added to boiling water, the water stops boiling and takes time to boil again.

Su3 The surface of a liquid is flat when settled. The liquid can move and change shape. Drips of a liquid will join the main body of the liquid and cannot be separated again. Different liquids flow at different speeds.

Su4 When solid chocolate is heated, it changes to liquid chocolate. Margarine and wax behave similarly. All three change back from liquid to solid when cooled. The solid wax and chocolate retain the shape of the container in which they cooled. Cooking oil will solidify if cooled sufficiently (refrigerated).

Su5 The shape of an egg determines the way it rolls. The shell is solid. The yolk and white are liquid. When an egg is boiled, it changes in colour and from liquid to solid. The change is irreversible.

Su6 Sugar behaves in some ways like a liquid. It is made up of many small solid pieces. When added to water and stirred, it apparently disappears. The taste of the water is changed. The sugar has dissolved. Several types of sugar and salt dissolve in water.

Su7 Plastic can be transparent or opaque. Plastic containers can be rigid or flexible. Glass containers are always rigid. Containers are made from material suited to their purpose.

Pets

P1 When water is poured (e.g. on to gravel in a fish tank), it exerts a force. The force can be spread in various ways (e.g. by using a saucer). Water weed is intended to grow in water. It changes in appearance when it is transferred from air to water.

P2 Goldfish have particular features on their bodies. Fins can be moved in particular ways; scales overlap in a particular direction suited to the flow of water past them as the fish moves.

P3 Budgerigars have particular features on their bodies. Feathers are of various sizes and overlap in a particular direction. Budgerigars move in particular ways. They seem to hear, although ears cannot be seen. A budgerigar's behaviour when offered a selection of foods can be observed.

P4 Budgerigar toys illustrate different kinds of motion – swinging, rocking, rolling. Objects can be sorted according to how they move.

P5 Different materials make different sounds when tapped. The surfaces on which they are placed can affect the sounds produced. Materials may be identified by the sound they make. Sounds can differ in pitch.

P6 The body of a small animal (mammal) has particular features. It has certain similarities to and differences from the goldfish and the budgerigar. We can investigate the animal's behaviour in various circumstances.

The sweet shop

Sw1 Sweets and sweet papers can be many different colours and different shades of one colour. Some sweets and sweet papers are translucent: light can be shone through the coloured sweet or sweet paper on to white paper to give a patch of that colour. Light can be shone through a coloured sweet paper on to an object thus apparently changing its colour.

Sw2 Sweets have various flavours. The sweets change as they are sucked. A boiled sweet will become soft and sticky in hot water. Strands of the sweet will harden quickly when cooled.

Sw3 Sweets of different types have different weights. The same weight of sweets will contain fewer heavy sweets than light sweets.

Sw4 When cooking, ingredients may need to be weighed. Ground almonds contain oil. An investigation can be set up to find out whether colour affects taste (e.g. different colours of marzipan).

The post

Pt1 Regular 3D shapes have a number of curved and flat surfaces. Some faces are identical. A regular 3D shape may be opened out flat to form a net composed of regular 2D shapes.

Pt2 Regular 3D shapes will pass through spaces of different shapes and sizes depending on which way round they are presented.

Pt3 Some regular 3D shapes will fit together without leaving spaces, while others will not. The same applies to 2D shapes.

Pt4 Size is not necessarily related to weight. Some large objects are lighter than smaller ones.

Jobs in the kitchen

K1 In cooking, ingredients may need to be weighed. Scone mixture must be heated to cook it. It changes in appearance and texture when cooked. The addition of baking powder makes the mixture rise during cooking and alters the texture of the scone produced.

K2 Baking powder, sugar and salt have some features in common and some differences. When added to water, baking powder produces bubbles, while the others do not. Warm water speeds up the reaction.

K3 Cold and hot water have different effects on greasy plates. Solid margarine melts and floats when hot water is added; washing up liquid, solid soap and washing powder each change the margarine differently when added to the mixture. We can investigate which cleanser is most convenient.

K4 Many shades and tints are classed as red. Some red substances have a smell, others do not. Some will mark fabric. The cause of the mark may be identified by colour and smell. Some marks wash out of fabric more easily than others.

K5 Water will boil when heated. We can tell when it is boiling by observing its behaviour. A tea bag may have little holes in it. Inside are small pieces of various shapes and shades of brown. Boiling water changes colour when poured over the tea bag or on to loose tea. The tea leaves change in appearance, texture and temperature. Something from the tea leaves dissolves but the rest of the tea leaf does not dissolve. 'Instant' tea may be the part of the tea leaf which dissolves.

K6 We use a variety of materials to cover walls. In a kitchen, the material used may be required to resist a variety of stains. Some types of surface are easier to clean without damage than others. We can investigate which surfaces are satisfactory.

K7 Some paper towels are thicker than others, some contain more layers and some are more absorbent. We can find out by investigation which absorbs water best.

Teachers' Book B: Level 2

Easter

E1 Many flowers are yellow in colour. The flowers of one type have particular features in common. Surrounding temperature affects the rate at which cut flowers in tight bud, given water, open and eventually die.

E2 When paste powder is added to water, the mixture thickens. When inflated, balloons change in certain ways and remain the same in other respects. Newspaper changes when soaked with paste, and changes again as it dries out. The reflection of a hemisphere placed on a mirror will make it appear to be a complete sphere.

E3 Seed potatoes may have shoots and roots growing from them. If placed in damp soil, they will grow into potato plants.

E4 Seed peas given water on a paper towel will grow roots and shoots. The shoots grow upwards and the roots grow downwards.

E5 Tomatoes and peppers contain seeds. The fresh seeds are different in some ways from the seeds bought in packets. Fresh and packet seeds may be planted and their progress compared.

E6 When sweet corn seeds are planted,the surrounding temperature will affect their rate of germination and growth.

E7 When cucumber seeds are planted, the amount of light will affect the growth of the young plants.

Police

Po1 Objects may be identified by describing their properties and attributes.

Po2 People have unique features. They may be identified by describing details of their appearance.

Po3 A reflection of one hand or foot in a mirror looks like the other hand or foot. Hands have a palm and a back which differ in some respects. Fingerprints can be made using an ink pad. Each child's fingerprints are different from the other children's in some details.

Po4 Torches can be taken apart. They have a battery, switch and bulb. The batteries must be placed in a particular direction to make the bulb light when the switch is on. A bulb will only light when certain materials are placed across a gap in the circuit connecting it to a battery.

The firefighter

F1 New wood from trees has bark; the type of tree it comes from determines the characteristics of the bark. The wood inside has patterns in it. It can be flexible and it is damp. Burning changes the colour and texture of the wood. Burnt wood is not flexible. It will mark other objects.

F2 Children can move along the ground in many ways. Some ways are faster than others: the speed can be compared by racing. The competitors must all start and finish at the same places, and they must all start at the same time. Speed can also be compared by timing over a set distance. The less time taken, the faster the speed.

F3 The fasteners on clothes can affect the time it takes to get dressed. By comparing times taken, we can check whether practice improves performance.

F4 When we blow, air comes out. It is invisible but we can feel it. It moves things, and it forms bubbles under water. We breathe air in and out of our chests through our noses or mouths. Our chests change size as we breathe. We can measure how much air we breathe out by catching the air in a jar under water.

F5 The conditions for using a siphon to transfer water from one place to another are explored. The siphon tube, which can go up and down, must be full of water. The flow of water depends on the relative positions of the upper reservoir and the lower end of the siphon tube.

F6 We can find out which is the shortest route between two points by measuring length. We can find out which is the quickest route by measuring time taken.

Milk

M1 A milk straw is a cylinder. We can suck and blow air through it. If one end is covered, it prevents this. If one end of a straw full of milk is covered, the milk will not run out.

M2 Milk can be bought in different shaped bottles. Bottles that look very different may hold the same amount of milk. Some bottle tops need a bottle opener to remove them. The bottle opener uses a combination of pressing down and pulling up. Sterilised milk stays fresh longer than pasteurised milk. Pasteurised milk will stay fresh longer at a cooler temperature.

M3 Milk is a liquid. It can be heated and it will boil. If vinegar is added to hot milk, solid pieces form in the liquid. These curds can be separated from the liquid (whey) by various methods. If bread is soaked in milk and put in a warm place, moulds will form. Moulds will also grow on some cheeses.

M4 Milk bottles are transparent. We can see other objects through them. The appearance of the object changes very little when seen through the bottle. Water is transparent. We can see objects through it. The appearance of an object changes in various ways when seen through a bottle full of water.

The park

Pa1 We climb up the steps of a park slide and slide down the smooth ramp. It requires more effort (energy) to go up than down. Our feet will slide differently on a surface depending on the soles of our footwear. A surface can be made more or less slippery by putting other substances on to it, e.g. oil or chalk.

Pa2 A roundabout is circular. It rotates horizontally and its centre remains in the same place. Some circular objects can be rolled. They rotate vertically and the centre moves along, staying the same distance from the ground.

Pa3 A bead suspended on a short string will swing backwards and forwards at a faster rate than a bead suspended on a longer string. 'Pushing' it harder does not affect this.

Pa4 A pretend see-saw can be made to balance by adjusting the objects placed on either end.

Pa5 Cups and plates can be made from various materials including metal, plastic, pottery and paper. Picnic items need to have certain characteristics, e.g. they need to be unbreakable and light in weight, and so they are made from materials which have these properties. Items made from metal, plastic and pottery can be immersed in water for washing without damage. Paper changes in water and paper items cannot be washed and used again.

Pa6 If an object is placed on a horizontal mirror, its reflection appears to be upside down. Reflections can be seen in various shiny surfaces. The shape of the surface affects the reflection. A wet, painted paper can be folded and opened to make a pattern so that one half resembles the reflection of the other.

Pa7 Water can leave a tap at different rates. The force of the water feels very different when the tap is full on compared with when the water only drips from the tap. A squeezy bottle can be used to make water move in drips and jets. The more force that is applied to the bottle, the more force the water has.

Teachers' Book C: Level 1

In the garden

G1 Many vegetables are the roots of plants and they have certain features in common. If a wet paper towel is left exposed to the air it will dry; the water goes into the air. The same happens with a slice of root vegetable. As it dries, it loses weight and shrinks in size. If a root vegetable is placed with its base in coloured water, the colour will travel through the root to its top.

G2 Fresh celery is rigid and will snap. It contains moisture. Celery deprived of water will become limp. If various parts of the celery are immersed in coloured water, only the celery with its base in water will show the colour rising up the stem to the leaves. A stem of celery which has been split, so that one part can be placed in water of one colour and the other part in another colour, will show one colour reaching certain leaf parts and the other colour reaching other parts.

G3 Dandelion seeds all share the same features. They can be planted and they will grow into dandelion plants. They fall through the air more slowly than some other seeds. They will travel in a draught and their particular formation helps them to do this. This is the way in which new plants grow where there were none before.

G4 Some trees have seeds. The seeds from one type of tree share the same features. Some types of tree seed fall more slowly than others. A test can be carried out to show this. The rate of fall seems to be related to the shape rather than the weight of the seeds.

G5 Blackberries change in colour and texture as they ripen. The colour from ripe blackberries will stain skin. If left, mould will grow on the ripe fruit. Investigations can be set up to find out which factors affect the rate at which mould grows on the fruit. Other ripe fruits behave in a similar manner.

G6 The leaf patterns inside a red cabbage can be observed when the cabbage is cut open in various directions. When cold water is added to some red cabbage and hot water is added to other red cabbage, the hot water changes colour more than the cold. When red cabbage is boiled in water with a piece of white cotton, the white cotton changes colour. The colour can be changed again by adding vinegar. The colour of the cloth will fade quickly if the cloth is left in the sun.

Hallowe'en

Hn1 A balloon is made of rubber. It can be stretched in various ways and will resume its original size when released. Air is used to stretch the balloon when it is blown up. It will only stretch so far, and then the rubber splits. An inflated balloon has a curved 3D shape which can be measured in various ways. We can set up an investigation to compare the force with which different pumps blow out air.

Hn2 Different types of paper absorb water paint differently. Paper can be treated with other substances, e.g. oil, fat or wax, to reduce its absorbency.

Hn3 The consistency of water changes when cellulose paste is added. Newspaper can be added to the mixture and it will absorb water. The resulting mixture is a type of papier mâché which can be used for models. As it dries, it loses weight and becomes hard. We can set up an investigation to compare this with papier mâché made with other white powders, e.g. salt, sugar or flour, instead of cellulose paste powder.

Hn4 We can observe the behaviour of small animals and record this over a period of time. We can put them in an environment offering light and dark areas and check at intervals how many animals are in each. Some small animals seem to prefer dark areas.

Hn5 A magnet will attract some objects and not others. All the objects it attracts are metal, but it does not attract all metal objects. If a paper clip is touching the magnet, the paper clip will attract another paper clip. The magnet will attract a paper clip through a sheet of paper. We can investigate the strength of different magnets by using this information.

Celebrations

Ce1 A piece of clay can be modelled. If all the clay is used, the shape can be changed while the weight remains the same. Clay loses weight and becomes harder as it dries. We can set up an investigation to discover which factors affect the rate at which clay dries.

Ce2 Candles are made of wax. The flame of a candle has certain features and behaves in certain ways. Wax melts and becomes liquid when heated. As it cools, it becomes solid again. It will melt and solidify repeatedly if heated and cooled. Wax can be various colours. Two colours of liquid wax can be mixed to form a new colour.

Ce3 Candles can be made by pouring liquid wax around a wick and cooling it to make the wax solidify. We can set up an investigation to discover whether the size, shape, or colour of a candle affects the size, shape or colour of the flame.

Ce4 We can set up investigations to compare the properties of the modelling materials clay, plasticine, and flour and salt dough. Plasticine becomes softer when warmed, while clay and dough dry out, losing weight and becoming hard. Water left on a saucer will eventually evaporate, while oil on a saucer will not.

Ce5 The colour of light produced by a torch can be changed by shining it through different colours of cellophane. If two differently coloured lights are shone on a white screen and overlap, the colour produced may not be the same as that produced if the two colours were mixed in paint.

Jobs in the house

Hs1 Bottles and tins have lids which open in various ways. Some can be opened by hand; others need a tool. If a screwdriver is used as a lever, the force is applied to the lever in one direction and the lever forces the object in the opposite direction. Using a lever of similar type, less effort is required to lift a weight if pressure is applied to the longer arm of the lever with the weight on the shorter arm than vice versa.

A balance with one arm longer than the other will require less weight on the longer than the shorter arm for the two to be equal.

Hs2 When two objects are suspended from a beam, as in a mobile, the beam will balance at a point nearer the heavier object than the lighter object. The distance of the hanging objects from the beam does not affect this.

Hs3 Ellipses can be drawn by holding a pencil in a loop of string around two fixed nails. The nearer together the nails are fixed, the 'fatter' the ellipse. The centre of gravity of a 2D card shape can be found. If the card is suspended at this point it will hang flat.

Hs4 The material used for a pinboard needs to be fairly soft. We can investigate the suitability of various samples of board and wall covering for this.

Hs5 Many different sounds may be heard around the house. An investigation can be set up to discover whether adults or children are better at identifying household sounds.

The newsagent

N1 Strings, cords and ropes can be of various thicknesses and made up in various ways. An investigation can be set up to compare the different breaking strengths of thin strings.

N2 Paper can be of various thicknesses, texture and colours. The various papers behave differently when creased or wet. Investigations can be set up to discover which papers tear more easily than others.

N3 Some papers are stiffer than others. A test can be arranged to compare the relative stiffness of a range of papers.

N4 An investigation can be set up to compare the efficiency of various rubber erasers when used on different types of paper marked with a range of pens and pencils.

N5 An ink colour may be made up of several colours. Chromatography can be used to separate the various colours.

Sports and games

Sg1 A nylon swimming costume holds less water than a similar cotton costume. The amount of water held is equivalent to the difference in weight of the dry and wet costume. Investigations can be set up to find out which dries more quickly, and which conditions affect the rate of drying.

Sg2 Various types of float can be used as aids to swimming. They each support different weights before sinking. They can be made to support different weights by presenting them to the water at differing angles.

Sg3 Balls are made in different sizes and weights. The size and weight can be measured. The largest is not necessarily the heaviest. The smallest is not necessarily the lightest. The impacts of balls when dropped on to wet sand can be compared by measuring the depths of the holes they make. An investigation can be set up to find which type of ball hits the sand hardest when dropped from a fixed height.

Sg4 Investigations can be set up to discover which of a collection of balls is the best bouncer.

Sg5 A test can be arranged to find out how good each child is at aiming a ball so that it will roll along the ground and hit a skittle. Various methods of improving aim can then be investigated.

Sg6 If a ball is rolled to bounce off a wall into a receptacle, and the rolling point and receptacle are equidistant from the wall, the ball should hit the wall at a point half way between the receptacle and the rolling point. The distance of the receptacle and rolling point from the wall can be varied, as long as they remain equal. The beam of a torch can be shone along the same path to be reflected by a mirror, so that it shines on the receptacle.

Teachers' Book C: Level 2

Transport

T1 Regular 3D shapes have particular numbers of curved and flat faces. The shapes affect the way in which they roll. Narrow cylinders can be rolled to follow curves by tilting the track. Wide cylinders cannot be steered in the same way. The wheels on vehicles are usually narrow cylinders.

T2 To move a scooter, one foot pushes against the ground and the other against the scooter. To move a pram or trolley, the feet push against the ground and the hands push against the pram or trolley. A loaded pram is harder to push. A load is easier to move by pushing on a pram or trolley than carrying by hand.

T3 To move a tricycle, the feet push against the pedals. In a fixed wheel tricycle, the pedals turn the front wheel which pushes against the ground. The other wheels roll along behind. In a chain tricycle, the pedals move the chain which turns the back wheels and then push against the ground. By turning one card wheel on a board, other wheels can be turned in various ways by linking them to the first wheel with a rubber band.

T4 A moving scooter can be stopped by pressing one foot against the ground. The more the foot grips the ground, the quicker the scooter stops. A brake block works by pressing against the wheel to stop it turning. Some materials used on a brake block grip more effectively than others and stop the wheel more quickly. The wheel becomes warm where the brake block presses.

T5 Given the same push, some toy lorries will travel further than others. Given the same push, a lorry will go further on the flat than uphill, and furthest downhill. Ramps and a device to give a 'standard push' can be made to investigate this.

T6 Some flat objects float. Some flat objects that sink can be made to float by changing their shape. Boats need to float and carry a cargo. An investigation can be set up to find the best shape for a toy boat so that it floats when empty and also when carrying a large cargo.

T7 More effort is required to move the hand through water palm first than edge on. Boats made from the same weight of plasticine will move differently through the water depending on their shape. The same is true of card boats.

Animals

A1 Sea water contains salt; fresh water, as found in ponds, does not. Frog spawn is found in fresh water. It follows a particular sequence of development through a tadpole stage to the adult frog. At each stage, behaviour can be observed and related to body features. Some body features are related to environment. The adult frogs will go on to produce more frog spawn.

A2 Spiders are found on land in many different habitats. They can be a variety of shapes, sizes and colours, but they all have particular features in common. Spiders produce a thread which they use to construct a web. The webs have a particular pattern, and trap food for the spiders.

A3 Caterpillars hatch out of eggs. They may need a specific type of food. They grow and can cast their skin. They all have particular body features in common. They follow a particular sequence of development though a pupa stage to adult moth or butterfly. The wings of the adult are mirror images of each other. The adult goes on to lay eggs and the sequence is repeated.

A4 Some ants live in soil. Many ants are found together in one place. They can move very quickly. In cool temperatures, the ants move more slowly. All ants have particular body features in common. We can observe their behaviour when presented with a variety of foods.

A5 Water snails can be found in ponds. They all have particular body features in common. They move in a particular way. From time to time, they open a tube on the surface of the water and appear to take in air. Snails may float or sink depending on how much air they are holding.

A6 Some animals live in a particular type of habitat. Others can live in a wide variety of habitats. This may be related to their food supply. Some animals have body features related to their environment. Animals of one type all have specific features in common by which they can be identified.

Fabrics

Fa1 Clothes wear out. The fabric may wear in particular places where rubbing occurs. An investigation can be set up to compare how quickly different types of fabric wear out when rubbed.

Fa2 Some fabrics tear more easily than others. A piece of fabric will tear in a particular direction, in relation to the weave. An investigation can be set up to compare the 'tearability' of different fabrics.

Fa3 Clothes may be worn to keep people warm. Some fabrics do this better than others. An investigation can be set up to compare how well different fabrics keep heat in.

Fa4 Dyes can be used to change the colour of fabrics. Different fabrics respond to dyes. Some fabrics will dye a deeper shade than others when treated similarly. Cotton and nylon can be distinguished by observing the results of dyeing.

Fa5 Water-based dyes will only be effective on fabric which absorbs water. Fabric treated with various waterproofing materials will not dye effectively. A pattern can be produced by treating certain parts of a piece of fabric in this way and then dyeing the fabric. Only the untreated parts will change colour.

The farm

Fm1 A layer of cream forms at the top of milk in a bottle. The cream can be removed; it is thicker than the remaining milk. The cream will turn to butter when shaken, but the skimmed milk will not.

Fm2 Rice and barley absorb some of the boiling water as they are cooked. They increase in volume and weight and change in texture. The changes in weight and volume can be measured. The number of grains of rice or barley does not increase.

Fm3 Flour is made by grinding wheat seeds to a powder. Grinding is best accomplished by rubbing between two hard surfaces.

Fm4 The food contained in the wheat seeds is intended for the young plant which could grow from the seed. This is also true of barley. The number of seeds produced on a plant grown from one wheat or barley seed can be investigated. The seed contains enough food for the young plant to start growing, but to continue it needs soil to provide food.

Fm5 Bread can be made using flour in various ways. When yeast is added, the dough will rise. Only dough containing yeast rises in this way. The yeast appears to produce bubbles in the dough. The volume of a loaf can be measured. Bread made with yeast is very different in volume and texture from bread made without yeast. How much the bread rises depends on the amount of yeast added.

Weather

We1 The shadow of an object falls on the side of the object which is opposite to the sun. During the day, the relative positions of the sun and a stationary object change, and the shadow position changes correspondingly. The height of the sun above the horizon affects the length of shadow. At the same time on different days, the shadow will fall in the same place. It is possible to make a shadow clock.

We2 Investigations can be set up to discover the conditions needed for fading to occur.

We3 Water left exposed to the air will evaporate. Investigations can be set up to discover the conditions which aid evaporation.

We4 Some substances dissolve in water. When the water they are added to evaporates, the substance is left behind. Investigations can be set up to discover the effect on the rate of evaporation of adding soluble substances to the water.

We5 The amount of rainfall each day can be measured and a record kept. The record will show that the amount can differ from one day to another. The apparatus used to collect and measure rain must be constructed in a particular way. This is a rain gauge.

We6 Temperature can be measured using a thermometer. At any one time, temperatures may be different in different places. At different times, the temperature may vary in the same place. A record can be kept to show changes in temperature.

We7 Wind direction and speed can be observed in various ways. A daily record can be kept to show changes. When a combined record showing rainfall, temperature, wind speed and direction, and general conditions is kept, patterns in the weather may begin to emerge.

Extension D Language in science

The relationship between science and language for young children is twofold. Firstly, the rich variety of experiences which science offers requires a wide range of language to describe it, to comment on it and to report it. Secondly, if the observations and information acquired are to be understood, language is the means by which teachers and pupils can explore their common experience and extract from it their individual understanding.

In the early activities in *Longman Scienceworld*, we rely almost completely on spoken language. Most of the children will not yet have come to grips with the intricacies of the written word, so that teachers will be seeking ways of encouraging children to talk about what they are doing and what they are observing. Much of the talk will be among themselves (or even to themselves). A lot of the talk will involve the teacher who can take the opportunity to help the children to develop their language usage in different ways.

Using language to understand science is very much concerned with spoken language, even after children have a firm grasp of reading and writing. The spoken word is much closer to our thinking than the other language modes. It allows for the expression of the doubts and uncertainties which the various observations and puzzles of scientific activity present. We can um and ah and change our minds and say, 'Do you mean this or is this what you really mean?' We can listen to statements reflecting increasing understanding, and again question these. Everyone must make sense of an experience in his or her way. The interpretation of a new experience depends on the previous experiences which a person brings with him or her. One of the tasks of the teacher in introducing science is to help children explore the new experiences and relate these to themselves. An open-minded approach will help teachers quickly to become aware that there are no subject barriers in children's minds. Experiences from a wide variety of sources will often be brought together in interpreting these new experiences of science. This linking enables children to make sense of their new science experiences.

As the children's language skills develop and they begin to read and write, science activities provide a wide range of contexts for different kinds of writing, ranging from the descriptive to reporting sequential events. Suggestions have been made for this within the Science activities themselves and sometimes in the Further activities.

For the third infant year, it was decided that books for the children to read would be more appropriate than another *Starter Book* for teachers. One of the most important aspects of learning to read is wanting to read and going on wanting to read. Children of this age might not be able to tackle the reading of practical instructions, so these have been confined to the teacher's books. (Material which the children could read could be produced, but the children would still be teacher dependent for setting up activities, and this might simply make their reading frustrating.)

There are many simple science and technology related books available for young readers and many of them can be used as background material. They should be viewed with caution, however, if they are attempting to present scientific 'facts'.

Books about people and their jobs and occupations are likely to provide related reading of interest to children. The Ladybird series *People who help us* is a good example of this.

Longman Scienceworld does not have a sex bias and girls and boys should be able to relate to it equally well; however, teachers will have to look carefully at items such as reading books in the classroom if that lack of bias is to be preserved. The proportion of information books which are sex-stereotyped is still high, unfortunately.

Each child must arrive at his or her own understanding, and language is an important means by which understanding is derived from experience. Every opportunity for children to express their thinking and interact orally with each other should be seized upon. Science activities provide a rich source of such opportunities.

Extension E Using mathematics in science

Teaching mathematical concepts is not a direct objective of this science scheme but many opportunities do arise to use mathematical skills in a purposeful way. In particular, the concepts and skills associated with shape, length, weight and capacity are important in science as they are in mathematics and these have been included as appropriate. For quantities and shape, detailed suggestions are given throughout the scheme for their practical inclusion. The same consideration has been given to number work, but specific reference to this has not been made since teachers will recognise many instances where the practical situation provides excellent opportunities to reinforce the work being done in mathematics. Care has been taken to ensure that the work suggested closely matches the developmental stages normally covered in infant work. The details of these stages related to the science levels are shown in Table 2 on page 108.

The work is specifically tied in with the stages suggested in the *Nuffield Maths 5–11* scheme, and for teachers using this scheme Table 4 shows the links. By no means are all the skills and concepts covered in these *Nuffield Maths 5–11* chapters practised, but where mathematics work is included it does not exceed the demands of these chapters. Whatever mathematics scheme is being used, teachers will wish to respond to the needs of particular children; for most children the activities suggested are at the appropriate level, and will provide a purposeful enrichment of their normal mathematics programme.

Table 4

Science through infant topics		**Nuffield Maths 5–11** **Quantities and shape**	
Year 1	Level 1	L1:1 L1:2 S1:1 S1:2 S1:3 W1:1 W1:2 T1:1 T1:2 C1:1	*Teachers' Handbook 1*
	Level 2	L1:3 L1:4 C1:2 C1:3 C1:4	*Teachers' Handbook 1*
Year 2	Level 1	L1:5 L1:6 W1:3 W1:4 T1:3 T1:4 C1:5	*Teachers' Handbook 1*
	Level 2	S2:1 S2:2 S2:3 S2:4 T2:1 T2:2 T2:3	*Teachers' Handbook 2*
Year 3	Level 1	L2:1 L2:2 S2:5 W2:1 W2:2	*Teachers' Handbook 2*
	Level 2	L2:3 L2:4 L2:5 W2:3 T2:4 T2:5 T2:6 C2:1 C2:2 C2:3 C2:4	*Teachers' Handbook 2*

The numbering in this table is the same as is used in the Contents pages in the *Nuffield Maths 5–11 Teachers' Handbooks*.

Extension F The development of technological ability and understanding (Making and doing)

A lot has been written about technology and what it is. For many non-specialist teachers, the picture which emerges is a daunting one; how can they translate the grand ideas into action? *Longman Scienceworld* tries to demystify technology and suggest activities which will enable children to acquire some technological skills. The children should have opportunities to investigate in situations where they really do need the information which the scientific investigation can produce.

Firstly, what do we mean by technology, and more importantly what do we mean by technology in the Making and doing activities suggested? Technology is a way of thinking which is useful in solving problems of a particular kind. Generally, these problems are expressions of some particular need. In real life, these problems may be very complex and complicated. In the classroom, where our concern is with how to set about solving the problems, our examples are simpler. For example, one of the first problems is 'Can you make a bag to carry fruit home from the fruit shop?' Another feature of technological problems which this illustrates is that they do not have right and wrong answers: some solutions are just better and some are worse. Often, one solution will be better in some ways than another and worse in other ways, and there has to be a balancing of desirables and undesirables. There is a strong element of optimisation.

Another salient feature of technological problem solving is that we have to think about the problem from all sorts of points of view. For example, in making a bag, we have to think first of all about what the bag must do – what properties it should have. It will have to carry a fairly heavy weight, it may get wet and it must not collapse if it does, it must look attractive and the cheaper it is the better. So, even with this simple problem, we are able to pursue a variety of channels – the scientific, the aesthetic and the economic. It really is important that the material used is strong enough for the job, even when it is wet. A fully technological approach would require the setting up of scientific investigations to produce the information we need. However, the scientific investigation is only being used to support the technological problem solving activity. That is how scientific activity is related to technological activity: it provides vital information which is fed into the problem solving process, along with the information which comes from looking at the problem with the eye of the artist or that of the economist.

Sophisticated technological problem solving is very demanding: children can only be introduced to the ideas and be helped to acquire in some measure the skills needed to set about a task. As soon as the task is within the children's grasp, they should use their increasing scientific skills to produce information needed to make decisions within the problem solving sequence. It should be clear that the kind of scientific information required will depend on the problem and the materials which might be used. A question about what kind of paper to use or whether plastic sheet would be better than paper can be answered from the scientific viewpoint by setting up an appropriate investigation. For some problems, the children might need information about whether to use wood or metal, or what kind of wood or metal. Again, the information can come from a scientific investigation. How to make something move is another question which can be tackled, or how to cut a sleeve so that the arm can move freely requires an investigation of how our limbs work. All these are examples of scientific investigation being used within the context of technological problem solving.

Technological problem solving or Making and doing can best be tackled systematically and in each of the activities suggested, the same structured but simple approach has been used. It is not intended, however, that this should be regarded as prescriptive; rather, it is indicative.

1 The problem
The statement of the problem to be solved.

2 Exploring the problem
Examining the nature of the problem and identifying the various facets of it; being quite sure that the nature of the problem is understood; ensuring that the problem statement expresses the need.

3 Ideas for solving the problem
a) Producing ideas without, at this stage, being concerned with whether they are practical; thinking creatively and openly; letting original thinking loose; brainstorming.
b) Sifting the ideas; looking for obvious snags; comparing the ideas.
c) Deciding which idea to pursue.

4 Making
Planning how to implement the chosen solution; collecting and, if necessary, investigating methods of construction and materials. (Of course, it is possible that unforeseen snags will be found which will require that the solution chosen should be reconsidered. This illustrates another aspect of technological problem solving – it is not a straightforward sequence. As the problem and its solution are pursued, there will be snags, new bits of information and new ideas which will require that steps be retraced and new and different decisions made.)

Finally, craft skills are exercised in the making of the solution. The skills of young children will be limited and imperfect but the aim is that they should produce their solution to the best of their ability. Often, the idea will be far better than its execution. Our main interest is in the development of technological thinking. At this stage, lack of craftsmanship is, therefore, a secondary consideration although teachers will undoubtedly wish to give children every help and encouragement to improve their craft skills. Equally, teachers will be concerned to ensure that every child experiences success, however modest.

5 Evaluating
Does the chosen solution solve the problem? In the light of experience, would a different solution have been implemented? Might any of the ideas which were rejected have been better? Do the children want to try again? How have other people tackled similar problems?

At first, children will not find it easy to evaluate their own work. Looking critically comes with maturity and for young children the sense of the product being right because it is a personal achievement is understandably overwhelming. Later, the children are able to look at their own work and the work of others more circumspectly, and then the teacher can (by question and discussion) help children to look at their own work and the work of others in a more analytical fashion. They are able to learn from each other and support each other's thinking. It is a field rich in opportunities.

Monitoring making and doing activity

It has not been suggested that teachers should attempt to record formally the development of children's making and doing skills; however, it may be useful to have in mind some questions which will help in monitoring the children's progress. More importantly, the questions may be of assistance in guiding the children's work. The questions are to some extent ordered so that they indicate a developing competency, but they should be regarded as no more than indicative. Tackling making and doing problems has so many facets that it is not possible to identify a right way or even a best way.

It is difficult also to suggest how children will progress. Some will move slowly, some rapidly. Young children can be surprisingly innovative and imaginative, particularly when they are interacting with construction materials. However, the level of thinking suggested by some of the questions is sophisticated and may be reached by only a few children. Nevertheless, the questions will provide a useful guide to progress in making and doing activity.

1 The problem
2 Exploring the problem
Do the children make little or no attempt to explore the problem?
Do they ask one or two isolated questions?
Do their questions go beyond what is immediately apparent?
Do the children begin to ask questions more systematically and to identify criteria which must be met?
Do the children, as a matter of course, ask a wide range of pertinent questions and assemble the criteria thus identified in an ordered manner?
Can the children reframe the statement of the problem if the criteria identified indicate that this is necessary?
3 Ideas for solving the problem – choosing a solution to implement
Do the children provide no ideas of their own and wait for ideas to be provided?
Do they produce no ideas of their own but respond to and develop ideas that are provided?
Do they produce one or two ideas of their own?
Do they think freely and creatively if they are encouraged to do so?
Do they attempt to evaluate ideas according to their understanding of the problem?
Are they able to evaluate the ideas in relation to the material and skill resources which are available?
4 Making
(The development of the ability to produce the chosen solution will depend on the nature of the artefacts being produced. Craft skills appropriate to the materials being used will be developed. Their development will relate closely to the development of attitudes to the work, as well as to the understanding and knowledge associated with the materials and solution chosen.)
Do the children choose appropriate materials?
Do they work neatly and safely with these materials?
Do the children use appropriate tools in the correct manner, thinking of their own safety and that of others?
Do they work accurately?
Do they use materials imaginatively?
Are they able to improvise?
5 Evaluating
Do the children make no attempt to evaluate their own work?
Do they attempt to evaluate their own work in some measure?
Do they view their own work with some detachment and examine it with some degree of analysis?
Do they consider criticisms of their own work by others?
Do the children look at their products critically and consider whether they meet the criteria identified in exploring the problem?
Are they able to suggest how the product might be improved?

Extension G People and their jobs and occupations

On page 102, you will find this statement:
'Science is used in society in all sorts of ways. People use it in their work and hobbies. Everyone is confronted with it in everyday life.'
A variety of people who do different work and have different hobbies are introduced in the scheme, in order to show how science is important for them all. The kinds of work and hobbies they have were chosen with the following criteria in mind:

1 relevance to children of this age range and breadth of experience;
2 the relative importance of science in the particular work or hobby;
3 potential as a context for the development of science activities and understanding of ideas.

'Work' refers not only to paid work but also to all that work which is given little recognition because it is not financially rewarded. Therefore, the word 'job' has been used to signify paid work and 'occupation' to signify unpaid work. What are jobs for some are occupations or hobbies for others, and this might have to be pointed out. Here are parts of the original lists:

Jobs
School caretaker, school cook, lollipop man or lady, policeman or woman, detective, forensic scientist, firefighter, optician, hairdresser, health visitor, school doctor, general practitioner, nurse, dentist, medical auxiliary, engineer (aeronautical, electrical, electronic, etc.), chemist (plastics, fibres, food, etc.), pharmacist, public analyst, gardener, electrician, joiner, painter, decorator, motor mechanic, shop assistant, jeweller.

Occupations
Housewife, mother, father, DIY activities . . .

Hobbies
Fishing, flower arranging, pottery, athletics, pop music, playing the guitar (piano, violin, etc.), swimming, games . . .

It was after drawing up the lists that it became apparent that a good opportunity would be missed if there was no discussion about what jobs, occupations and hobbies are and what people do when they are pursuing their various interests. What is it that makes people want to do these things? What is it that makes them worthwhile?

Below are points which the children should be made aware of; these points have been used in drawing up the suggestions for discussions. The points listed are very basic ones because very many children have little idea about jobs and occupations. Often, even parents do not talk to their children about the work they do in their jobs and occupations.

1 People work.
2 Sometimes work is done in return for money (jobs). Sometimes work is unpaid (occupations).
3 Different people do different jobs and follow different occupations.
4 The work of some people helps us directly.
5 The work of some people helps us indirectly – they work behind the scenes.
6 Some work is done just during the day. Some work has to be done at special times.
7 Some work has to be done all the time.
8 Some jobs are not very pleasant but they serve the community.
9 People take pride in their work.
10 People may need special knowledge, expertise and skills in their work and hobbies.
11 People have to acquire the special knowledge, expertise and skills which they need.
12 People only work in jobs for part of the time.

13 When people are not working at jobs, they do other things and follow other occupations and hobbies which they enjoy.
14 Sometimes, people's enjoyment depends on the jobs being done by other people.
15 What is a job for one person may be an occupation or hobby for another.
16 People use scientific information in their jobs, occupations and hobbies.
17 People need to use a scientific viewpoint in their jobs, occupations and hobbies.

Extension H Recording progress in science

There are two aspects of children's progress which should be recorded:

1 their experience of scientific ideas – ideas which they have encountered in the activities;

2 their progress in acquiring the skills being developed in the activities.

Ongoing accurate records are an essential part of ensuring that children's experience of science is progressive and developmental; to assist teachers in keeping records, sets of pupils' *Record Sheets* are available. There is a *Record Sheet* for each level so that a complete record of progress can be maintained for each pupil and accompany him or her from one class to the next.

Experience of scientific ideas

The science concepts and ideas covered in the topic activities are shown in Table 3 in Extension B of *Science through Infant Topics, Teachers' Books A, B and C*. The experiences provided by each of the activities are described briefly in Extension C (*Teachers' Books A, B* and *C*).

Science skills

The science skills developed in the scheme are shown in Table 2 in Extension A (*Teachers' Books A, B* and *C*).

On the back of each *Record Sheet*, the skill levels which the children should ideally have reached by the end of Levels 1 and 2 are described. On the front of the *Record Sheets* the skills are listed accompanied by a series of boxes. The boxes cover a range of comments, from 'not yet able' for children who are a long way off reaching the described skill level to 'competently' for those children who can perform in the manner described. In between, the boxes allow you to make qualified responses (ticking as appropriate), matching the child's ability to the skill description.

There is a bar in the line of boxes at a point which might represent a reasonable level of competence to be achieved by all children.

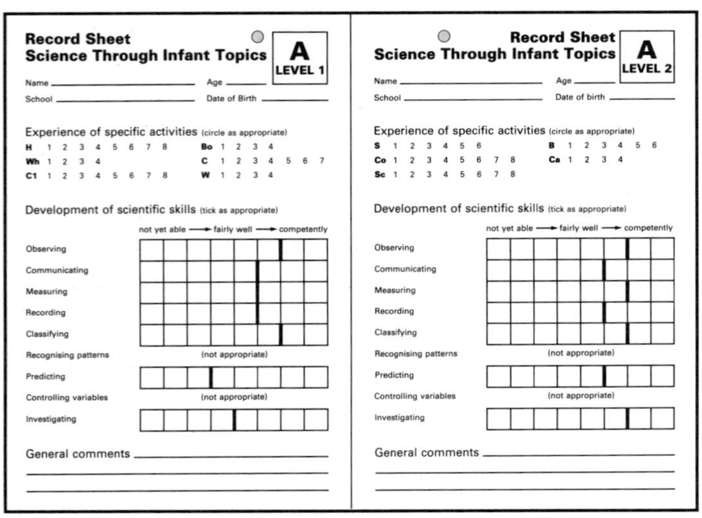

Record Sheet
Science Through Infant Topics — A LEVEL 1

Name ______ Age ______
School ______ Date of Birth ______

Experience of specific activities (circle as appropriate)

H	1	2	3	4	5	6	7	8	**Bo**	1	2	3	4			
Wh	1	2	3	4					**C**	1	2	3	4	5	6	7
C1	1	2	3	4	5	6	7	8	**W**	1	2	3	4			

Development of scientific skills (tick as appropriate)

not yet able → fairly well → competently

Observing
Communicating
Measuring
Recording
Classifying
Recognising patterns (not appropriate)
Predicting
Controlling variables (not appropriate)
Investigating

General comments ______

Record Sheet
Science Through Infant Topics — A LEVEL 2

Name ______ Age ______
School ______ Date of birth ______

Experience of specific activities (circle as appropriate)

S	1	2	3	4	5	6			**B**	1	2	3	4	5	6
Co	1	2	3	4	5	6	7	8	**Ca**	1	2	3	4		
Sc	1	2	3	4	5	6	7	8							

Development of scientific skills (tick as appropriate)

not yet able → fairly well → competently

Observing
Communicating
Measuring
Recording
Classifying
Recognising patterns (not appropriate)
Predicting
Controlling variables (not appropriate)
Investigating

General comments ______

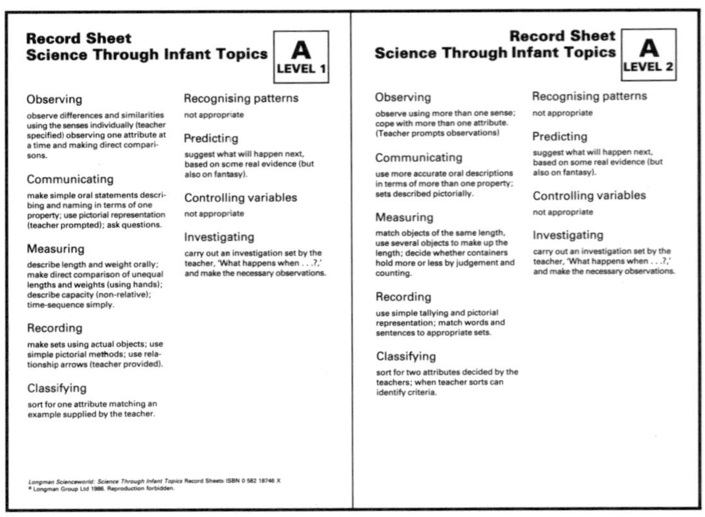

Record Sheet
Science Through Infant Topics — A LEVEL 1

Observing
observe differences and similarities using the senses individually (teacher specified) observing one attribute at a time and making direct comparisons.

Communicating
make simple oral statements describing and naming in terms of one property; use pictorial representation (teacher prompted); ask questions.

Measuring
describe length and weight orally; make direct comparison of unequal lengths and weights (using hands); describe capacity (non-relative); time-sequence simply.

Recording
make sets using actual objects; use simple pictorial methods; use relationship arrows (teacher provided).

Classifying
sort for one attribute matching an example supplied by the teacher.

Recognising patterns
not appropriate

Predicting
suggest what will happen next, based on some real evidence (but also on fantasy).

Controlling variables
not appropriate

Investigating
carry out an investigation set by the teacher, 'What happens when . . .?,' and make the necessary observations.

Longman Scienceworld: Science Through Infant Topics Record Sheets ISBN 0 582 18746 X
© Longman Group Ltd 1986. Reproduction forbidden.

Record Sheet
Science Through Infant Topics — A LEVEL 2

Observing
observe using more than one sense; cope with more than one attribute. (Teacher prompts observations)

Communicating
use more accurate oral descriptions in terms of more than one property; sets described pictorially.

Measuring
match objects of the same length, use several objects to make up the length; decide whether containers hold more or less by judgement and counting.

Recording
use simple tallying and pictorial representation; match words and sentences to appropriate sets.

Classifying
sort for two attributes decided by the teachers; when teacher sorts can identify criteria.

Recognising patterns
not appropriate

Predicting
suggest what will happen next, based on some real evidence (but also on fantasy).

Controlling variables
not appropriate

Investigating
carry out an investigation set by the teacher, 'What happens when . . .?,' and make the necessary observations.

Extension I Classroom organisation

Preparation

Before each half term, you might find it a good idea to decide which topics and which specific activities you intend to cover, go through the equipment required (Extension J, page 141) and also read the 'You need' section for each of your activities. Then you can collect together the items you need and look for any you do not have immediately to hand.

You may find it useful also to make up boxes for the activities so that you have everything in one place. Boxes can contain unique items, common items and a note of any other items which need to be collected from elsewhere to complete the set of equipment.

Another method of organisation is to keep a card index, with a card for each activity. This could list the items required for the activity and say where they are to be found. Coloured cards for special items which may need to be located well in advance could be put in 'early warning' positions, so that you have enough time to prepare.

Before embarking on an activity with the children, you will need to read the notes in the *Teachers' Book* carefully so that you are familiar with the objectives and the approach. As you become increasingly accustomed to using the scheme, you may be tempted to skim through the notes: this is not advisable as you may miss important details referring to secondary objectives. Often, the odd question or comment is particularly significant. Also, the detail is intended to guide you in making the gradual change of approach which the children's developing skills and confidence require.

Organising the work

Although some of the activities will lend themselves to a class lesson or discussion, most of the activities are intended for groups of four to eight children. This way of working is familiar to most infant teachers, as are the two practical problems which arise: how to organise the rest of the class so that you can spend some relatively uninterrupted time with one group; and how to prevent the children in the rest of the class observing what is going on so that when their turn comes they already know what it is all about. They may see the result before the problem. Many teachers will have found their own solutions; if you are still searching for an answer, you might like to consider the following suggestions.

1 **How can you organise the class so that you are free to work with a small group?**

a) Use other people

You may have time when a helper employed in the school works with you in the classroom. This may be a trained person, e.g. approved by the National Nursery Examination Board, or an ancillary helper. You can concentrate on your science group while your helper monitors the work of the rest of the children and deals with any minor difficulties.

If you work in an open plan or semi-open plan building you may be able to organise team teaching, so that groups are shared unevenly between staff at certain times, allowing a small science group to be formed.

Finally, you may be able to organise volunteer help which will free you to concentrate on your science group.

b) If you have no help

You can arrange your class so that children are working on some less teacher intensive activities while you are working with your science group. Make a list of activities which the children can do without a lot of help. These may include some of the following, depending on the children's ages and abilities:

Free play with apparatus and/or materials prior to or following their more structured use, e.g. sand, water, paint, construction toys, etc.

Reading for enjoyment at a level that the children can cope with easily.

Matching and fitting activities which are self-correcting.
Practising skills for improved neatness or learning useful facts, e.g. handwriting, number bonds, etc.
Making observational drawings of materials which are used for an activity.
Some craft activities can be pursued once the basic skills have been acquired, e.g. weaving, knitting, etc.

2 **How can you arrange your class so that the children do not know the outcome of the science activities before they do them?**
Arrange your classroom furniture to form a bay or bays. This allows a variety of work to go on without one thing interfering with another. It can also make the room look more interesting, with opportunities for good display related to specific aspects of the children's work.
When a new activity is introduced, choose a different group each time to be the first to do it.
Use corridors, wide entrances or any other nearby spaces which can be supervised properly and where you do not get in anyone's way, but where the science group can work without acting like a magnet for everyone else.
It may be possible for groups of older children to tackle different activities and then come together as a class to explain to the rest of the class what they did and what they found out.

Keeping records and evaluating work

The pupils' *Record Sheets* for the scheme are described on page 138. These are quite easy to keep and require just a little time to be spent at the end of each level. However, as you carry out the work with the children, you will find it helpful to note down briefly their reactions and responses to the work. You can prepare a rough table which includes the names of the children in the group, the various objectives of the activity, and headings such as 'involvement' or 'enthusiasm'. You can quickly tick, cross or comment in your own shorthand as the activity progresses. Your rough table might look like this:

Names	Sorting by size	Sorting by colour	Involvement	Comments
John	✗	✓ could match to mine	✓	No idea of longer/shorter
Steven	✓	✓	?	too easy
Jane	✓	✓ knew names	✓	found it easy
Amanda	✗	✓ matched	✓	Needs longer/shorter

This will be helpful in filling in the *Record Sheets* and in planning the next work. In this case, John and Amanda are going to need more 'longer/shorter' experiences; Steven and Jane may be able to join another group and miss some of the activities concerned with colour and size.

It should now be easier with this developmental scheme to match a child's work to his or her particular needs.

Extension J Equipment and techniques

Part 1 Equipment, materials and storage

a) Equipment and materials

The science activities described do not require very much specialised equipment or apparatus. All the activities can be carried out in the classroom, in its vicinity or in the playground. For a number of activities, access to water and a power point are required, while for a few others you need a refrigerator or an oven for a short time. Much of what you need will already be in school and most of the rest can be borrowed from home, although you will no doubt find it more convenient to establish a store of the more commonly used items in school. The problem of storage is discussed in the next section.

The materials and equipment which you will need for the infant years are listed on the following pages. Any additional requirements for a particular activity are listed in the description of the activity.

Classroom equipment and materials
The following equipment and supplies which are normally required in infant teaching should be included:

Apparatus and equipment
construction sets (including Lego and Meccano)
water play apparatus (including watering cans, sieves, funnels, transparent plastic tubing and waterproof aprons)
sand play apparatus with fine dry sand
playhouse facilities
musical instruments (particularly percussion, including sleigh bells)

Consumable materials
a variety of paper (including kitchen, blotting, tissue, crêpe and sugar papers)
drawing and colouring materials (including chalk, wax crayons, drawing charcoal and an ink pad)
modelling materials (including plasticine and clay)
adhesives (including polyvinyl adhesive)
paper clips (wire and brass)
string, twine of various kinds
rubber bands
adhesive labels
Blutak
sellotape
wallpaper paste
drinking straws and art straws

General household equipment and materials
cling film
aluminium foil
polythene bags (small and large rolls)
greaseproof paper
brown wrapping paper
paper towels (kitchen roll)

tissues
thin plastic sheet (dry cleaning covers, shop bags, etc.)
black dustbin liners
parcel tape
cocktail sticks
needles and pins
cotton and threads
safety pins
stapler

Kitchen equipment and supplies
a large electric hot plate (big enough to accommodate two glass pans; you could substitute other means of heating which would not be as safe or as satisfactory; you could regard this as the one big investment you need to make.)
two or three glass pans (coffee making flasks could also be used. Glass laboratory beakers can be substituted but they are more fragile.)
a variety of bowls, jugs, plates, dishes,etc. (of various shapes, sizes, materials, e.g. plastic, pottery, stainless steel, aluminium, heatproof glass; some identical pairs and some sets would be useful. Most of these can be brought from home as required. However, you may feel it necessary to make some purchases to provide variety and matching pairs, and to cater for the needs of two groups who want things at the same time.)
a variety of cups and beakers (various shapes, sizes, materials, e.g. transparent and opaque plastic, pottery, paper, heatproof glass, etc.)
a variety of cutlery (metal and plastic, of different sizes)
a collection of cooking implements (wooden spoons, tin openers, bottle openers, perforated spoons, sieves, colanders, rolling pins, pastry cutters, funnels, etc.)
a collection of cooking equipment (baking tray, patty/tart/bun tins, mixing bowl, pastry boards, kitchen scales)
a tablecloth
trays (metal and non-metal)
ice cube tray

Foodstuffs
flour
rice
sugar (granulated, caster, icing, crystal)
salt
cooking oil
food colouring

Garden equipment and supplies
potting compost (peat based for convenience)

Workshop equipment and supplies
hammers (three sizes)
screwdrivers (three or four different lengths)
nails (a range of at least three head sizes and lengths; different metals – iron, brass, zinc; same sizes in different metals where possible.)
screws (a range of at least three head sizes and lengths; different metals – steel, brass, aluminium; same sizes in different metals where possible.)
small saws

Junk
A major requirement for a class of children who are enthusiastically pursuing scientific and technological activities is a large, varied, motivating and never-ending supply of junk. A stock of junk should include:
newspapers and magazines
plastic sheet and bags (all sizes, all thicknesses)
paper of all kinds (wallpaper particularly)
corrugated cardboard
jars and bottles with and without screw caps (all shapes and sizes, glass

and plastic, rigid and squeezy)
soap or hand cream dispensers
egg boxes
cheese boxes
cuboid boxes (large and small; with and without lids; plastic, wood, cardboard, metal)
sweet jars (plastic, preferably)
plastic food trays
plastic cartons (yoghurt, margarine, etc.)
aluminium foil dishes, trays and cartons
pieces of fabric (any shape or size; any fibre type, colour or texture)
pieces of floor coverings (cork, vinyl, tiles of all kinds, carpet)
cardboard tube (toilet rolls, kitchen rolls)
expanded polystyrene (pieces of block, tile, packaging, etc.)
bottle tops
plastic beer glasses (transparent – one pint)
plastic cups and beakers (transparent, opaque, expanded polystyrene, double sided)
pieces of wood (particularly soft wood of small cross-section)
metal
plastic

Collecting junk
Every teacher can use parents, friends, the school kitchen and local shops as a rich supply of containers, boxes and the like. Particularly useful to remember are:
wine shops – the strongest cardboard containers with useful compartments, some packing materials;
furniture shops – large cardboard containers, large sheets of strong plastic, bubble plastic packing sheets;
white goods suppliers – large cardboard cartons, polystyrene packaging;
DIY shops – bits and off-cuts of all sorts of materials;
paint and wallpaper shops – out-of-date pattern books, colour cards, damaged polystyrene tiles, odd rolls of wallpaper, etc;
timber merchants – off-cuts of all kinds of wood cross-sections, lengths of soft wood which children can saw (dowel rod, lathe), different kinds of wood;
monumental mason – bits both rough and polished of a variety of stone, marble and granite.

Less often considered or exploited as a source of junk are local companies, particularly manufacturing companies. They produce all sorts of material which is waste for them but of value to schools. Companies do not want waste material left lying around so it is quickly destroyed if it does not find a better home.

Why not see if you can come to an arrangement with local companies, and put some of their junk to good use? You probably pass companies on your way to school and there may be some in the area surrounding the school. You could write to them or, better still, call in. Most people will be glad to help in some way and you will have found a reason to make contact and establish a link between your school and the company. That can bear fruit in all sorts of ways: inviting the people from the company to visit your school; you and maybe the children visiting the company; more information about people and their jobs; more examples of people using science; and more ideas for topic work.

Science equipment
magnifying glasses (a large, flexible arm, table mounted, magnifying glass is useful. Hand lenses should be readily available, and there is a range of magnifiers for observing specimens – some form the lids of small specimen boxes.)
binocular microscope (invaluable item)
large mirror (to put flat on the table)
small hand mirrors
large and small standard magnets
one or two pairs of strong magnets (Alnico or similar)

torch bulbs
torch batteries
plastic covered bell wire
bulb holders
crocodile clips

} to make electric circuit

tape recorder
camera
two thermometers
(marked in degrees Celsius)

Mathematics apparatus
sorting circles
2D and 3D plastic/wooden shapes (large and small)
2D templates for regular shapes
30 cm rulers (unmarked and marked 10 cm, 20 cm and 30 cm)
metre sticks (unmarked and marked)
one litre and half litre measuring jars
balance scales
bucket balance
callipers

Certain other apparatus is used during the scheme:

Year 1	Year 2	Year 3
poleido blocks	posting box	set of weights 10 g–1 kg
coloured beads and laces	matrix diagram	several gram weights 1 g–10 g
sorting trays	sorting tree	tape measures
large arrows	egg timer	minute timer
	clock	
	card arrows	

b) Storage

Central storage or classroom storage
Various problems arise in planning how to store science equipment and materials. Firstly, a decision has to be taken as to whether to establish a central store or whether to store equipment and materials in each classroom. This will depend on the particular circumstances of your own school but certain requirements and considerations will be common. Infrequently used specialised equipment is certainly better kept in a central store to which all teachers have access. For more generally used small scale equipment and materials it makes sense to arrange storage in individual classrooms; however, it is most important that someone should make a record of what is where, and that everyone concerned has access to this record. The person who keeps the record should also be responsible for ensuring that equipment is maintained in a serviceable condition and that materials are replaced.

Activity boxes
It may be advantageous to collect together the equipment needed for a particular activity and to put it in its own labelled box so that it is available for anyone wishing to use that activity. The box can contain specific items and a note of anything else that is needed to complete the set of equipment for that activity.

Various boxes, trays and cartons made from card or plastic can be purchased commercially but there is a wide range of useful containers available free from a variety of sources. Shoe shops can provide a variety of smaller boxes while greengrocers have stacking boxes, e.g. tomato boxes, which can be most useful.

Pupil access to materials
The biggest headache is trying to make satisfactory arrangements for the storage of equipment, material and junk to which pupils should have access. It requires considerable thought to devise a system which gives encouraging and necessary freedom of access but at the same time affords reasonable security for equipment.

Junk in particular takes up a lot of room and needs to be neatly stored if it is not to overflow in all directions. Again, commercially produced storage boxes, bins and containers can be attractive but strong cardboard boxes, e.g. wine shop boxes, can be stacked between solid walls or pieces of furniture to form a storage range. They can be placed in the classroom or in a wide corridor – but do check that you are not contravening fire or safety regulations.

A storage range

Small items can be stored in plastic containers which have had a corner cut away. They are free, look tidy and are easy to store side by side on a shelf.

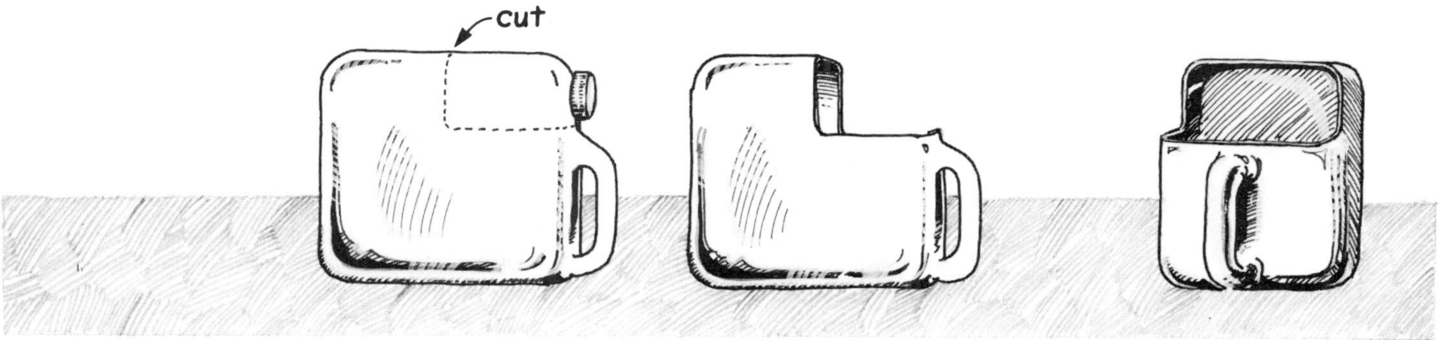

Plastic container used for storage

The important thing is that the materials are to hand and that children are not held up for want of a jam jar of the right size or a yoghurt carton. Children, like teachers, will appreciate a system which is maintained in an orderly fashion so that everyone knows where things should be and finds that they are there. That in itself is good education.

Part 2 Techniques

a) Growing plants and seeds

A number of activities involve growing plants and seeds. These are particularly rewarding activities not only because of the scientific/observational interest but also because they give children the opportunity to take individual responsibility for the care of a living thing. Below are some very basic guidelines which will help to ensure success. If you want more detailed information you should consult a gardening book or a local garden centre.

Compost
Seeds and plants need something to grow in. In the garden, they grow in soil but in the confinement of a pot or box they are likely to flourish better if planted in a specially prepared compost. There are basically two different types of compost: peat-based or loamless (various brands, e.g. Levington's), and loam-based (John Innes composts, which are sold made up under many trade names).

Each type of compost has different grades, depending on whether it is intended for seed-sowing, small plants in small pots or large plants in large pots. There are also general purpose composts. For classroom use, you will find a peat-based general purpose compost most suitable and convenient. The peat-based composts are clean to use and light in weight for their bulk. It should be noted, however, that if plants are to be grown on for more than two or three months, feeding is necessary. Peat itself does not contain plant nutrients and the compost relies on added substances, which need to be replaced as the plant grows.

Growing plants

Pots or boxes for plant growing must have good drainage: yoghurt cartons etc. should have holes punched in their bases, and the pots should not be left to stand in puddles of water. Plastic food trays are useful for standing pots on. Virtually anything can be used as a container provided it has good drainage. Most plants object strongly to having their roots water-logged and more plants probably die of over-watering than under-watering. Generally, if you have any doubt about when to water it is better for the plant actually to look as if it needs water than to give it too much. Some plants, however, do object to being allowed to go dry and plants which are flowering or growing freely usually require much more water than slow growing or dormant plants. Also, plants can cope with more water when they are in a warm place than when they are in a cold one.

Plants which like dry conditions, e.g. cacti and succulents (fleshy leaved plants), are best kept in clay pots (with a specially prepared compost) but most other plants are quite happy in plastic pots and general purpose compost.

Plants should be planted firmly with thumb pressure on the compost, but the compost should not be packed down. They should be fed with a liquid fertilizer (or other pot plant fertilizer) about once a fortnight.

Small plants need small pots and most flowering plants flower best if kept in pots which appear to be full of roots. Eventually, a plant will need repotting when it gets too big for its pot. Likely signs are that it stops growing, its pot seems very full of roots and it looks unhappy. Plants should only be repotted during the growing season and a plant should be transferred to a pot which is only slightly bigger than the old one. Before repotting, the plant should be on the dry side and the new compost should not be too wet since after repotting the plant should be carefully watered. Repotting is a shock process for plants and they need sympathetic treatment.

Repotting

Some plants like bright light and some prefer shade. Very few like strong direct sunlight and most hate draughts. Finding out where plants are happy is often a trial and error matter. Reference books will tell you whether a species of plant is a sun or shade lover and what temperature it requires, but after that it really is a case of trying the plant in different places until you find a spot where it is happy (i.e. grows, keeps its leaves and maintains a good leaf colour). If any plant is not thriving try moving it to various places in the room since even very small differences in the amount of light can affect the plant's well-being considerably.

Growing seeds

Seeds need warmth and moisture for germination. After germination, they also need light and ventilation. Seeds such as peas and beans which can be handled individually should be planted about 4 cm deep, in well moistened compost. Finer seeds should be nearer the surface, and very small seeds should be sprinkled on the surface of the moist compost and covered with a very thin layer of fine compost.

The seed pots or boxes should be covered with cling film and put in a warm place (but not in direct sun) with newspaper over the top. As soon as the seeds germinate, the newspaper and the cling film should be removed but a loose covering of plastic sheet may be useful in conserving moisture. Tiny seedlings need to be watered (sprayed) very gently. They need plenty of light but avoid direct sunlight in the early stages. For growing on instructions, you should consult the seed packet.

Sprouting bean shoots

Various kinds of seeds which can be used to produce bean sprouts can be obtained from health food stores. The following method produces good results.

The ideal container is a square fruit juice bottle but any similar wide-necked jar can be used. The mouth of the jar should be covered with a piece of muslin, surgical gauze or similar, held in place with a rubber band. To start the beans off, the jar is rinsed with water and most of the water drained out. About 1 level dessertspoonful of seed is put in the jar and tossed about, so that the wet seeds stick to the sides of the jar. With the muslin cover in place, the jar is put in a warm, dark cupboard.

The seeds or shoots should be washed with clean water and drained twice a day until the bean shoots are the desired length – about 4 to 6 cm. This will take only a few days, the exact time depending on the variety. You will find more information on the seed packet.

b) Keeping animals

Keeping animals in the classroom is very worthwhile not only as a focus for science activity but also as a source of pleasure and satisfaction for the children. Children can gain a great deal from having an animal to care for at school. The children should be responsible for the care of the animals, and great emphasis should be placed on the idea that these small creatures rely entirely on the children for their well-being.

There are a number of activities which allow the study of animals and fish but observation of the creatures and their behaviour should continue throughout the year. The animal cages and fish tanks should not become just part of the classroom furniture.

For details of housing, feeding and care of animals and fish you should consult one of the many specialised books or pamphlets which are available (see reference list). The following notes may help you in deciding which animals to keep.

Rabbits
They are particularly good for younger children – easy to handle, not easy to lose in a classroom as they are not too quick, they sit still long enough for the children to have a really good look at any particular feature, and they do not bite. However, they need a big hutch and as they are not completely indoor animals they need access to outdoor pens. They smell very little. Arranging for their care at weekends and holidays can be a problem. Rabbit hutches are not easily transportable.

Guinea pigs
As for rabbits, but they can live indoors all the time. They are ideal for younger children. They do not smell, they do not bite and the cage is small enough to transport easily to its 'holiday home'. If the cage is put on a sand tray the guinea pigs can be left to potter in and out and they develop very clean habits. They are nervous animals though, and can suffer from over handling.

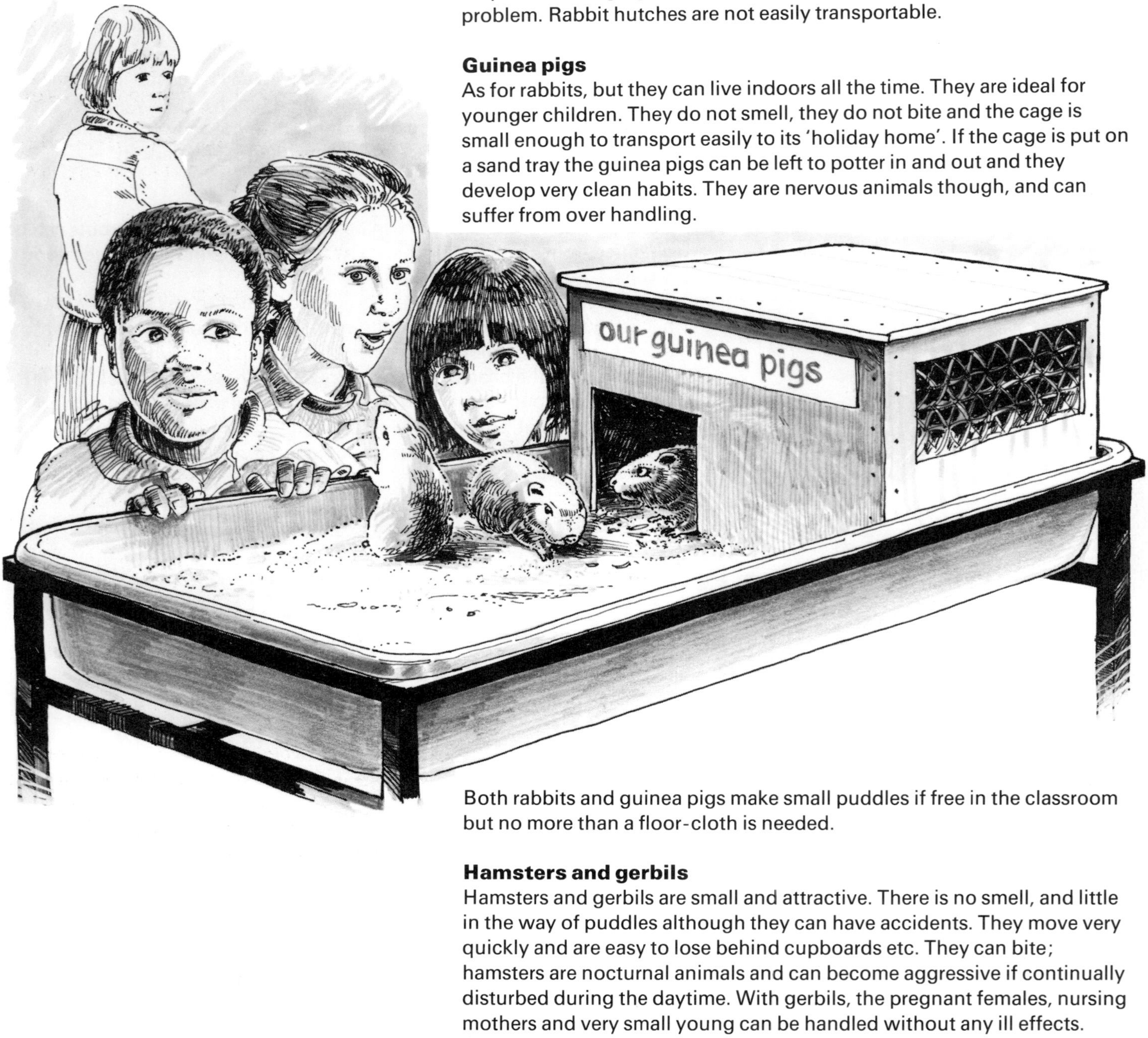

Both rabbits and guinea pigs make small puddles if free in the classroom but no more than a floor-cloth is needed.

Hamsters and gerbils
Hamsters and gerbils are small and attractive. There is no smell, and little in the way of puddles although they can have accidents. They move very quickly and are easy to lose behind cupboards etc. They can bite; hamsters are nocturnal animals and can become aggressive if continually disturbed during the daytime. With gerbils, the pregnant females, nursing mothers and very small young can be handled without any ill effects.

Rats
They are intelligent and make good pets. They appreciate spacious wooden housing where they can move easily (they can grow as large as a small rabbit), and explore their surroundings.

Mice
Mice are very appealing but they move very quickly and are easy for small children to lose. Unfortunately, they do smell.

Note:
1 Classroom animals can carry bacteria harmful to human beings and children must be taught to wash their hands after handling the animals and particularly before eating.

2 Monkeys, squirrels and other wild animals should not be kept as classroom pets because they constitute a health hazard.

3 Budgerigars can on rare occasions be carriers of psittacosis and for this reason it is best not to keep them in a classroom which is occupied all the time by the children. A secure, draught free position in a corridor or school hall where children can enjoy observing them without prolonged contact in a confined space may be a possibility.

Budgerigars should be purchased from a breeder with an established stock; problems seem to arise where birds are imported from the wild.

Some Local Education Authorities make specific recommendations about where the birds should be housed and others have banned them from schools, so you should check your own position. It is recommended that the birds are kept in pairs and housed in an aviary large enough for them to spread their wings and to provide an area of privacy.

For the science activities suggested in the scheme, you might like to borrow a budgerigar from a parent or friend if you do not already have one in school.

c) Simple electrical circuits

Below are some basic notes about simple electrical circuits of the kind used in torches.

In a torch, a battery and a bulb are joined by conducting material to form a circuit. A switch is incorporated so that the circuit can be closed and the bulb will light.

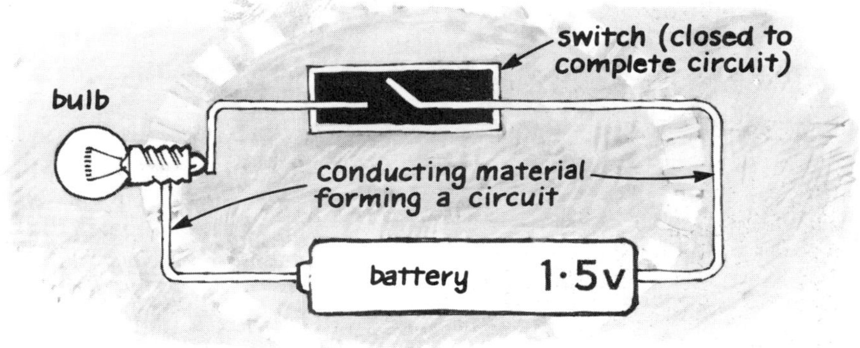

The battery

The battery is the electricity store. When a circuit is formed, the battery pushes the electricity through the circuit. How hard it pushes is measured in volts. The batteries which are used in torches are usually 1.5 volt batteries. If two are arranged inside the torch in line, the push is 3 volts. Batteries can be arranged in other ways so that the voltages are added. This battery is a 3 volt battery.

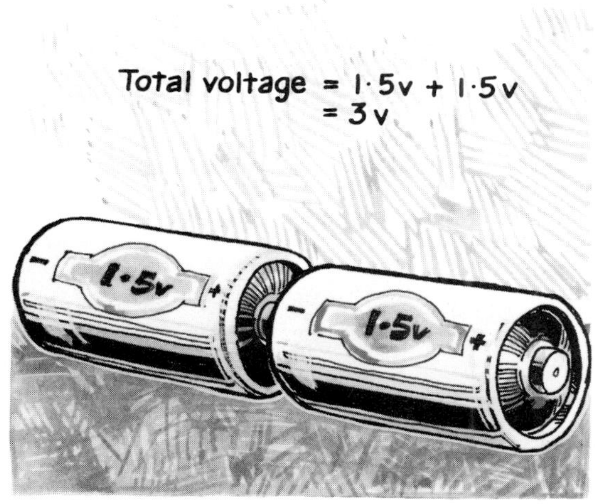

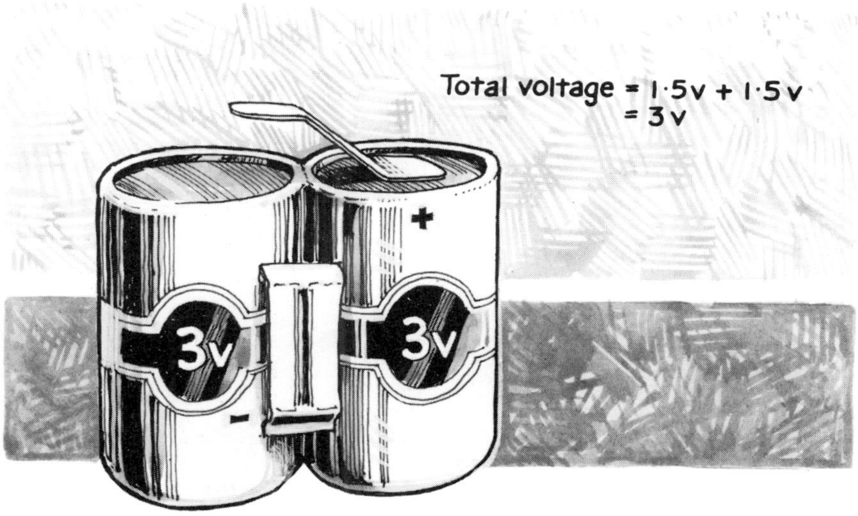

Batteries up to about 12 volts are quite safe for classroom use but for simple work you will not need more than a 3 volt battery.

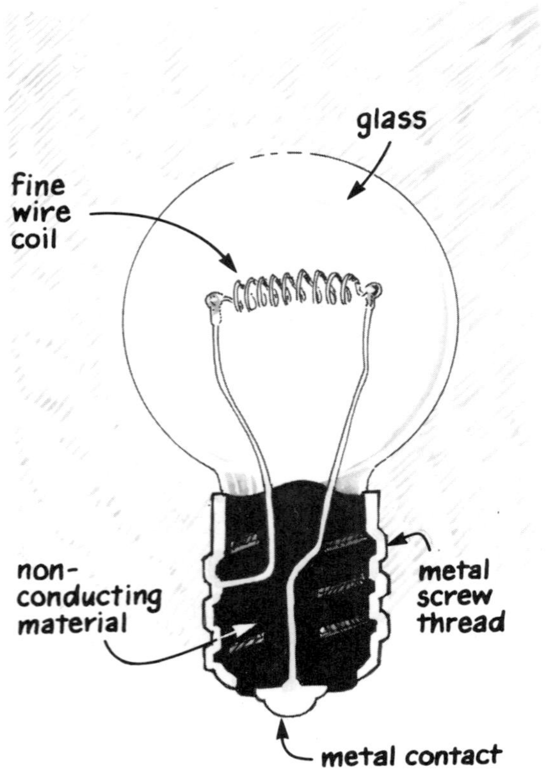

The bulb

A bulb looks like the drawing on the left.
The space inside the bulb contains no air and there is a very fine wire which is coiled and the ends fastened to the side and end of the bulb. (It is easier to see the coil in a normal clear light bulb.) When electricity passes through the bulb filament, it becomes extremely hot and glows white hot – and so gives out light. How brightly it glows depends partly on how hard the electricity is being pushed through, i.e. it depends on the voltage of the battery. Torch bulbs are rated according to the battery which will make them light up well, so they are labelled with a voltage; the voltage of the bulb should match the voltage of the battery within narrow limits. If the voltage of the battery is much above the voltage of the bulb, the filament in the bulb will become overheated and break. Always check that bulb and battery match (or nearly).

e.g. 1.25 volt bulb with 1.5 volt battery (maximum)
2.5 volt bulb with 3 volt battery (maximum)

The conducting material

The conducting material is always metal – wire, strip or even part of the torch case. The metal contact at the end of the bulb usually touches one terminal of the battery directly.

Note:

1 A material which is not a conductor is a non-conductor.
2 Arbitrarily, a very effective non-conductor is called an insulator.

The switch

In a torch, this is merely a mechanical means of making or breaking the circuit. If there is a physical gap in the circuit, the bulb can only be switched on if the gap is bridged by a conducting material.

The circuit

When the switch is closed there is a continuous path of conducting material from one terminal of the battery through the bulb and back to the other terminal of the battery. Only when the circuit is complete can a current flow and the bulb light up.

Setting up a circuit in the classroom

A 3 volt battery is suitable for making connections. The connections to it can be secured either by crocodile clips or paper clips. N.B. The covering at the ends of the wires must be removed so that connections are to bare wire.

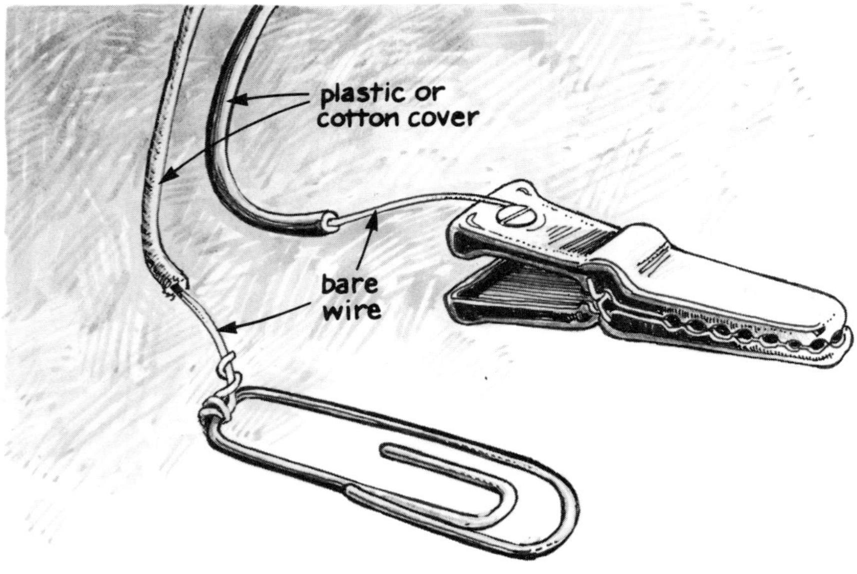

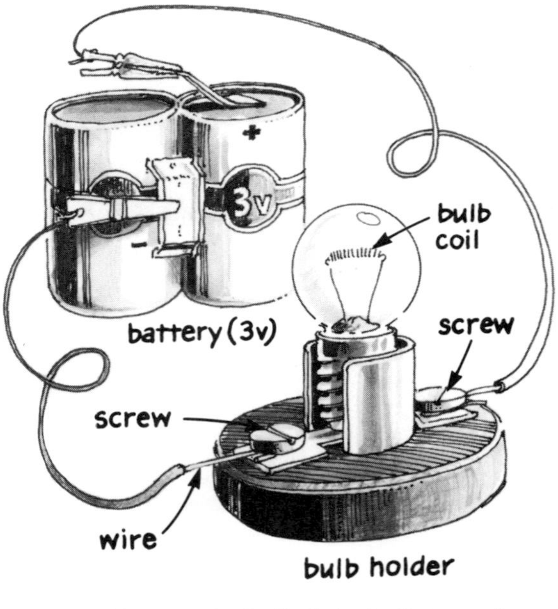

It is easier to make good connections to the bulb if the bulb is put into a bulb holder. The bulb holder takes the wire from one screw to one end of the bulb coil and the wire from the other screw goes to the other end of the bulb coil.

An elaborate switch is not necessary. Paper clips and drawing pins can be used for perfectly satisfactory switches.

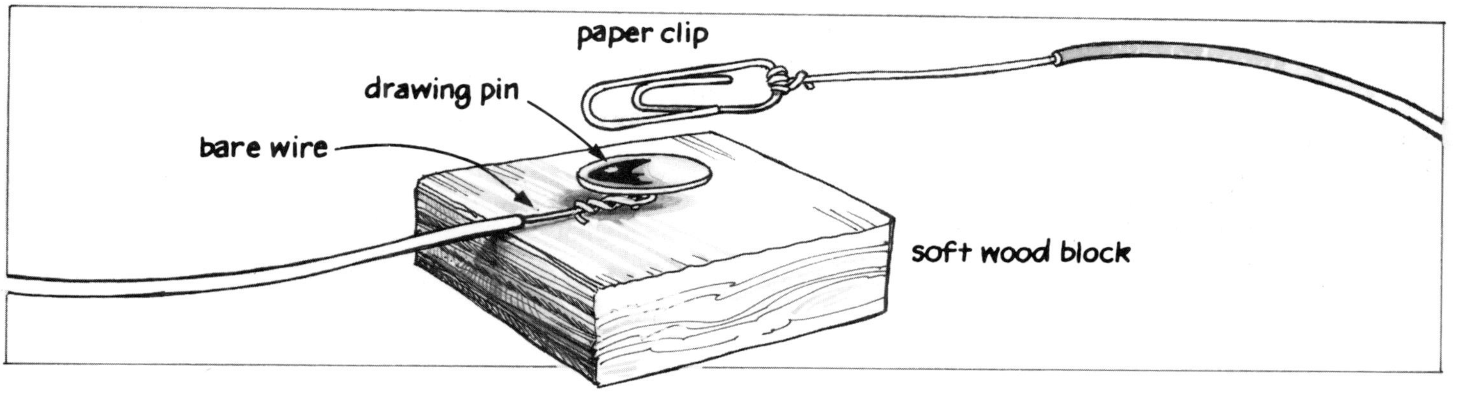

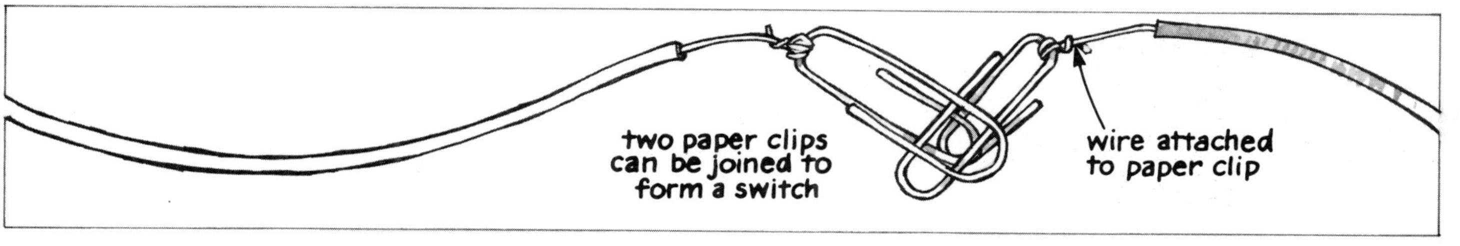

Some useful reference material

Teachers' books

School science policy
The DES Assessment of Performance Unit (APU) has published various reports and documents on science education. These include:
Science in Schools. Age 11: Report No. 3, DES 1984
Science Assessment Framework. Age 11: Report No. 4, HMSO 1984
Copies of these reports and others in the series are available from: The Association for Science Education, College Lane, Hatfield, Hertfordshire, AL10 9AA.

DES, *Science 5–16: A Statement of Policy*, HMSO 1985
Formulating a School Policy: with an Index to Science 5–13, (*Learning through Science Project*), Macdonald Educational 1980

Resources
Bainbridge J W, Stockdale R W and Wastnedge E R, *Junior Science Source Book*, Collins 1970
Science Resources for Primary and Middle Schools, (*Learning through Science Project*), Macdonald Educational 1982

Living things
Animals in Schools, 2nd edn, RSPCA 1985
Gregory V B A, *Keeping of Animals and Plants in School*, RSPCA 1985.
A variety of books, leaflets and posters on the care of animals and plants are available from the RSPCA and from the Schools Natural Science Society.
RSPCA publications from local pet shops or from Royal Society for the Prevention of Cruelty to Animals Education Department, Causeway, Horsham, West Sussex RH12 1HG.
Schools Natural Science Society publications from The Association for Science Education.

Animals and plants, Nuffield Junior Science Project, Collins 1967

People and their jobs and occupations
A source of excellent, well-presented information is the COIC (Careers and Occupational Information Centre), Moorfoot, Sheffield S1 4PQ. The *Working in* . . . series in particular provides bright, colourful material giving information for the teacher and attractive pictures for display. Local Education Authority careers service offices will be able to provide examples of this material.

More ideas for science activities and help with science teaching
Finch I, *Nature study and science*, Longman 1971
Kincaid D and Coles P S, *Science in a Topic* series, Hulton Educational 1973
Science 5–13 series, Macdonald Educational 1972
Teaching Primary Science series, Macdonald Educational 1975

Children's books

A variety of topics
Gulliford R, *Stop, look, listen, Teachers' booklet*
This booklet accompanies the television programme, *Stop, look, listen* and provides useful book lists for each topic covered in the series. The booklet can be ordered through Central Television, Central House, Broad Street, Birmingham B1 2JP.
Ivory L A, *Headstart* series, Burke 1970
Let's Go series, Franklyn Watts 1974
My First Library series, Macdonald Educational 1984
Pluckrose H (ed), *Small World* series, Hamish Hamilton 1979
Whitlock R and Heeks P, *Down on the Farm* series, Wayland 1984

Living things
Althea, *Life Cycle* series, Longman 1977
Althea, *Animals at Home* series, Dinosaur Publications 1981
Moon C, *In the Wild* series, Wayland 1983
Observing Nature series, Wayland 1980

People and their jobs and occupations
Stewart A, *Cherrystone* series, Hamish Hamilton 1983
Swayne D and Savage P, *I am* . . . series, Dent 1978
Egan (ed), *When I Grow Up* (Benjamin Books series), adapted from the Dutch by Jan Selby, CIO Publications 1975

More ideas for science activities
Kincaid D and Coles P S, *Read and Do* series, Arnold Wheaton 1981
Science Starters series, Macdonald Educational 1983

Index